christian family
guide to

Organizing Your Life

Series Editor: James S. Bell Jr.

by Jeff Davidson with Michael Clark

ALPHA

A member of Penguin Group (USA) Inc.

International Standard Book Number: 0-02864493-X
Library of Congress Catalog Card Number: 2003100694

05   04   03   8   7   6   5   4   3   2   1

Interpretation of the printing code: The rightmost number of the first series of numbers is the year of the book's printing; the rightmost number of the second series of numbers is the number of the book's printing. For example, a printing code of 03-1 shows that the first printing occurred in 2003.

Printed in the United States of America

Most Alpha books are available at special quantity discounts for bulk purchases for sales promotions, premiums, fund-raising, or educational use. Special books, or book excerpts, can also be created to fit specific needs.

For details, write: Special Markets; Alpha Books, 375 Hudson Street, New York, New York 10014.

Contents

Introduction

Getting organized may seem on the surface to be a personal and practical issue, and indeed it is both. You need to take personal responsibility for organizing the things you can touch and see around you, which involves, to a large extent, old-fashioned common sense and practicality. Yet the process of organization involves the spiritual dimension—the things you can't get a physical handle on—yet are nonetheless just as real. The impact it has on others also needs to be considered, especially as it relates to those most dear to you in your family.

Christian Family Guide to Organizing Your Life is a book that goes beyond its competitors by enhancing your spiritual and family life through organizational skills. Does this mean you can't be a good Christian if you aren't organized? We wouldn't go that far, but we will say that if you run your life in an organized fashion, a by-product will be an enhanced relationship with the Lord and with your spouse and kids.

We attempt to show you how biblical principles relate to organizational skills. As you become a more efficient and productive person, your family life as well as your work life will be richer and more satisfying.

Your motivation in getting more organized should first be to please God the Father and the Lord Jesus Christ, and second to serve others as the Word of God commands. Personal benefits should be third.

Though organization gives us greater control of our environment, we still must allow God to rule our circumstances. Proverbs 16:9 says, "We can make our plans, but the Lord determines our steps." So as you walk the road to being more organized, be humble and realize that he is the one ordering your steps, and so give him all the glory.

Maybe once upon a time it was easy, but today getting organized is no small feat. Among my friends, relatives, and associates, virtually everyone I know faces challenges when it comes to staying organized. Working adults caring for their parents are caught in a time bind and often let things pile up. Children today, of all ages, seem to be less capable of keeping their lives—let alone their rooms—in order.

Could it be that society in general is conducive to disorganization? Could it be that we are all confronted by so many items, so much information and communication, in the enormous effort required to address the chaos that our weeks, days, and hours have perceptively shortened? There is less time to get in control and stay in control.

The moment it seems as if you have your own little world in order, more enters it, making demands on your time, your energy, and your mental clarity. Books, documents, folders, magazines, newspapers, food items, household items, garments, work-related items, and everything in between pile up and overwhelm us all. We don't have enough time to read the Bible and the Christian books we so desire to read.

This book plots you a course past all the clutter to that hallowed ground where you feel and actually *are* in control of your house, your car, your office, and the other important places and spaces of your life.

Getting organized offers you many desirable advantages. The obvious benefits include being able to find things more easily, saving time, and helping you feel as if you are in control. Being organized can help you to take advantage of opportunities—social, professional, economic, and spiritual. Maintaining an effective calendar or scheduler means you have a greater probability of being on time to appointments and events and helps you schedule your time more wisely.

Being organized gives you more space, literally. You can accommodate what is new and make choices about what to retain. While possessions are not as important as your spirituality, your relationships, and the good deeds that you do, staying in control of your possessions nevertheless supports these important elements of your life.

In plain English, with a hint of mirth, this book takes you on a room by room, space by space review of all the places in your life that may be in need of organization, and it gives you an array of options for taking control. We mention in the text that it's similar to the way the Lord takes over your heart—one room at a time. Your long-term and continuing goal is to become comfortably organized so that you can better enjoy your life and those around you. You don't want to make becoming and staying organized a job in and of itself, with accompanying stresses and anxieties. Obsessive organization is not pretty!

Don't let the sheer amount of territory that this book covers bewilder you. No one can become organized in every aspect of life over night. The piles, the clutter, and the messes around you took time to form; correspondingly, it will take time to undo them.

In using this book, you don't have to read the chapters in order, and you certainly don't have to read the book from cover to cover. Turn to those chapters that address your most pressing organization issues. This might mean skipping to the chapter on your kitchen, or your bedroom, or someplace else. Focus on what currently "ails"; when you have mastered that area, turn to something else. By and by, as the days and weeks pass, you will gain a growing sense of control, feel more comfortable in your surroundings, and be energized to get organized in yet other places and spaces of your life.

Good luck on your journey to get organized. With this book, you have a valuable aid that will guide you every step of the way. May you reach that hallowed ground, and may the process of getting there be enjoyable. And may the time you save be spent in great fellowship with your family and with the Lord.

How This Book Is Organized

This book presents information in six parts.

Part 1, "When Did the Avalanche Begin?" opens the book by exploring some of the common denominators of disorganization then continues on with the basic notion that you are in control when it comes to maintaining an organized household. First you need to remove those items you don't want, need, or that simply represent household clutter.

In **Part 2, "Your Home Is Your Castle,"** we examine the kitchen, living and dining rooms, bathrooms, and bedrooms. We start in the kitchen because it serves as a place for family meeting, storage, studying, and leisure. Then we discuss maintaining an organized living room and dining room. We then tackle the bedrooms and bathrooms.

In **Part 3, "In and Around Your Home,"** we explore the other vital rooms inside your home beginning with the laundry room, moving on to the den, basement, and garage. We include recommendations for staying organized in the event of guests, when entertaining, when giving gifts, and even when managing a pet. And since you're always on the go, we also offer key tips for keeping your car organized.

Documents, documents, everywhere! **Part 4, "Organizing Your Vital Documents,"** focuses on the vital skill of managing papers and documents so that you can retrieve them when you need, fast. These very necessary organization techniques go a long way in keeping your home and home life organized.

We all could stand to better integrate the volumes of new information we receive daily. **Part 5, "Organizing New Information,"** will help you to become a master at identifying and ingesting new information so that it best serves you and your family.

Part 6, "Organizing in Everyday Life," offers specific guidance for staying organized in certain situations. For example, doing your taxes, purchasing appliances or electronic gadgets, or even handling service contracts, guarantees, or warrantees. This part will guide you to successful conclusion.

More Facts, Advice, and Serendipity

Extra bits of information are presented separately from the text in boxes. You will see three different kinds of these special boxes in each chapter of the book:

Divine Guidance

How would Jesus handle this? Maybe not the first thought that pops into your head when you're straightening and organizing, but maybe it should. These boxes give you a little bit of guidance and remind you that God *is* everywhere, in everything.

Caution Corner

Even simple tasks such as cleaning and organizing come with their share of potential missteps. These boxes will highlight some things to watch out for. From the reasons to organize to the way you do it, there often are only subtle differences between the right way and the wrong way.

That's the Spirit

These boxes contain faith-related inspiration and advice for organizing. This can be found in many sources, including the Bible and well-known Christian commentators.

Part 1

When Did the Avalanche Begin?

This short part opens the book by exploring some of the common denominators of disorganization that plague many a home and many a family. Its two chapters offer the basic notion that you are in control when it comes to maintaining an organized household and that there's no swifter method for getting organized than to remove first those items you don't want or need, or that simply represent household clutter.

Chapter 1

The Roots of Disorganization

Some people seem to actually be born organized. When you look at their desks, cars, and homes, everything seems to be in its place. The way some families schedule and complete projects or even make time for leisure seems to say, "We're organized." Conversely, others seem to have a knack for *disorganization*. All the spaces of their lives seem to be cluttered. Project files are all over the place. They never know where anything is.

Is being organized versus not being organized a matter of being born under a lucky star? Or do people who are organized engage in a few key behaviors that anybody can learn? In this chapter, we talk about where disorganization comes from and how you can deal with it—and even overcome it.

Who's in Charge?

The foundation for maintaining organization in your home and family life starts with the basic notion that you are in control. You steer the rudder, flip the switch, pull the lever, call the shots, and have the power within you to take steps to make your life more organized. Even if you have a highly demanding job and considerable professional and personal responsibilities, there are ways to make your life more organized.

Getting organized means different things to different people. For example, for some people getting organized means having ...

- A neater home.
- A reduction in stress.
- Fewer material goods.
- Fewer bills to pay.
- More time (specifically, more time over which you have control).
- Control over space (as in less clutter, less to clean, or less to maintain).
- Greater peace of mind.

Your quest for getting organized may encompass one or more of these notions, perhaps most of them, and maybe *all* of them.

That's the Spirit

Is there spiritual incentive to better organization? The Bible shows that change is inevitable, so be prepared. Ecclesiastes 3:1–8, in particular, explains how life is comprised of many seasons of activities and events. The legendary rock group The Byrds borrowed from that book for the 1965 hit "Turn, Turn, Turn." It begins with:

"There is a time for everything
and a season for every activity under heaven:
a time to be born and a time to die,
a time to plant and a time to uproot ...."

Change and Disorganization

With each passing year—and more specifically, each day, hour, minute, and second—an accelerating amount of information is generated on Earth and an accelerating number of technological breakthroughs are achieved. There has never been a generation in the history of the earth that has been besieged by more items competing for its time and attention than the generation in which you find yourself.

We've reached the point at which regulations, laws, news and information, and the technologies that we are expected to know or abide by are leaving many individuals overwhelmed and exhausted. The infrastructure that now holds society in place—the computer systems, the highways, the structures, and the energy that runs them all—are based on ever-sophisticated systems and technology.

Don't Regard Technology As a Cure-All

In Edward Tenner's book *Why Things Bite Back: Technology and the Revenge of Unintended Consequences,* the professor and historian notes one example after another of how the best-laid technological plans so often go astray. For example, as corporations turn to automation and put a PC on every desk, a fax machine in every corner, and a copier at the end of the hall, pundits predict that eventually we will gravitate to the paperless office. Yet, for the first 10 years of the true computer revolution, 1985 to 1995, the use of paper in the workplace more than tripled; it has increased more since 1995.

Dr. Tenner's research reveals that nearly every technological "breakthrough" comes complete with its own set of pitfalls. Athletic equipment, for example, was engineered to keep football games safer, but it actually prompted players to engage in more reckless plays. That resulted in more injuries per player and per team for more of the season than in previous years, when players had to suffer with inferior equipment.

Unnecessary Accumulations

Here are some tips to consider in light of Dr. Tenner's research, to help you beat back disorganization in your life. Take a walk through your house. Did you subscribe to a travel and leisure magazine with the notion of having more travel and leisure in your life? Now, however, you have magazines mounting up, and you've taken fewer trips than before you subscribed?

Perhaps you can chuck the issues, clear some space, and think about traveling closer to the time you're going to travel. Maybe you can even do without the magazine. The next time you're going to travel, bone up on your destination with one swift trip to the library a couple of weeks beforehand.

Now consider your subscriptions to technical publications. You wanted to be more adept at using your PC, so you began subscribing to some computer magazines. Lo and behold, what happened? You bought equipment and it didn't quite work the way you envisioned it to work. Some of it may be lying off to the side, barely used, if used at all.

When you view each new informational resource and technological tool as both beneficial and detrimental, you're in a far better position to keep things in perspective. For example, if you are in the market for a new cellular phone, you could make the purchase with predetermined rules of use, such as making calls only to loved ones and for crucial appointments, limiting calls to less than three minutes, and not listing your car phone number on business cards or brochures. Or, you might employ other ground rules.

For example, determine whether you need the "latest model." Did you trade in your old microwave with the basic dial for one with a new digital touch pad with multiple functions, most of which you've never explored? All the technological devices in your life have far more capabilities than their predecessors.

> **Divine Guidance**
>
> The crucial element to each new informational resource and technological tool is that you define your personal set of rules for using each tool. Naturally, your rules can change, but they're still your rules.

Many of them come with thick instruction manuals (so thick that you still can't figure out how to remove the flashing "12:00" sign). All of them have capabilities that you will not explore in this lifetime. Why not pick the item with the easiest instructions? Maybe the device doesn't do everything the more involved versions do, but if it does what you want easily, that's all you need.

Oversimplifying That Leads to Problems

Some "gurus" proclaim that the key to becoming and staying organized is to "simplify" every aspect of your life. For most people, however, whether holding an outside job or not, reducing your wardrobe to a subsistence level will yield only a temporary experience of getting organized. Initially, it will feel good when you look in your closet and see it uncluttered, with the few clothes that you truly enjoy wearing hanging there. What more do you need?

Caution Corner

You may not need two complete sets of silverware, but you certainly want more than a bare minimum three or four sets. The same is true of any other kitchen utensil and items in other parts of your house. You could probably get by with less, but not so few as to reinvite disorganization into your life at a future date.

Soon enough, when one item gets torn, another is in the wash, and something happens that requires your immediate presence, you'll find that paring down your clothes or credit cards or other elements of life beyond a sensible level is *not an act of getting organized, but an inconvenient emergency waiting to happen.*

Don't follow the gurus to absurdity. Taken one step further, by following the advice of some people, you might as well get rid of all your plates, since you can eat right out of pots and pans. Also, you need only one fork, one spoon, and one knife for each member of your family, and perhaps one more set for however many guests you think you might have at one sitting. Otherwise, everything else needs to go based on the admonitions of some.

Since you'll be living a simpler, more organized life, some say, you can probably bathe or shower less frequently. After all, you won't be entertaining as much, and you won't need to be in pristine hygienic condition as often. That will save on the water bill, soap, shampoo, and the number of washcloths that you end up throwing into the washing machine. You can quickly see where this kind of absurd logic is heading.

A Commitment Worth Making

If you enjoyed double the hours per day (which is, in effect, like having a clone of yourself), it's still not likely that you would be able to tend to everything that screams out for your attention. Perhaps with triple the hours in a day, a 72-hour day, your life could begin to take on a more organized nature, but don't count on it! If your life is disorganized now and you haven't mastered the fundamentals of getting organized, chances are good that it would be *even more disorganized* if your days were longer!

The sections that follow describe some tips to help you get off the dime, so to speak, and onto the special path that leads to getting more organized in *your* life.

Regard Your Quest As Worthy

If you've resolved to get organized in your life, then you're well on the road to its achievement. Some people choose to have a more organized life because they've been forced to. They've been laid off from work, they've received grim news from their physician, or circumstances have changed in their life so that major changes are in order. If you have chosen a more organized life, independent of external prompting, more power to you. In any case, the quest is worthwhile.

> **Divine Guidance**
>
> If you've resolved to make your life more organized, you're likely to be happier, more independent, and ultimately more comfortable, it's not necessarily less of a life—it's a different life.

Those who scoff at the notion of making their lives more organized might believe that the sacrifices are too great. Paradoxically, the opposite is true.

> **Divine Guidance**
>
> John Wesley (1703–1791), founder of the Methodist Church, had strong feelings on how Christians should live—which meant no wasted time. After seeing Oxford University students playing cards, he called them "a generation of triflers, triflers with God, triflers with one another, and triflers with [their] own souls." Wesley's perspective is, perhaps, extreme, but he was a crusader and you don't build denominations at the card table. A little recreation is healthy, just make sure you have a balanced hand.

Make Happiness and Contentment a Criterion

Attempting to keep up with the Joneses is inherently taxing. At its worst, it means always having the latest model car, the fastest computer with the biggest hard drive, the largest house, the most chic vacation home or vacation spot, and so on. It means maintaining a killer wardrobe, sending your children to exclusive schools, joining the right clubs, paying the large initiation fees, and making appearances. A life for those who are able to achieve such demonstrable levels of "success" can be all consuming. For many, it is a shallow, hollow existence, representing materialistic and symbolic success at best.

Unless you do work that makes you happy, have relationships that make you happy, and engage in hobbies and activities that make you happy, you're unmercifully consuming the time in your life. By striving for that which makes you happy, you're more productive, energetic, focused, and directed. You're able to give more of yourself to others, have more fulfilling experiences, and maintain more control of your life.

If you can muster the spiritual and emotional strength to let go of the trappings of success and instead focus on what is comfortable, rewarding, or enjoyable, your life will be that much more serene. A study of millionaires, for example, reports that most are unpretentious people who drive older cars, dress plainly, and long ago developed the habit of living within their means while saving at least 15 percent of their annual income.

Choose Good Health

If you want a more organized life, stay healthy! You'll have fewer trips to the hospital, fewer doctor visits, fewer bills, fewer needs for medication, fewer days away from work, and fewer times when people tell you what to take, what to eat, and when. Hereafter, err on the side of health.

> **Caution Corner**
>
> Too many people deplete their health in pursuit of wealth and then spend that wealth to try to regain their health. If ever there was a vicious circle, this is it! Why fall into it to begin with?

More often than not, choose what's good for you. If you have the opportunity to take a baked potato or fries with your entree, don't think twice about it. Take the baked potato every time—and if you can stand it, hold the butter. You have many options when it comes to nutrition and fitness. Your body is forgiving.

Even after years of abuse, if you quit smoking now, in as little as a few months your lungs will feel remarkably better. In as little as a year, many of the effects of long-term smoking dissipate. If you haven't suffered serious illness from smoking, you can become one of the healthiest people you know.

In One Fell Swoop

Take inventory of everything in your house that needs fixing or updating. This sounds like a little work, and it is. Examine your house or apartment room by room, and jot down everything that needs to be done. A leaky faucet? Write it down. Clear out a closet? Write it down. Sweep the garage floor? Write it down. You'll be left with perhaps a long list of stuff to do to get your house in the shape you want it to be.

You don't necessarily need to do everything on your list. Perhaps others in your household can help. Perhaps you can get part-time help at affordable rates. The point is, once and for all you have a list of everything that needs to be done. Instead of having a half-baked approximation of what you think needs to be done, you now have the true perspective. Knowledge is power. Having the whole list is a form of getting organized in itself. At least now you know what you're up against and can plan accordingly.

Whether better organization is completely new for you or an effort that you're renewing, it is an important transition. John Trent, noted Christian speaker and author of several books, including *Lifemapping,* defines transitions as "major movements in your life … that usher in a new season of life or a new way of relating, and close off the old."

Clothing Your Family

Unless you're an absolute whiz of a seamstress, round up every stitch of clothing you own that needs to be altered, taken up, taken down, stitched, sewn, mended, or otherwise altered and take it to your favorite tailor, all at once. Ask for your tailor's best volume rate. Then take your ticket and leave. For far less money than it would have cost you to buy comparable goods, you just updated your wardrobe in grand fashion and made your life a whole lot more organized.

If you do need to acquire new items of clothing, try to do so without breaking the bank. When clothes shopping, follow these tips to cut costs, save time, and stay organized:

- Don't buy an item of clothing before trying it on. On the hanger it might look great, but on you it might not be as flattering. Once you're home you will have less motivation to take it back, even if you won't ever wear it.

- Buy winter clothes in February and summer items, such as swimsuits, in September. The savings will be substantial. Though it's hard to imagine wearing a bikini when it's cold outside, you'll be glad you got it when summer rolls around again—and you can be sure that it will.

- Stick to classic styles that won't rapidly become "dated." You will save money in the long run. An expensive jacket that you wear dozens of times is worth more than a cheap dress that you wear once.

- Items that are "dry-clean only" may end up costing you much more money than the blouse or dress is worth. Always check the washing instruction labels before you commit to buying.

Divine Guidance

Jot down the amount you've saved after a shopping expedition, taking into account coupons, store specials, and other savings, and watch the cost-saving total rise. This will help you to enjoy the results of your cost-cutting efforts. Seeing the numbers add up will encourage you to save even more.

- Look in your wardrobe and assess what you wear regularly and could use extras of, perhaps in different colors. Plan what you are going to buy according to what you need. Incorporate as many mix-and-match pieces as you can.

- Take a sewing course and learn to make simple clothes. You can become more adventurous with time. Considering how much material they require, infants' and children's clothing is expensive. Learn to make their clothes yourself to save money, and let your child wear them with pride.

Seek and Ye Shall Have It Delivered

Do you realize that Federal Express will come to your door to pick up a package, as will UPS or any of the express delivery services? You don't have to be in business. You don't even have to be a volume user. Some dry cleaners may even be willing to pick up and deliver if you do enough business with them. Some offer outright delivery.

Increasingly, in every community, there are product and service providers who recognize the profitable value of capturing your business by offering pick-up and delivery services. If the spirit moves you, why not put a sticker on your phone that says, "Remember to ask if they pick up and/or deliver." Thereafter, every time you make a call, you'll be prompted to ask this oh-so-important question.

It *Is* Better to Give …

Round up everything you won't use again. Some early Saturday morning, following a wonderful night of sleep, arise and go through your home from top to bottom on a reconnaissance mission. Your mission is to round up all the clothes and every other item that's been taking up space that you're not likely to use again (see Chapter 2).

What kind of items? Books and magazines, records (if you still have them), cassettes or CDs that you don't listen to, knickknacks, mementos, games, appliances, equipment, and anything else you haven't touched in a year or more that you can part with unemotionally.

More, More, More

Even if you're standing there minding your own business, life is becoming more chaotic. It is not necessarily a function, per se, of you aging or of having more responsibility, a bigger mortgage or higher rent, more children, more responsibilities, or more of anything in your life.

Merely being born into this generation at this time all but guarantees that you will face a never-ending stream of distractions within your home, when you leave your door, on the highway, at work, and everywhere in between. Acknowledging this fundamental reality is one of the most basic and effective steps for achieving redress.

If you're up against the wall, for example, and are facing a tough challenge, you want to employ language that will help you rather than leave you in a quandary. When beset by disorganization, rather than ask yourself "What *can* I do?" ask yourself "What *will* I do?" Then get out a piece of paper and start writing down whatever answers come to you.

Rather than asking how you *can* make time for both your family and your business, ask yourself how you *will* make time for your family and your business. Even a generic type of question such as "What can I do about this issue?" can be converted into a more powerful inquiry that will readily prompt answers within you when it is stated as "How will I handle this issue?"

Less Is More

As society all around you grows more complex, that's all the more reason for you to practice the worthy goal of getting and staying organized. Rent fewer videos per week from the video store, but make them higher-quality videos. Read fewer professional publications, but make them higher-quality publications. Eat less, but make it higher-quality foods. In nearly every aspect of your life, you have the opportunity to turn less into more by choosing to focus on higher-quality experiences.

Behavior that's rewarded is repeated. Even self-generated behavior—things you decide to do all by yourself—that's rewarded is repeated. If you undertake some of the tips suggested here to achieve some immediate measure of getting organized and experience the benefits, you may be prompted to undertake others.

Chapter 2

Stop Being a Prisoner in Your Own Home

One of the wonderful things about making your family life more organized is that it doesn't cost a lot or require a great deal of time. You can chip away at the disorganization in your life a little at a time and still achieve great results. As with any worthwhile endeavor, some general guidelines and prevailing notions that have proven themselves effective are worth learning and adopting.

Decollecting

If you've been in your present home for as little as two years, chances are good that you've already accumulated more things than you can easily dust or perhaps even keep organized. These things lie around keeping you from feeling a sense of comfort or order. For some people it's Hummels. For others it's souvenir plates. For yet others it's licensed merchandise, like beer steins that say "Go Broncos."

Regardless of what's taking up valuable space in your house and crowding the tops of your mantles, shelves, tables, ledges, and other furniture, it may be time to round up the excess.

Here's how to deal with your vast accumulations.

> **Divine Guidance**
>
> There is no faster way to get organized than to first clear out what you don't want or need to retain. You are the primary force preventing disorganization from engulfing you. Whether it's a collection or simply piles of stuff, consider that anything you retain is potentially hazardous to a more organized life.

Unmomentous Events

Face it, you don't need a memento or knickknack for every other event in your life. Sure, some items had their moments, but this is now. By boxing up the outdated and the excess and living without them in your visual field for several months, you give yourself the opportunity to reclaim the spaces in your home or apartment. You achieve an early and easy win in this manner and experience the mounting realization that you can make your life more organized.

After several months, again revisit the box and critically examine each item. If you can't bear to part with something, consider this written permission to reinsert it back into your home. You always have the option of boxing the items, having a yard sale, or simply giving the items away.

> **Divine Guidance**
>
> The ancient Oriental wisdom of dividing—and hence, conquering—one's opponent is as applicable now as it was in the days of antiquity.

No matter what piles have accumulated in your life, such as excess clothing that threatens to overtake all your closet space, you have the ability to regain control. You can reclaim your space by taking bold and decisive steps to make your life more organized.

Best of the Best

In every collection there are some items that you can remove without sentiment. Suppose you're a stamp or a coin collector and your collection has gotten unduly large. What if you were to focus on the most rare, most valuable, most beautiful, or most pleasing items in your collection—the best of the best—with an eye on retaining those and selling, trading, or donating the rest? Could you gather the mundane parts of your collection and trade them for something valuable?

Do the task and be done. In coin collecting, you could group some of the rolls of pennies, nickels, dimes, or quarters from more common dates, for example, and sell or swap them for a single more rare and more valuable coin. The value of your collection would remain the same, while its volume would greatly decline. The same is true of a stamp collection, baseball cards, old magazines, or whatever else you've chosen to collect.

Pack Rat No More

There's no need to have all your clothes crammed into your closets all year long (see Chapter 7). If spring is coming, pack away all your winter clothes. With the first frost, it's a safe bet that you can stow all your summer clothes.

You may already rotate your wardrobe with the seasons, and you can do the same with garden utensils, athletic equipment, toys, and anything else in your possession that you employ only during particular times of the year. The hour or so that it takes to put your possessions into "seasonal holding bins" is more than offset by the freed-up space and sense of simplicity you gain thereafter.

That's the Spirit

Most people know of Jesus' warning about acquiring riches: "Again I tell you, it is easier for a camel to go through the eye of a needle than for a rich man to enter the kingdom of God." (Matthew 19:24) The verse describes the path into walled cities in biblical times that led to narrow gates called needles. Camels overloaded with packs had trouble squeezing through. So, whether you're rich and need to learn that you can't take it with you, or you need to shed some belongings, becoming better organized will do you good.

When Multiples Make Sense

If you wear contact lenses, you know the value of using multiple stations. You know to keep extra saline solution and storage containers at the various stations in life: your desk, car, and health club locker. Hence, you are always prepared without having to carry these materials.

Store frequently used items in multiple locations. Ask yourself what else can be stored at multiple stations, freeing yourself of the responsibility to carry or be concerned with it. Pens, note pads, calendars? What is inexpensive, often used, and easily missed, such as a comb or brush, a note pad, or even the kids' medicine? Anything that you *need* at various checkpoints in your life is best stored there. Think of it as a squirrel finding a choice acorn that he happened to stash earlier when he instinctively knew that he might be hungry later. Placing small items in multiple stations is a variation on dividing and conquering.

Rotation Sensations

One of the most effective ways to stay in control of your possessions is to engage in a form of replacement. For example, you probably have a collection of about 24 videos that you've accumulated over the years. Some are copies of your favorite movies, and others are presidential speeches or sports contests. When you are about to videotape some other program, use one of the existing 24 tapes and copy over it. You can do it—there is 1 video out of those 24, if not 5 or 10, that you can live without, particularly something that you haven't looked at since you taped it six years ago!

As long as you keep your collection at around 24 videos, or whatever you deem to be a reasonable number, you'll avoid spending any more money on videotapes, you'll control the spaces in your life, and you'll even be a role model to others in households that are becoming overrun by "collections."

 **Divine Guidance**

A role model is a person who, as a result of position, expertise, actions, or personality, serves as an example of good, productive, or effective conduct.

The technique works best when the items are small and relatively inexpensive, tend to accumulate quickly, and contain no one item of particular importance to you. The principle also works well when you can readily copy over, reuse, or relabel existing items such as a video or cassette tape. Then you can restore them on your own without taking a lot of time and effort, making additional purchases, or relying on others.

Keep the Recipients in Mind

Identify other parties who could benefit from what you have to offer. Whether it's clothes, books, games, toys, sports equipment, appliances, or knickknacks, somebody out there right in your own community would greatly appreciate what you have to offer.

For example, when giving away clothes, consider your relatives. Does your brother or sister have children younger than yours who would benefit from a big box of toddler clothing? Does your second cousin once removed have an elderly parent living in her home who is no longer fashion-minded and would greatly appreciate your five old cardigan sweaters?

Boxes to Fill

As you go through your closets, drawers, shelves, and storage areas, fill up boxes with target recipients in mind. It's far easier to fill up the box if you've already identified who will be receiving it. A home for the elderly? A school? Street people?

If you have a particular charity to which you'll make your donation, and if that charity will give you a gift letter to include in your income tax returns, then you benefit again.

Some newspapers publish annual guides or special features listing such groups as well. If you call your local newspaper's archives desk, someone there may be able to get the right issue or list into your hands for little or no fee. Some charitable organizations themselves maintain a roster of other such local organizations.

> **Divine Guidance**
>
> Obtain a list of all the groups in your community that accept donations of household goods. The local branch of the United Way often maintains a roster of all such community groups, including addresses and phone numbers. You can also check them out at http:// national.unitedway.org.

Support Your Local Library

Did you receive books as gifts years ago that you have never touched and have no idea when you ever will? Do some books that you have read no longer have any connection to you? Many town libraries, particularly those in small towns, face severe budget crunches. The cost of new books continues to climb. Therefore, the books that you have to donate to your local library are most welcome.

The books don't need to be in top condition, but if they are, it helps. The library will issue you a gift letter, perhaps even happily, that you can use at the end of the year when compiling your taxes if you itemize them using Schedule A.

> **Caution Corner**
>
> You don't need to clean the clothes that you donate because these operations wash and disinfect everything they receive. As a decent person, though, you probably will clean them first, won't you?

Salvation Army and Goodwill

A branch of the Salvation Army or Goodwill can be found in nearly every community. Both organizations are routinely listed in your local telephone book and telephone information directory. If you haven't made a donation to such a group before, all you need to do is box or bag up old clothes and other items. Then simply drop them off, preferably during hours that the establishment is open for business.

The easiest maneuver is to drop off your box and be gone, although you may also ask for a gift letter to use for completing your taxes.

School Days

All schools today face budget challenges. The elementary school in your neighborhood could use a helping hand in the form of books, magazines, paper, pens, pencils, rulers, or any type of writing or desk equipment. Do you have wall posters suitable for a school building? How about charts, maps, or historical memorabilia?

Schools also need globes, educational puzzles, and video and cassette tapes (which can be copied over for their own purposes).

Glasses to Go

Give your old glasses to the Lion's Club. This group collects old glasses, with or without the lenses intact. If your prescription has changed in the last couple of years and you're still holding on to an older pair of glasses that you never use, go ahead and donate them.

> **Divine Guidance**
>
> You can be happy with fewer possessions in your life. You are not attached to them.

You may free up only a tiny portion of some drawer or shelf space, but you're achieving another easy win on the road to organizing your family and yourself. You're demonstrating that you don't need to steep yourself in excess.

Bank on This

In many communities, the fire department, community shelter, or other charitable organization maintains a food bank. Considering all the stuff cluttering your kitchen cabinets, surely there is some canned item you haven't touched in a while, are not likely to use, and hence can donate. The same applies to other dry, packaged, never-opened goods you have on hand.

Take three minutes to peruse your kitchen cabinet drawers and pantry shelves right now. Round up everything you know you're not likely to consume in the near or intermediate future.

Russell J. Clinchy (1893–1981), a former Congregational minister, noted in his *Essays on Liberty* that charity is "a purely personal matter; an act voluntarily performed by one person for another; an act of faith in God and His commandments for governing our relationships with our fellow men."

In God's House

Churches can use the most mundane and ordinary donations, such as cleaning supplies, sheets, pillowcases, towels, and even rags. All places of worship can directly consume such items themselves or hold rummage sales and raise money from their sale. They are always looking out for the needy in the community. Churches can also use gardening and lawn supplies and equipment.

As you survey your attic, house, basement, garage, and tool shed, don't make a value judgment as to whether these groups will appreciate your donation. Grab everything you know you're not going to use and donate it. Let them dispense and allocate the items however they want.

Support for the Red Cross

At this moment, some region of the world is experiencing a flood, earthquake, hurricane, tornado, tsunami, drought, famine, or epidemic. The Red Cross is always in need of sheets, blankets, pillows, pillowcases, towels, washcloths, bath mats, bathrobes, pajamas, and anything else you can prune from your overloaded collection.

The Red Cross can also use all types of games, toys, and gadgets. If your tiny village has been racked by some natural disaster, you've lost everything, and you're eight years old, even the smallest toy from some well-wishing stranger halfway around the globe can bring comfort.

Community Groups

Round up all your old computer parts. Someplace in your community there is an art center, a youth center, a visitors' center, a historical society, or some other such group that can use your old computer, printer, modem, or monitor. Such groups can also put to great use an old fax machine, old TV, old telephone, or any old thing that is still in good working condition. This suggestion never gets old.

Get Clear, Feel Great

Once you clear out portions of your home, car, and office, you gain the feeling of space and ease, control and simplicity. What do you do with the spaces you've created? For one thing, you don't fill them up again with more clutter or things that will re-clutter your life. Here are some suggestions for what you can do to have a plethora of clearings in your life:

- Maintain some slack in your file drawers, desk drawers, closets, kitchen cabinets, and pantry, and on the shelves, mantles, and ledges in your life. There's no trick to filling up these spaces. Keeping them unencumbered requires a discipline all but unknown to the great masses of people in society today.

- Visit a local nursery or home center superstore, and pick up a couple of low-maintenance houseplants. The taller, the better. Install these in the spaces previously consumed by clutter. Plants can go directly on the floor (with a flower pot) or on a table. Give them sunlight, water them, talk to them if you will, and, all the while, keep your life more organized.

- Arrange your furniture so that *less* covers *more*. Discard pieces that you do not favor, and move the remaining furniture around so that it appears to occupy as much of the room as the greater number of items previously did. Does every square yard of floor space have to be covered? Does every open wall space have to have something in front of it? Make sure you free up window areas, doorways, and entrances.

In no time at all you will get used to having less, as previously you were used to having more.

That's the Spirit

It's impossible to match the example set by Jesus, who held no possessions except for the clothes he wore. But as Christians, we should remember his simple advice offered in Luke 12:15: "Then he said to them, 'Watch out! Be on your guard against all kinds of greed; a man's life does not consist in the abundance of his possessions.'"

Reconsider Before You Buy

On the path to organizing your home and your life, your decollecting needs to be matched by prudent "collecting." Whether you're shopping in a mall, thumbing through a catalog, or listening to an enticing offer from a door-to-door salesperson (there are fewer of these as time goes on), ask yourself the basic question "Do I need this?" Often the answer is, "No, I don't need it."

Then ask yourself "Do I want it?" In some cases you might concede, "Yes, I'd like that," but after a while, would it bring you any great joy? Often the answer is, "No, it would be of passing interest."

If you're confronted with an item of discernible value, ask yourself further probing questions. If you bought the item, would it make a difference in your life? Would it save labor or time, or yield peace of mind? If so, consider buying it.

Then ask, "Will it pay for itself shortly?" If it's a high-priced item but it easily pays for itself within a year (and perhaps far sooner) *and* there are immediate recognizable benefits, take the plunge.

Next, ask yourself, "What are my options?" Often the alternative to buying something new is using something else that you *already have* that costs you nothing more.

Ask yourself, "What else accomplishes the same ends?" Before you buy an electric can opener, for example, have you considered testing new mechanical can openers? Some are available for $3 or less and work so well that lids practically glide off. If you have arthritis, the electric ones make perfect sense. If you're otherwise adept, the low-cost substitute does the same job.

> **Divine Guidance**
>
> If an item pays for itself the first, second, or third time you'll use it, and if you'll use it several times within a few months, go ahead and purchase it.

The same principle applies when shopping for an alarm clock. Do you need a souped-up, overloaded, combination radio, alarm, snooze button, timer, extra-large display, built-in phone, and who knows what else? There are so many gadgets, so many instructions, so little time. Identify your major need—perhaps a good quality alarm with an overly large red, lighted display so that you can see the time without your glasses, and nothing more. If so, pay less and sleep just as soundly.

By safeguarding at the start what enters your home, you avoid having to engage in most of the exercises discussed in this chapter. Whether it's small items, clothing, larger items such as home furnishings, or paper and documents, be vigilant about what you choose to retain: Evaluate and then reevaluate what crosses your path before making your decision.

Part 2

Your Home Is
Your Castle

In this large part, we examine the major rooms in your household, including your kitchen, living and dining rooms, bathrooms, and bedrooms, with an eye on what can be done to keep these vital spaces organized, streamlined, and ready to serve you and your family. We start in the kitchen, devoting two chapters to it because, more than just an arena for food preparation, the kitchen serves as a place for family meetings, storage, studying, and even leisure. Thereafter, we discuss how to determine which style fits you and your family so that you can maintain an organized living room and dining room. We also tackle the bedrooms and the bathroom, which of all rooms seems to get disorganized the fastest.

Chapter 3

Organizing Your Kitchen

Of all the rooms in your home, the kitchen is unique. In addition to being the center for food preparation, the kitchen is an area for family meetings, storage, studying, and even playing. Traditionally, television shows use the kitchen as a background for many of their most emotional scenes.

You likely will spend more time working in and cleaning your kitchen than any other room in the house. Compared to your grandma's kitchen, today's kitchen is high-tech, which can be overwhelming if you don't have time to study 20- to 60-page instruction manuals for the new appliances (for example, how do you set this thing to bake?). To make your kitchen simpler, stay with what you know and what makes you and your family comfortable.

We'll devote two chapters to this vital area, since there are so many organizational issues to cover!

Optimal Appliance Arrangements

If you're about to move into a home or if you have discretion over the kitchen layout, this section is for you. What is the most efficient layout for your kitchen? To answer this question, take into account what you use most in the kitchen. The stove, refrigerator, and sink are the most commonly used appliances for people with a full-size kitchen. So it's necessary to minimize the distances between these three without crowding, which makes it more difficult to work efficiently.

The Work Triangle

The preferred layout is commonly called the "work triangle." The work triangle puts the refrigerator, stove, and sink at the points in the triangle, making it easier to reach each when you're preparing meals.

If you have a small kitchen, one advantage that you have over others is that there is less area to clean after a meal is prepared. If your kitchen is larger, you can still achieve the same effect with the work triangle. Since the majority of food preparation is done in one area, there is only one area to clean. This will lessen the overall amount of time you spend in the kitchen so that you can move on to more enjoyable tasks.

> **That's the Spirit**
>
> God is everywhere, but because some places, such as the kitchen, seem so utilitarian, we don't think about God as being there much. But location shouldn't matter if you want to be closer to God at all times. The Christian Chefs Fellowship (check them out online at www.christianchefs.org) suggests a simple prayer to keep God in your heart no matter where you are: "Be joyful always; pray continually; give thanks in all circumstances, for this is God's will for you in Christ Jesus." (1 Thessalonians 5:16–18)

Add in the Microwave

When arranging your kitchen, consider your microwave oven in the equation. If you have the standard, free-standing, on-the-counter variety of microwave, avoid putting your microwave on your counter beside the stove. Generally, this area is needed for food preparation. With the microwave taking up considerable space, it will be difficult to fix meals without something getting in your way. Place your microwave closer to the refrigerator, or if counter space is limited, put the microwave on a cart.

Move your microwave left or right, or backward or forward, to see what you gain or lose in terms of ease of use, more counter space, and easier cleanup. Perhaps you can mount it under a cabinet or over the stove. Maybe you'll find that where you originally had it was best. In any case, it's good to know!

Utilitarian Organization

If you've sorted through things that you don't utilize in your kitchen and have moved seldom-used items out of the way, you have accomplished something that few others have. Give yourself a pat on the back, and get prepared to go to the next level. Now that you have more space, it's time to make the best use of the space. Whether it be the stove or the floor, you'll save time if you use the space as efficiently as possible.

> **Divine Guidance**
>
> Most stoves have a storage area at the bottom. This is a convenient place for you to put pots and pans. If bending is not your favorite activity, put your commonly used pots and pans in cupboards close to the stove.

Large decorative pots take up an enormous amount of space, and sometimes stacking these pots can scratch the coating or chip the porcelain. If your refrigerator is not enclosed in the wall, store some of these pots above it. This provides a nice decorative touch to your kitchen and keeps things out of the way but within arm's reach.

Utensils at Hand

If you have a particularly useful or favorite frying pan, keep it close to the stove so that it's easily accessible when you need it. It's also beneficial to keep large spoons and cutlery near the stove for stirring and turning over foods when cooking. Believe it or not, you can end up traveling the equivalent of 120 miles a year in the kitchen by preparing an average of two meals a day!

In Reach Is Best

If you're short, don't waste your time putting items on high shelves. It's potentially hazardous, and it wastes your time! There may not always be a tall person around to reach things for you. Put the items that you use less frequently, or that are used more frequently by taller people, on the higher shelves.

Divine Guidance

If you have a specific area where you store bakeware, stack it with the least used items on the bottom and the items that are used more frequently on top. You'll save time and effort by having the most used pans nearby when you need them.

If your cupboards or shelves are high, it makes sense to install cup holders underneath your cupboard. Coffee mugs and tea cups consume lots of space in your cupboard, so you have lots of space to free up.

Recipe Tips at Hand

If you or your family enjoys one or two favorite recipes, tape those recipes to the inside of your cupboard door. This way you don't waste time looking through a bunch of loose recipes or trying to remember which cookbook has a particular recipe. Be careful with this one—no need to turn your cupboard door into a bulletin board. A few recipes may be all you need and all you ever use.

Counter Power

Whether you have a small amount of counter space or counters from one end of your kitchen to another, leaving them with less mess is a good way to increase productivity and decrease aggravation when you're baking or cleaning. Choose an easy-to-clean surface, such as Formica. It's durable and comes in a variety of colors and textures.

You actually can purchase cabinets and design your kitchen close to the comfortable working height of the primary user. This may not be practical if redecorating isn't in your budget. If this appeals to you, you will not only be more comfortable, but you'll also work more efficiently day in and day out, for as long as you live in your current home. If this isn't an option, make the best use of the space you do have.

That's the Spirit

Your counters say a lot about you. And since kitchens inevitably become gathering places for any get-together in the home, many people will see those counters. Christians don't need a quota of crosses or Bibles for every few feet of counter space. But a kitchen Bible is a good idea; as a general rule, let hospitality be your guide. "Be joyful in hope, patient in affliction, faithful in prayer. Share with God's people who are in need. Practice hospitality." (Romans 12:12–13)

Here are a few more suggestions:

- **Barren counters.** In most households, blenders and mixers are stored on the counter in the kitchen. Unless you rival Betty Crocker in the volume of cakes and pies you bake each day, it's probably not necessary to store them on your counter. According to some studies, the ideal length of counter space for preparing meals is 72 inches or more. Put these small appliances in a cabinet out of the way.

- **Counter safety.** When a fire breaks out, you don't have any time to think! Have a fully functional fire extinguisher handy in case a grease fire or other small fire breaks out in your kitchen. You can purchase smaller models that sit on the counter near the stove. Making this simple and easy purchase could save lives.

Caution Corner

Contact your local fire department to find out where you can have your fire extinguisher recharged. Make sure that it's recharged after every use.

- **Splish splash.** Install a back splash from the top of your stove all the way up to the cabinet. One large, smooth surface of plastic laminate (or whatever your counter material is) will save precious minutes every day. Avoid paint or wallpaper for back splashes that aren't durable.

Cupboard Know-How

Can you ever have enough cupboard and storage space? Where else could you put all of the duplicate electric can openers and hand mixers that you received as wedding gifts? What about the tons of casserole dishes that you received when you moved into your first apartment? Aside from having a huge yard sale or giving away the duplicates as gifts, the answer lies in your kitchen storage areas.

When making the most efficient use of the cupboards and shelves in your home, ensure that you have enough space for all the necessities for you and your family. Along with pots, pans, dishes, and cups, you may need to use your cupboard or shelves for food storage if you don't have a pantry. The large cereal boxes, along with all the convenience foods such as macaroni and cheese, snacks, cookies, soft drinks, and the like, take up huge amounts of space and can be a stacking nightmare.

Replacement 101

When you buy new pots, pans, or cookie sheets, throw away the old ones. Abandon any strange attachment you may have to a five-year-old cookie sheet that is permanently stained beyond hope. Invest in quality cookware so that you don't have to replace items as often. When you do buy new pots and pans, give the old ones to friends or relatives who may be starting out and can use them.

If you have far more pots in your cupboard than burners on your stove, get rid of some pots. However, be careful to keep at least one pot of each common size near the stove in case you have to cook for a larger crowd. Store your lids together in a separate area from your pots. Your pots will stack easier without them. Some discount-retail stores sell round plastic containers that can be attached to the inside of a cabinet door to store lids.

> **Divine Guidance**
>
> The next time your can opener, toaster, or hand mixer wears out, buy a model that can hang from the bottom of your cupboard. These are great space savers. Make sure you hang them securely so they don't fall. Also avoid hanging heavy appliances underneath cabinets. In this case, opt for the standalone variety.

Is the Kitchen the Right Place?

Many things that you stored in your cupboards aren't actually needed in the kitchen. Infrequently used china, elaborate serving trays, and utensils (whose value confounds you) take up valuable cupboard and shelf space. If you have so many pans stored in the bottom of your stove that it takes 10 minutes to open the drawer and dig through to find the right one, perhaps you have too many pans down there! Similarly, if getting a pot out of an overhead cabinet starts a shower of pots, pans, lids, dishes, and Tupperware, you have too many things stored in the overhead cabinet!

> **Caution Corner**
>
> Sometime during all of the reorganization, things will break. Be ready. If any one simple thing can cause even a devout Christian to lose her cool, it's breaking an expensive crystal heirloom. Say a prayer before you begin. Ask God for safety first, ask for strength to keep up with the difficult task at hand, and then ask for peace in case anything else slips and falls. By doing that, you'll realize that even the most prized possession is merely another piece of the physical world.

If you have sets of crystal, china, or serving platters that are seldom used, move these items to other storage areas to free up cupboard and shelf space for more commonly used items. As a rule of thumb, if you don't use a particular item at least once a month, it probably doesn't need to be stored in the kitchen.

No Dumping Grounds

Your mate or kids may use the kitchen as a dumping ground for books, toys, and other supplies. Make every effort to put things in their proper place after they're used. You may run into the problem of not having enough space in the "proper place." Wherever you decide to keep the items, they shouldn't go in the kitchen.

If there isn't enough free capacity in your child's room for extra toys or school supplies, (see Chapter 8), consider buying him a desk or storage cabinet. When items are dumped in the kitchen, valuable counter space is taken up with things that don't belong. Hence, you're then forced to pick up or rearrange your space, which wastes your time.

Organized Drawers

Look in all your kitchen drawers. Which one is the monster drawer? You know which one—the drawer that you have to spend 10 minutes sorting through to find the ice cream scoop, or the drawer that has every utensil imaginable. Is all this necessary? If you have a small kitchen, a well-organized drawer can provide you with more helpful space. The key is getting organized, which, knowing what you're up against, may take a while.

> **Divine Guidance**
>
> For some reason, people hate to throw out knives. Generally, you need only three knives: an 10-inch chef's knife, a paring knife, and a 10-inch serrated-edged slicing knife. Buy top-quality brands, since you only need three. Top brands stay sharper and last longer.

Rule Your Utensils

Many discount retail stores sell plastic cutlery trays. If you don't have one, get one. Most of these are simple and have space for forks, knives, and spoons, with a few other compartments. If you want something fancier, you can probably find what you're looking for at larger department stores, but why bother?

Only the rare guest or house guests may ever have occasion to open your utensils drawer. Even so, they're not likely to draw any conclusions about your worthiness as a human because you use a plastic cutlery tray.

Junk Drawer Be Gone

Have you ever been cleaning out a closet or drawer, only to find something that you needed last week or something that you forgot you had? Still worse, did you make the mistake of buying a brand new item, only to find the same thing stuck in the back of the drawer? Avoid the problem altogether by resisting the urge to be a "junk-drawer junkie."

Typically, junk drawers are created when there seemingly is no other place to put items. There is no need for a junk drawer in your kitchen because there is no need for junk in your kitchen. Buttons, paper clips, nails, screws, and pennies are examples of things carelessly thrown in junk drawers. Instead of taking the time to properly store items, it's tempting to throw them in a drawer to hide them.

If you have many drawers, you may store items that are not junk in drawers where they don't belong. If it happens to be a precious memento or some remarkable piece of art that your kid made at camp (remember the ever popular clay ashtray?), put the item in a special place, not in a junk drawer!

Tools in a Tool Room

While we're at it, kitchen drawers are not the place for a bunch of tools. Keep them in the toolbox instead. If you want to have a few tools in the kitchen, a screwdriver and hammer are perhaps handy to have around. On the other hand, a socket set is not necessary.

Obtain a drawer divider so that your drawer is not damaged or scratched by the tools. You may also keep small amounts of nails, screws, or washers in small cups or small sections of the drawer divider. This is an easy way to make sure you have a nail (short of buying a pack of 100) whenever you want to hang a picture or move decorations.

That's the Spirit

If you can succeed in the tedious chore of organizing kitchen utensils, you can overcome your spiritual weaknesses. Just look at those weaknesses with the same sort of disdain that you might view a cluttered counter or disorganized drawer. When you clear away the clutter and the things you don't need—in the kitchen and in your faith—you find that you're near or at the victory stage. Philippians 4:13 says, "For I can do everything with the help of Christ, who gives me the strength I need."

Divide Your Drawers and Conquer

Many other utensils are stored in drawers other than forks, knives, and spoons. Corkscrews, mixing spoons, spatulas, and ice cream scoops are all thrown into utensil drawers.

Here are a few suggestions:

- **Drawer dividers.** Along with the plastic cutlery trays, drawer dividers work well in organizing these odd utensils to save you some time. These can be purchased at most discount retail stores. Thereafter, every time you open the utensil drawer and you don't have to hunt around for what you want, you remain organized with little effort.

- **Too many utensils.** Put a pegboard on the back of your pantry or cupboard door, and hang some of your larger utensils on the peg board. Utensils such as wire whisks, large ladles, and large spoons and forks work well in this situation and save you some drawer space.

- **Tablecloths.** Instead of stacking (and potentially mashing) your tablecloths into a kitchen drawer, consider storing them elsewhere, such as a linen closet. You probably don't use tablecloths on a daily basis, so get them out of your way! Storing them in a drawer makes it difficult to look for a specific tablecloth and takes up valuable drawer space. And as soon as you pull out a tablecloth, everything else in the drawer falls out as well.

- **Plastic wrap.** Instead of keeping your plastic wrap, aluminum foil, wax paper, and plastic bags in your cupboard or pantry, put these in a drawer under your counter so that they are accessible when you need them. These are commonly used items in the kitchen; you shouldn't have to stop what you're doing and walk over to the pantry to get one of them.

- **Coupons.** Instead of putting your coupons in a drawer in no order, purchase a coupon organizer—or better yet, make one yourself. You can do this by sectioning a folder into categories, such as meats, drinks, frozen items, and so on. When you clip your coupons, put them in the appropriate category in your organizer. This will save time when you're looking for a coupon and will help keep the number of outdated coupons to less than a couple hundred.

Take Advantage of Deep Drawers

Deep drawers can be used in interesting ways to free up some extra space in your cupboards or pantry. You may choose to relocate your recipe books. Deeper drawers can be used to house recipe books, loose recipes (in a folder!), instruction manuals, and warranty information on appliances or electronic equipment. This way, you don't have to take up space in personal files or boxes with warranty information that you may never need. It's also a good place to keep a quick recipe cookbook (check out *The Complete Idiot's Guide to 20-Minute Meals*, Alpha Books, 2002) so that you're not in the kitchen all day long.

You can also use deep drawers to hold recyclables, such as newspapers or magazines. For instance, in his book *The Smart Kitchen*, David Goldbeck suggests installing small cleats inside the drawer. "Attach a piece of twine or sturdy string to the cleats, long enough to lay across the bottom of the drawer," he says. "When the drawer is filled with newspapers you want to recycle, untie the string and tie the newspapers up for easy disposal into recycling bins."

A similar principle applies to aluminum cans. Line a sturdy box (that will fit in the deep drawer) with a heavyweight plastic bag, and put your crushed aluminum cans in the box until it's full. Put a twist tie on the bag and dispose of it in an appropriate recycling bin.

With so much activity in one place, it's important that your kitchen be organized, safe, and practical. In Chapter 4, we continue with even more ways to keep this vital family room organized!

More Tips for Organizing Your Kitchen

As we've discussed, the kitchen is often the central meeting place of your home and, hence, the area in which organization can most significantly benefit the Christian family. Because the kitchen is such a fundamental part of your home, this room, unlike all others, merits two chapters! In this chapter, we'll delve into specialty areas such as the pantry, offer tips on supermarket shopping, present cool ideas for using your refrigerator, and much more!

The Pantry

The pantry is one of the all-time greatest inventions, along with electric lights, sliced bread, indoor plumbing, and disposable diapers. Some people have no choice but to use their cupboards for food storage. If you're lucky enough to have a pantry, great storage opportunities await.

Divine Guidance

If your family is small or if you have many pantry shelves, consider allocating a shelf to each person. With separate shelves for each person, there will be less confusion and fewer arguments over who ate all the peanut butter. Also consider each person's height. Give the tall people the highest shelves—it will make life simpler.

Make Some More Space

The first time you looked in your pantry when you moved into your house, you may have thought, "I'll never fill up all those shelves." How long did it take to discover that pantry space is not unlimited? It doesn't take long to fill an empty space, but there are constructive ways of doing it.

If your pantry has only a few shelves, add some plastic-covered wire shelves to the door. These shelves generally are wide and deep enough only for canned goods, although there are some wider shelves to hold boxes of pasta. Add these shelves near the bottom so that you can close the pantry door without difficulty. This is an easy way to add a lot of extra storage space.

Pare Down Your Pantry

It's tempting to "stick" things in the pantry, especially if you know you're going to need them later, but avoid stocking your pantry with many of these items. Even though the pantry is an incredible space-saver for some families, be careful not to overload it with things that don't need to be there, such as batteries, a flashlight, and coupons.

If possible, designate your pantry for food only. If it takes more than 5 to 10 seconds to get an item out of the pantry, take a seat because here is some sobering news: your pantry is overstocked.

Divine Guidance

Disorganized or not, your pantry can help build your faith. As you look at the food, be aware that many people have much less—including the people who don't have pantries. So as you destock your overstocked pantry, make arrangements to give the excess to your church for an upcoming food drive. Remember how God feels about giving: "The King will reply, 'I tell you the truth, whatever you did for one of the least of these brothers of mine, you did for me.'" (Matthew 25:40)

Apples with Apples

You're probably in a hurry to unload your groceries, but instead of putting items wherever there is an empty spot, put similar items together. That is, put the canned foods, such as soup, together; put the cereal together; put the pasta together; and so on. A little organization in stocking your shelves will save you from having to search for the can of pork and beans that you know you bought during your last grocery trip.

> **Divine Guidance**
>
> If the containers are a tight squeeze, try putting them in the garage or another area that's convenient for you.

The inside of a pantry or cupboard door can be equipped with lightweight shelves or dividers deep enough to hold your boxes of kitchen trash bags or garbage bags. Small plastic bags, plastic wrap, aluminum foil, and wax paper also can be stored here.

The pantry is a good place to store recyclables as well. Containers for aluminum cans and plastic bottles can be stored in the bottom of your pantry, if the pantry is deep enough and space allows.

Is Bulk Always Best?

Unless you have a large family, you may not need to buy in bulk. Although there are cost savings on certain products, don't buy something if you don't need it. Remember when you get home, that 50-pound box of cereal has to go somewhere! Do you want to have 50 pounds of powdered milk sitting in your pantry for half the time you live in your home?

> **Caution Corner**
>
> Although you store mostly dry goods in your pantry, some of these do have expiration dates! Put new items behind the old ones to avoid this problem.

Occasionally, the grocery store or market runs a good sale on items that you and your family consume periodically. In this instance, purchase the items and place them in the back of the pantry so that they are out of the way. If necessary, you may want to prepare a "backup" pantry in the basement or garage for items that aren't used often.

Use It or Lose It

Use the oldest canned food items first. If you're dying to try the new brand of spaghetti sauce you just bought, resist using it before the other jar of sauce that has been stored in your pantry for one month and a half.

Super-Duper Supermarket Shopping

How many times a week do you go to the supermarket? You probably don't need to be going as often as you do; the time you spend commuting to and from the supermarket is valuable. This is time that you could spend doing something else. Also, consider wear and tear on your car. Those little trips add up to many trips to the gas pump.

With all that time and money wasted, why do you go so often? Maybe it's the joy of fighting for a parking place after you and everyone else in town get off work. Maybe you crave a new challenge. Whatever the reason, here are some ways to avoid frequent shopping trips.

Preparation and Planning

When you go to the supermarket without a list, you can be tempted to buy items you don't need. Before you leave for the store, take a few minutes to look through your shelves or pantry to see what you need from the store. Then add a few items that you or your family wants.

Divine Guidance

Never shop when you are hungry. If you're hungry, go home and eat. Aside from buying three boxes of cookies, an inevitable purchase, you'll waste money on things you don't need, and they'll take up too much precious space in the pantry.

Review any coupons that you've diligently clipped from the Sunday paper. It's a pity to buy an item at the supermarket when you've left the coupon at home.

If a nonperishable item isn't on your list, sometimes it's hard to resist a good bargain on something that you know you'll use in the next few weeks. If you have enough room to store it, go ahead—but first ask yourself the following questions: "Is it truly a bargain? Will I use it, or am I wasting money?"

Caution Corner

People often treat church as the place to go when they're hungry for help. Devout Christians have a close relationship with God and pray throughout the day. But many people, Christians included, do this when they're worried or grieving, or when they need something from God. The one-sided relationship many people have with God is, at best, ineffective for them, according to Larry Crabb, founder of the Institute of Bible Counseling and author of *Finding God*. "Until our passion for finding God exceeds all other passions … we will not find him as deeply as he longs to be found. He will not reveal himself to us in those wonderful glimpses of his love or in that quiet reassurance that he is with us."

Organize and Win

Learn to make the most of your local grocery store trip. The average family's grocery bill could be notably lower with a few simple shopping skills:

- Get to know the usual prices of goods as you shop, and then you won't be fooled by sales or specials that simply lower the price of already marked-up items. Some 15 to 20 percent of items highlighted in specials actually represent back-to-normal prices that won't save you anything.

- Plan your weekly menus around the sales and specials at your local stores. Low prices often are announced in the Sunday paper. Arrange your meals to include the bargain foods.

> **Divine Guidance**
>
> Many of the store brands are very similar to the big name brands, but some are not. Give them a try to find out which ones your family likes best.

- Look past the packaging, and you will discover that store-brand versions of national brands are often as good and 15 to 20 percent cheaper. Avoid the big names: You'll be paying extra for all the advertising costs—and you won't lose anything with the store's brand.

- Don't assume that the biggest pack is the biggest bargain. Check the price per ounce information marked, and buy the pack with the lowest price per ounce.

- Patronizing only one store means that you may lose out on savings occurring in other stores. This is what stores intend to happen; they lure you in with the sales and then hope you will give them back the money in your other purchases. So visit other stores and take advantage of their sale items. With such shopping rotation, you'll hit more bargains and keep more cash. Of course, shopping multiple stores means more time spent grocery shopping. So read the inserts in the Sunday paper before jumping into your car.

Shop for the Immediate Future

If you're cooking for the holidays, stock up on as much as you can ahead of time. You can never find a bag of ice on the Fourth of July, you can hardly find the good candy on Halloween, and you can barely find chocolate and coconut on Christmas Eve. Also, stores have the nagging tendency of jacking up the prices of these highly demanded products closer to the holidays. Buyer beware!

Take advantage of five-day forecasts. What does this have to do with grocery shopping? If it looks like bad weather may be approaching, stock up on needed items. Don't wait until it starts sleeting and snowing to go buy a gallon of milk. The store is likely to be out, and you also want to avoid the masses who waited until the last minute. Instead, you want to be sitting by a fire eating soup.

Cool Principles for Your Refrigerator

Your refrigerator is the most commonly used appliance in your home. One way to make it last a long time is to avoid changing the temperature dial in your refrigerator often. This leads to extra work for the compressor and shortens its life.

Decide on the best temperature setting for your food, and leave it there. Although some refrigerators can last 10 to 20 years, a bit of preventive maintenance and good sense can make your refrigerator and your food last longer.

Many people forget about the junk and dust that accumulate underneath the refrigerator until all of their food is spoiled and they get an expensive repair bill because the fridge stopped working. Not cleaning your refrigerator's coils can cause a 25 percent decrease in efficiency.

Caution Corner

The Maytag Corporation reports that a full freezer will remain frozen for about 48 hours, while items in the refrigerator will keep for 4 to 6 hours. Keeping the doors closed will keep the refrigerator cool.

Heloise in *Good Housekeeping* suggests, "Get a yard stick and tie a sock to the end of it. Slip it underneath the refrigerator and move it from side to side. This cleans the dust off of the refrigerator coil." If the coil on your refrigerator is in the back, pull or roll your refrigerator out enough so that you can get the yard stick behind it.

What about the inevitable power outage? Instead of opening the doors to your refrigerator or freezer during a power outage to see if your ice cream has melted, keep the doors closed. The longer you can keep food cool, the less likely you'll have to pack items in ice before the power is restored.

More Fridge Tips

By grouping similar items, like milk and juice, your refrigerator can serve you better. You won't have to hunt for the right item. Condiments should go in the side compartments, together with salad dressing. Milk, juice, and soft drinks should go on a shelf of their own located farther back in the refrigerator, while cheeses and sandwich meat should go in a separate drawer.

Here is a principle revisited from the pantry section: Put your newly refrigerated items behind the older ones. Nothing is worse than wasting a large portion of milk. This happens when someone opens a new gallon before the old one was empty. Be careful with this, though! Milk should be put on the coldest shelf well inside the refrigerator. Still, don't let the older gallon get wasted. Also, many a good food item has gone to the "refrigerator in the sky" because it was carelessly hidden behind the orange juice and subsequently forgotten.

Avoid storing leftovers in metal or enamel containers and cookware. In time, the salts and acids in the food can damage the container's surface. Worse yet, metal containers can cause food to spoil quickly and possibly can lead to health problems for you and your family.

If your refrigerator smells like the onions you threw out two weeks ago, don't feel bad. It happens to all of us. Just when you think it's safe to open the refrigerator door, whoa, the stench slaps you in the face. The easiest way to prevent this and provide you and your family with more storage space is to clean out your refrigerator every once in a while.

That's the Spirit

Just for the record, onions are perishables. To perish means to be destroyed or ruined, to die. Food is to nonperishable as human is to … immortality. Ask people if they want to be immortal both in this life and the next, and they'll give you a strange and confused look before walking away. But that's the heavenly deal we're offered through Jesus. Using food as a metaphor, Jesus described how humans can have immortality: "The bread of heaven gives life to everyone who eats it. I am the living bread that came down out of heaven. Anyone who eats this bread will live forever; this bread is my flesh, offered so the world may live." (John 6:50–51)

Be a Clean Machine

Have you ever thought that cleaning can be a wasteful activity? You do it once, and you have to turn around and do it again. And then there's an entire aisle at the grocery store full of cleaning products to choose from. Which one do you use?

The next time you shop, it's a sure bet that you're going to spend too much on cleaning products. To save a little money, follow some of these tips that use materials you probably already have in your kitchen.

Stain Removal

For grease stains on your counters, use rubbing alcohol to clean the stain instead of paying $3 for the fancy kitchen cleaner. Simply pour a small amount of alcohol on a sponge or rag, and rub the stain until it's gone. The rubbing alcohol disinfects the counters at the same time.

> **Divine Guidance**
>
> Nail polish remover can quickly and easily remove those black grease marks left by your shoes on vinyl flooring.

One of the easiest ways to remove Easter egg dye (or other types of dyes) from a counter is to clean the stain with fingernail polish remover as soon as possible. Be careful, though: If you have a special finish or type of counter top, polish remover may damage your finish. Be sure to test the polish remover on an inconspicuous part of the counter first.

Crumb Control

For crumbs and small particles on the floor, the easiest way to clean them is to put an old pillowcase or towel around the end of a broom, secure it with a rubber band, and sweep. Dampen the pillowcase with a small amount of water to pick up all the tiny crumbs.

Dirty drip bowls under your stove burners are a potential fire hazard. Most manufacturers recommend washing drip bowls in the dishwasher on the top rack. Don't scrub the bowls with abrasives or scouring pads; this can damage the coating. Newer model ovens have the raisable heating elements that are a snap to clean.

Cleaning Appliances

There's no need to spend vast sums when cleaning your kitchen appliances and utensils. Indeed, some appliances clean themselves. Be careful, however, because the interiors of some small appliances are delicate and can be scratched or corroded if an abrasive cleanser is used.

Instead of using strong cleaners, use some of nature's remedies for cleaning your kitchen equipment:

- The Vinegar Institute in Atlanta recommends cleaning the dishwasher once a week with vinegar to remove the hard-water stains and films: "Place 1 cup of vinegar in the bottom of the dishwasher and run it through one cycle. You can also put glassware in at the same time. Your glassware will come out shiny and bright."

- If you have an old lemon, cut it into small pieces and run it through the garbage disposal to freshen your drain. Also, if you're going on vacation, cut a lemon in half and leave half sitting out on a saucer in your kitchen to prevent the house from smelling like a shut-up house. Place the other half in a room at the opposite end of the house.

The Heat Is On

Self-cleaning ovens are common, but some people are leery of the high temperatures required. If your stove couldn't handle it, it wouldn't be designed to be self-cleaning in the first place. Be wary, however, of a common oven-cleaning technique: using oven cleaners or using in a spray can. You don't want to employ any type of cleaning aid in a self-cleaning oven. Once the oven finish wears thin, the oven won't clean at all!

Divine Guidance

Keep in mind that your microwave will actually cook better if it is clean, it won't be trying to recook the food caked on the inside surfaces!

Microwaves can be one of the dirtiest appliances in the kitchen. Unfortunately, after food has splattered on the sides and cooked there for a few minutes, cleaning it off can be a major chore. To clean and sanitize the microwave, boil 1 cup of water in your microwave for 10 minutes. Carefully remove the bowl after it has cooled and wipe the microwave walls clean.

Glassware and Silver

Along with appliances and kitchen surfaces, kitchen utensils and glassware need to be cleaned and disinfected. Most people keep silver items in a safe place and use them sparingly. Unfortunately, there's usually some polishing that needs to be done before they can be used. Since polishes are expensive, use some preventative maintenance with your kitchen items.

If you have glassware or crystal vases that have hard-water stains (lime deposits) in the bottom, rinse the glassware with vinegar, and promptly rinse with water and wipe dry. Don't let vinegar dry on fine glassware, however: It may etch the glass, especially in carved patterns and crevices.

If there are stains in the bottom of some of your small jars or bottles, pour a handful of rice in the jar, add some warm water and detergent, and shake. The rice does a good job cleaning (beach sand works well for this, too). Make sure you wash the jar thoroughly after cleaning with sand or rice: The rice has starch in it, which will leave a ring around some jars.

The Kitchen As Message Center

Let's explore the modern phenomena of "Kitchen as family message center."

Have you ever walked into someone's kitchen and been unable to see the refrigerator? Perhaps this is because it's covered with magnets, memos, reminders, message boards, and every picture the kid has drawn since she was five. That's not to offend anyone who has artwork all over his refrigerator—it's a nice gesture for parents to hang a child's artwork where everyone in the family can see it.

Sometimes the refrigerator door can turn into a bulletin board, though. This is a tenuous way, at best, to stay organized.

A Refrigerator Door, Not a Message Board

You can put an appointment reminder on the refrigerator door and days later not notice it anymore. Everyone has experienced this at one time or another. Instead of hanging doctor or dentist appointment reminder cards on the refrigerator, write down the appointment on a calendar or in a datebook.

If datebooks are not your thing, or if you have many items to keep track of, consider creating a tickler file for every month or week of the month (see Chapter 17). A tickler file is a file system designed to give you a place to chronologically park items related to forthcoming issues and to remind you when you need to deal with such issues. Place letters, business correspondence, and appointment reminders in the appropriate file. Refer to these files often so you don't forget important dates.

For example, Jenna, a mother of two, had a reminder card for a dental appointment hanging on her refrigerator for several months. Although she saw it every day, after a while, she didn't pay attention to it anymore. Sure enough, she forgot the appointment.

That's the Spirit

Ever thought of making an appointment with God? Don't limit spiritual behavior or awareness to a specific time frame, but do block out a half-hour or an hour each day to do nothing but pray and commune with God. It might sound extreme—if you're one of those folks who go to church only when you feel you're in need—but try it and see if your day isn't changed; see if your outlook isn't different toward the events of your day.

Post Messages in Strategic Locations

If lights or appliances need to be turned off at certain times of the day and household members or co-workers frequently forget this, post a note in your family message center area. Then post a specific label on the spot to increase the probability that the proper action will be taken. Whether you use a computer and label paper, or merely handwrite a note on a Post-It pad, leave notes near the stations of your life that help to keep things in control.

Create notes around your home to help other occupants know the proper times to take proper action. Change the appearance of labels to keep the message fresh. After a while, the notes become part of the environment and people don't notice them anymore. In that case, change their color or use stars or other symbols to draw attention to them.

Miniaturize, If You Must

Around the holidays or on birthdays, people often hang cards or decorations on refrigerators using magnets. Avoid this habit. If the decoration is heavy, it's probably going to fall down the first time you open the door.

If you insist on using the fridge as a message center, use a small message board. This is a convenient way to convey messages to other family members if it's used correctly. Make sure to erase your message after you check it. If the message board is never erased, no one will notice the new messages—that's the essence of disorganization!

As you've seen, with a little forethought and planning, keeping the kitchen organized does not have to be a huge undertaking. Now we'll explore the other rooms in your home.

Organizing Your Living and Dining Rooms

For today's busy families, it's rare to get everyone together in one place at one time. Indeed, you may be among the millions who see their families only in the evening, when things are winding down.

The living room and dining room areas assume different roles for different families. From the kids' entertainment activities to the old recliner where everyone races to sit, the living room represents your family and its collective habits. The key to keeping your living area organized, neat, and clean is to determine which "style" fits your family's interests.

Make a More Functional Foyer

The front door of most homes opens into the living room or foyer. Use this area to help organize your day's activities. This may save time when you're late for work and to help keep your kids organized for school. If you and your family use your back door more often, the tips in this section can apply to the area around that door also.

Imagine waking up in the morning to find that you're late for work. You rush around and start to panic when you can't find your car keys. On top of that, your child can't find his spelling book. One way to avoid this is to keep an out-table beside your front door. This table is only for items going out, not for things coming in.

The Out-Table

Before you go to bed at night, put your car keys, umbrella, grocery list, kids' books, or whatever you'll need the next day on the out-table. When you are ready to leave the next morning, everything will be waiting for you.

> **Caution Corner**
>
> Make sure you clear the out-table each day so that it doesn't become semi-permanent storage.

If you have a drawer under your out-table, store gloves and scarves there as the weather gets cooler. Keeping these items in a drawer in your out-table will keep them accessible when they are needed. If the out-table does not have a drawer, store them in a cabinet or closet near the front door. Don't leave them on the out-table unless it is particularly roomy. Otherwise, you diminish the effectiveness of using an out-table in the first place.

> **Divine Guidance**
>
> The Christian Booksellers Association acknowledges that $1.5 billion of its $4 billion in sales comes in gifts and products for home decor. Terry Willits, author of *Simply SenseSational Decorating*, favors subtle decor. "If we have Bible verse plaques all over the place," Willits said, "it might make an unbeliever uncomfortable." Instead, Willits keeps a verse on her desk and a prayer on the bedroom wall.

The Coat Rack

Consider hanging a coat rack near the front door. Everyone's coats will be accessible, and you won't have to run back upstairs to find them. Also, this prevents lightweight jackets from getting wrinkled as so easily happens when they're stuffed in a closet with many other items.

You know your day's starting badly when it's pouring outside and your umbrella is in the car (and you don't have an attached garage or covered walkway to your car). If your coat rack accommodates umbrellas, keep them there. Or, keep a container or umbrella organizer near the door so that you have a convenient place to keep umbrellas when they're needed. This is also a convenient place to put a wet umbrella when you come in so that you don't track water through the house.

The Foyer Mirage

You can create the appearance of a foyer even if you don't have one. If your front door opens into your living room, you can create the effect of having a foyer by placing a large screen, piece of furniture, or plant beside the doorway.

> **Divine Guidance**
>
> A "false foyer" is a simple way to add a decorative touch, and it prevents your out-table from looking out of place if it's standing all alone by the door.

> **Divine Guidance**
>
> You could also use end tables instead of a coffee table. Generally, end tables are placed closer to the sofa or chair. This can protect the end tables from being scratched.

The Coffee Table

A coffee table takes a beating. Your kids may sneak in and use it as a footrest, or it may get constantly bumped when people walk around it. If you want your coffee table to last, the following tips will help to avoid ruining it before its time.

- Put a coaster under your drink when you set it on the coffee table. Napkins aren't a good substitute. Even if your coffee table has a protective finish on it, it may not be protected from excess wetness. Using a coaster can save you money and keep your tabletop looking new.

- Allow enough legroom between the table and the sofa that people can walk around without hitting it. You need at least 12 inches between the sofa and the coffee table—and more to accommodate legroom for tall family members.

- If one leg of your coffee table is shorter than the others, put some plastic wood or wood putty on wax paper. Then put the short leg of the table on top of that. After the plastic wood or wood putty dries, smooth it down with sandpaper to the point at which the length is now the same length as the others. Alternatively, you can cover the short leg with a rubber cap (if you don't mind one leg looking different) or glue a button or rubber washer to the bottom of the table leg.

Rally 'Round the Fireplace

Nothing seems cozier than huddling around the fireplace on a cold winter's evening. People are drawn to a fireplace because of the warmth and feeling of relaxation it provides. Indeed, a fireplace is practical because if your power goes off during a winter storm, you and your family will have heat and will be able to cook over the fire.

Be aware that an open fireplace can draw more heat out of your house than it gives off into your home, hence sending your cash up in smoke. Cast-iron inserts can keep more of the heat inside your house and can markedly improve the efficiency of your fireplace. These are small plugs that help retain and steer heat back toward you. If you have more than one fireplace in your home, install inserts in both fireplaces.

If you prefer the natural look of your fireplace, install glass doors on your fireplace. The doors prevent the heat inside your house from being drawn up the chimney. This is also a way to close off the fire before you go to bed.

The fireplace is a focal point in your living area. Even if you don't use your fireplace for heating, it's a designer's dream. It provides a versatile backdrop to different types of accents and decorations. From the fancy formality of the living room to the casual atmosphere of the den, the fireplace can be used to accent virtually any decor. As you decorate around the fireplace, maintain order.

When artwork or portraits are hung above your mantle, your fireplace becomes the center of attention. If you have high ceilings, you might want to hang larger artwork above the mantle. A mirror also works well, giving the illusion of more space and providing another decorating opportunity. In many homes, sconces or small pictures surround both sides of a mirror. Don't be afraid to let the natural beauty of your fireplace stand alone.

Caution Corner

Having a fireplace also holds the distinct potential for adding chores—lingering ashes and soot, tricky cleanup problems, and safety concerns.

For a small living room, a few simple items on the mantle or a clock over the mantle will suffice. You don't need pictures and portraits from mantle to ceiling when you have a small living room. This will tend to make the room off-balance, which may prompt you to add more pictures on opposite walls. This compounds the problem and overcrowds your living room.

Put Safety First

Fire is a powerful force. One minute you can be relaxing in front of the fire, and the next minute your home might be in flames. You face potential harm each time you start a fire in your home. Making sure your fireplace is properly maintained can help prevent a disaster and increase your peace of mind.

Have your chimney checked annually before you begin using your fireplace. Also make sure the firebox has no cracks. If you're not sure of what you're doing, have a professional inspect for ashes, corrosion, and interesting items such as birds' nests that don't belong there. Spending the money on a professional who knows what to look for can save your life.

Creosote, a gummy, flammable substance similar in appearance to tar, can build up in your fireplace and flue after continual use. Creosote buildup is promoted by burning paper products and raw wood. Burning well-dried wood is one of the best ways to prevent creosote. If you have creosote, don't attempt to remove it yourself; the stuff is sticky and entirely crummy to deal with, and you probably won't get it all. Hire a professional to do this.

Install smoke detectors in all your hallways and on all floors of your home. If you have a fireplace, purchase a carbon monoxide detector as well. As you may know, carbon monoxide is a colorless and odorless gas. Faulty heating devices, such as clogged fireplaces, can emit this gas into your home. As with the smoke detectors, put carbon monoxide detectors on every floor in your home and near the bedrooms.

Fire extinguishers should be kept on each floor in your home, in the kitchen, and near the fireplace. Make sure the extinguisher is recharged after every use. Contact your local fire department for information on recharging your fire extinguisher. You can also purchase one-time-use extinguishers for kitchens and to mount on walls. They cost about $20 at any hardware or home center outlet.

Caution Corner

A single spark can ignite any combustible material (paper, clothing, or plastic). Keep a fully functional fire extinguisher on hand in the case of an emergency.

The Dreaded Magazine/Newspaper Rack

The contents of a magazine rack can grow at a rack-clogging pace unless you take steps to clear it out as you go. Unfortunately, many people don't do this. Magazines pile up. When you get around to cleaning, you've got a lot of outdated magazine issues to deal with.

If you've already looked through a magazine and found nothing of interest, dispose of it. Either throw it away, put it with the recyclables, or give it to a friend. If you stick to this habit, you won't have to go through bunches of magazines to figure out why you kept them and if you still need them.

If you've found an article in a magazine that you want to keep, cut it out and dispose of the rest of the magazine. If it's a recipe, put it in your recipe file or cookbook. If it's an article for your child, give it to your child. Keep your articles in an organized folder in a desk drawer—that is, allocate them all to their end destination as soon as you comfortably can. If you clip many articles, go through your file once a month and discard articles that are no longer relevant.

Divine Guidance

What do you do with those articles on faith that you've saved for years? The ones that jumped out at you because they were about you. Look them over again and write down key elements to remember in a notebook if you want, but expect that God will give you the inspiration you need—when you need it. It's not a sacrilege to throw out Christian material but try to give it to a friend to help her walk with God.

Carpet Care

Your carpet handles all the traffic that occurs in your living room, den, or dining room. Whether you have an old or new carpet, it takes a lot of abuse from you and your family. When guests walk into your room, the carpet is one of the first things that catches their eye. You don't want their first impression to be, "Don't they ever clean the carpet around here?"

Here are some suggestions for making your carpet last longer:

- Buy quality carpet for your living room. Indeed, this room is lived in, traveled through, and played in quite a bit. A lower-grade carpet will not hold up and will cost you more money in the long run. Nylon and polyester carpets last longer and are more durable.

- Avoid putting wool carpet in highly traveled areas. The first time something is spilled on it, you will have a chore cleaning it. When people track dirt, mud, and other unmentionable things onto your carpet, you'll face a dirt minefield and a perpetually incomplete task!

- Avoid white or cream carpets. Even if you and your family are ultra careful, these colors will get too dirty too fast. Sure, they look fantastic in the Carpet Emporium showroom, but when you get home, eventually you're hounded by the reality that light-colored carpeting shows dirt much more than darker colors. If you prefer a lighter color due to the color scheme in your living area, try a tan or beige that will hide the dirt and stains better. The extra cleanings necessary with a white carpet waste your time and cost you money.

- Vigorously request that your family members remove their shoes when they enter the house. Hey, doormats don't catch everything. Dirt and mud are your carpet's worst enemies. The more that's tracked in, the dingier your carpet gets. This leads to you know what: more cleaning, more time, and more money.

- Rearrange your furniture every six months to a year, to even out areas that are traveled often. Areas around entrances, sofas, and recliners tend to be crushed quickly due to the heavy amount of activity.

- Don't put down a high-pile carpet in your living room. Lori Tietz of the National Safety Council recommends using a shorter-pile carpet: "Rather than standing straight up, long pile tends to lie over, providing a smoother surface that's easier to slip on. It's easier to get high heels tangled in the longer pile." The last thing you want during a dinner party is for someone to slip and spill a drink or get hurt.

Divine Guidance

It makes good sense also to put sturdy foam pads under heavy furniture to prevent crushing your carpet. After you have moved your furniture, you can place an ice cube in the matted down carpet spot and it will revert back to normal much faster.

Hardwood Floors and Rugs

Hardwood floors are durable but, like carpets, also need some TLC. Hardwood floors serve well in areas of heavy traffic, such as your foyer and eating areas, but keeping wood floors in good condition can be a gargantuan task. Were you looking for more work to do?

Fortunately, taking small steps to protect the floors goes a long way. One of the easiest and most effective ways of protecting your hardwoods is to partially cover them with decorative rugs. Larger rugs can be costly, so stick with smaller throw rugs and area rugs in places where you'll want to make frequent changes.

Put tightly looped rugs in areas where many people walk. These areas include your foyer and your kitchen. Avoid using rugs with outer fringes. The fringes get pulled and tugged, and they eventually unravel. Tightly looped rugs will resist crushing and save money in the long run. For high-traffic areas, a darker-colored area rug or a print will hide dirt and stains better.

Divine Guidance

Different rugs can be used every season to give your room a new look and your home a festive atmosphere around the holidays.

An unsecured rug can be an invitation to a fall. Many discount and hardware stores sell adhesive strips that you can stick or glue on the back of your rugs so they will stay in place. However, if you apply an adhesive glue directly to the back of your rug and glue seeps out, it can damage the finish on your wood flooring. Turn the rug upside down until the glue dries completely.

That's the Spirit

What's the "glue" of your faith? Can it seep out and cause more harm than good? You go to church every week, and that shows your faith: Keep the Sabbath and honor God. That's your glue, right? But you lean on the horn when you drive, you speed, and you cut people off. You play fast and loose with professional ethics. To hold on in a world of temptation, glue must come from inside. "Only one thing delights him—people who fear him and put their faith in his unfailing love," says Os Hillman, author of seven books including *Today God Is First.*

If you need a larger rug or if you're looking for something ornate, consider an Oriental rug. You can find simple or elaborate designs that can hide dirt better than light carpet and give your room a stylish look. You may want to limit costly Oriental rugs to rooms that aren't used as much (but are perhaps in view), to protect them from accidents, such as spilled drinks. Oriental rugs are more expensive to clean due to the wool content. These rugs generally work well in the dining room.

If you choose to leave the natural beauty of your wood flooring exposed, use casters or felt underneath furniture. If you don't resort to such protection, wood flooring can be damaged or at least scuffed when your chairs slide back and forth. Beat-up, scuffed up floors require more maintenance.

When you carry hot items from the kitchen to the dining room, spills can damage unprotected wood. Polyurethane finishes provide good protection and can withstand higher temperatures. Also try to avoid subjecting your hardwood floors to high-heeled shoes. The pressure can make indentations in the finish.

Saving Space in the Dining Room

If you rarely use your dining room, you may consider it wasted space. Many people don't have a dining room, yet seem to function quite nicely. Conversely, some people use their dining rooms frequently, either for entertaining or for dinner with the family. If you have a dining room, how do you use the space? Are you a frequent entertainer, or are you thinking of using the space for another purpose? Here are some tips that may help you make better use of the space:

Caution Corner

Dining room tables and chairs are expensive purchases, but when taken care of appropriately, they can stay in good condition for years. A good way to protect your table surface from scratches is to use a table cover or tablecloth. Avoid placing vases or other decorative items on an unprotected table; they may leave marks or scratches.

- If you use your dining room quite a bit, make your next table an expandable one. By adding table leaves, you can seat as many people as necessary. Allow at least 32 inches between the edge of your dining room table and the nearest wall or piece of furniture. This gives enough room for your guests to move their chairs back. Later, you can shorten the table to increase the space in your dining room. This makes it easier to walk around your dining room table.

- If you plan to place a rug under your dining room table, buy one that is large enough that when your guests move their chairs back, the chairs are still on the rug. A rug that is too small may catch your guest's chairs or cause them to trip or to spill food or drinks. Sliding the chairs also may scratch hardwood floors.

You may only need a few accessories in your dining room to achieve the utility and style you want. Sometimes the difficult part is not what to put in the dining room, but how to arrange it and take care of it. Here are some easy ways to accentuate and take care of the accents in this area:

- Fine china is considerably more costly than everyday china or kitchenware, so show it off! China can be displayed in a china cabinet for utility purposes and as a decorative showpiece. Many china cabinets have drawers or cupboards for extra storage of more place settings. Drawers can also be used to house flatware, placemats, or tablecloths. Candles can be stored in a drawer divider in your china cabinet as well. Use a drawer divider so that wax doesn't damage the inside of your drawers.

- Also employ those little round wax guards with your candlesticks to make sure wax doesn't run down on your crystal, brass, or silver candlesticks.

- Candles provide a certain ambiance that's hard to duplicate with artificial lighting. You could add a candelabra, which invariably enhances the style of your dining room. Whether employing candelabra or candlesticks, use paper shades so that wax doesn't drip onto your dining room table.

- Buffets are also a good option if you don't have room for a full hutch or china cabinet. They can be especially handy if you want to serve the meals on them.

Divine Guidance

If you don't have a candelabra, install a dimmer switch in the dining room. Very bright light in the dining room may make guests uncomfortable. With a dimmer, you can control the lighting for each occasion.

If you need more storage room for holiday dinnerware or other serving utensils, install a corner cupboard or sideboard. Corner cupboards provide good storage space without taking up too much floor space. If you already have a china cabinet in your dining room, this may be your best alternative when looking for more storage space.

By maintaining a little order and employing some of the tips and tricks presented in this chapter, you can actually use your living room and dining room for their original purpose: living and dining.

Taking Charge of the Bathroom

Despite its status as one of the smallest rooms in your home, the bathroom seems to get "out of order" in a hurry! Your bathroom might not be that large, but it contains the necessities. How do you go about organizing the bathroom to make it less cluttered and more efficient for you and your family? Read on to find out how this chapter will help you take charge of your bathroom.

One Section at a Time

Do you spend 10 minutes looking through cabinets or the medicine chest for an item you know is there? You may want to approach your bathroom by sections and see if each is optimally organized in a constructive manner. For example …

- Can you reach every item you need?

- Do you have to look all over for what you need?

- Does having to clean the bathroom make you want to hide, not because it's so dirty, but because you have to rearrange everything just to clean the counter?

Ideally, your bathroom should serve as a functional haven. It's an area where you and your family can replenish yourselves. As such, the bathroom should be one of the least cluttered rooms in your home. When you're getting ready in the morning, you need space to maneuver. If too many things are in the way, your chances increase of knocking over items and breaking them. A little organization in the form of sorting, cleaning, and moving should do the trick and leave your bathroom in meticulous order.

Saving Space o'er the Sink

Chances are good that you don't have too much storage space in the bathroom over the sink, so you need to use it for storing important things that you and your family use often.

If you have shelves or cabinets in your bathroom, you may think of them as the ideal places to store items that you don't need often or that you can fill with unnecessary items.

Divine Guidance

Because it's the "necessary" room, the bathroom gets short shrift in spiritual considerations. Don't hang a black velvet version of *The Last Supper*, but use little touches. Slip a smaller, palm-size New Testament into one of your organizing baskets. A cross or crucifix might not feel comfortable, but art of a soaring dove or a framed copy of a favorite Psalm or Proverb tastefully proclaims your faith.

If you have only one bathroom, sharing the same space can become quite complicated. A husband may ask his wife, "Do you need all that makeup?" His wife's response might be, "Does all of your shaving stuff have to stay out all the time?" Your mission becomes arranging things so that everyone who uses your bathroom has enough storage room for the things he or she needs.

If you have limited shelf space in your bathroom, you might end up keeping some items around the sink. In this case, store these items in organized baskets that hang from the wall or ceiling. If your hanging baskets are filled to overflowing, another small basket or container can sit on top of the toilet tank. In addition to saving space, these baskets can add a decorative touch to your bathroom.

... And Under the Sink

If you have a stand-up or wall-mounted sink with no shelves or cabinets underneath, there may be little you can do with this space. Storing things here will only make your bathroom more cluttered and unsightly.

If you have a cabinet or shelves under your sink, keeping this area organized can help you save time in the morning when you're getting ready or at other times throughout the day.

Bathroom drawers tend to get almost as messy and cluttered as kitchen drawers. Drawer dividers can be purchased from most discount stores and come in a variety of sizes. You can use drawer dividers to consolidate your bathroom items, such as brushes, makeup, razors, and nail files. This is also a good place to store nail polish bottles together so they won't get knocked over.

Consider installing a Lazy Susan in a cabinet under your sink. Lazy Susans revolve 360 degrees, so you can keep your bathroom items on it and merely give it a spin to quickly have any item at your touch. This item is available in the kitchenware section of department stores (although you'd be using it under your sink). Avoid using a wooden Lazy Susan because plastic works best in the bathroom. If shampoo, rubbing alcohol, or another product is spilled, it will be easier to clean and won't damage your cabinet.

> **Divine Guidance**
>
> If you also keep towels and washcloths in your cabinet, install a barrier—some type of plastic or wood divider—between the towels and other items. This prevents the towels from tipping over and knocking everything down.

If a Lazy Susan or shelf is not practical for you, put the items that you use on a daily basis in the front of the under-the-sink cabinet. Keep other items that you may need only once or twice a week closer to the back.

Ready-made Storage System

You may have a wall-mounted sink with no storage underneath. In this case, you can purchase a ready-made storage system, a mini-cabinet or mini-set of drawers, that sits on the floor and fits under the sink plumbing. These systems may have fold-out doors with small divided shelves to hold extra toiletries. Or perhaps you can find open mini-shelving units that sit on the floor and still fit under your sink.

You can purchase small, plastic-covered wire racks for the back of the cabinet door. Small items such as soap, razors, brushes, or other necessities can be stored here. Avoid putting heavy items in this wire rack so that you don't do damage to your cabinet door. Shaving cream, shampoo, and other liquid products belong in a sturdy cabinet.

You can also purchase ready-made storage units that go over the toilet. These are very handy and offer lots of storage space.

With a Large Vanity

If there is a vanity in your bathroom, put only large items in the cabinet under the sink. Large items such as hair dryers, personal hygiene products, and toilet paper will be easier to find, and you won't have to worry about knocking over smaller items. Keep the smaller items, such as makeup, in a vanity drawer.

Caution Corner

With children around, be sure you store your cleaners in an area other than under the sink. Also make sure that all the lids are on tight so there is no spills.

Keep particular cleaning items for bathroom use in the bathroom, if you have the room. You can purchase plastic caddies from most discount retail stores. Be careful with this.

Hang It Up

What else can you do to save some space and make your bathroom easy to use if you've taken up all of your cabinet and traditional storage area? When you're in a hurry, you're likely to want items to be at your fingertips. You don't want to encounter clutter or waste time cleaning up. Having the capability to do so is not as far-fetched as it might sound.

By placing frequently used items close by instead of storing them in a cabinet, you can do what you came in to do and still be out of the bathroom and out the door in no time.

That's the Spirit

Is cleaning the water closet a downer? It might be hard to find joy in bathroom cleaning, but it could be worse. The Bible holds hundreds of verses that include the word *clean*, most found in Leviticus and concerning animal use or personal hygiene. Managing a case of mildew in biblical days was quite an adventure: "The owner of the house must go and tell the priest, 'I have seen something that looks like mildew in my house.' The priest is to order the house to be emptied before he goes in to examine the mildew, so that nothing in the house will be pronounced unclean." (Leviticus 14:35–36)

Improvise to Organize

Hang a shoe bag on the back of your bathroom door, the kind that has compartments for many pairs of shoes. These bags are generally made of a mesh type of material that you can see through, which makes it easier to find what you're seeking. The compartments are big enough to hold soap, cotton balls, disposable razors, and such. This saves space in your cabinets and makes getting a hold of some items more convenient.

Instead of keeping your hair dryer or curling iron in a cabinet or under a sink, mount it to the wall. Some of these appliances come with wall mounts in the packaging. If yours did not, many hardware stores carry the appropriate equipment; some even carry wall-mountable caddies for a hair dryer, curling iron, and hot rollers. Be careful not to mount these items too close to the sink.

Hooks and Racks

You never know when company will drop by or when a family member will have a guest. It's always wise to leave your bathrobe in the bathroom so that you will have it when you need it most. Purchase some plastic hooks to hang either on the back of the bathroom door or by the shower, for example.

When you moved into your home, most likely there was a towel rack hanging in each of your bathrooms. Consider adding a smaller rack above or below the existing rack. A two-tiered towel rack will allow you to hang twice as many towels in virtually the same space. If you convert all your towel racks to the two-tiered system, you'll maximize this space in your bathroom.

Organizing the Bath and Shower Area

Bathing Beauty says … if you have a large family, you probably have observed that the bathtub and shower get cluttered post haste. Things could stay organized so much easier if everyone used the same shampoos and other products! This may never happen in your family. Still, if you don't take some control over this space, the shower or bathtub will turn into a hazardous area.

Divine Guidance

If bath time for your small children turns into a free-for-all with toys scattered from one end of the bathroom to another, put all the toys in a mesh bag and hang the bag from the bathtub faucet. Items can drip dry while being contained.

Shower Caddies

The people in your household most likely use different items in the shower. So what about giving each person his or her own portable shower caddy? This way three different shampoos and conditioners, two different soaps, and three different types of razors won't be crowding the shower or bathtub. Each person can take his or her caddy in at bath time.

If you have a small family, a small caddy that hangs over the shower head may suffice. These caddies are generally large enough to hold shampoo, conditioner, shaving cream, soap, and a razor.

Vertical Storage Bar

A bathtub-shower combination allows the option of installing a tension-mounted vertical storage bar. These generally have three shelves on which you can store your bathroom necessities and even attach a shower mirror. Having as many shelves as there are bathroom users is ideal. Give the tallest person the tallest shelf and so on, and ensure that all items are placed so they can't fall out when you take a shower.

Soap, razors, loofah sponges, and other lightweight items that might not stay put on a shelf can be placed right in front of you without taking up space beside the tub when you use a bathtub tray that rests on each side of the tub.

Divine Guidance

Many Bible passages address cleaning, as in personal hygiene and processing animals for slaughter. While cleanliness is important, "godliness" is about much more …. In 1 Timothy 2:1–3, Paul says, "I urge, then, first of all, that requests, prayers, intercession, and thanksgiving be made for everyone for kings and all those in authority, that we may live peaceful and quiet lives in all godliness and holiness. This is good, and pleases God our Savior."

Linen Closet Organization Tips

Generally avoid putting anything in your linen closet other than towels, linens, and extra bathroom items. The linen closet has a specific function that doesn't include serving as the household catchall. The linen closet's function is to store your linens and bathroom accessories in an organized manner so that all you need to do is open the door and, behold, everything you need is at your fingertips.

Avoid stowing frequently used items on high shelves. If towels and washcloths will be retrieved from the linen closet every day or every other day, it makes sense to make them accessible to everyone who needs them, including short people and smaller children.

Store all of same size towels together, and instead of folding them and stacking each towel on top of the one other, roll your towels in jellyroll fashion. Folding and stacking towels is slow and takes up too much space. High piles tip over, which leaves you having to refold some of the towels. Rolling your towels is fast, prevents them from tipping over, and actually saves you time and space.

Your linen closet can contain a variety of other things besides towels. Obviously wash clothes go here as well as do actual linens, possibly bed sheets, pillowcases, and anything else that is not easily stored within the bedroom. Ensure that your linen closet is not overflowing with bathroom supplies, rather make it complement the organization management you have applied to the bathroom, simply housing those items for which there is no additional room in the bathroom. Consider the following:

- Some of the larger items that you use in the bathroom such as a hair dryer or other electrical devices that cannot be stored easily in the bathroom logically might find their way to the linen closet.

- Employ small boxes to keep a variety of supplies neatly organized such as extra soap, shampoo, toothpaste, and various personal hygiene items.

- Use the height of shelves to determine what goes where. For example, if you have small children and you want them to be able to reach washclothes these would go on lower shelves.

- Alternatively, if there were items that children should not be touching these would go on the highest shelves.

Some people use the far reaches of the linen closet to store extra supplies and closer to the front of each shelf they stack their towels, wash clothes, bed sheets, or pillow cases. When you open the linen closet, only fabric items appear. It may seem like a small point, put sometimes visually arranging the closet is as helpful as anything you can do to maintain the feeling of being in control.

Organizing the Other Bathroom Items

If you've done your best to organize your bathroom storage space but some essential items still have no home, what can you do with them? Perhaps you have a nearby linen closet. Store the extra items here. The secondary linen closet's function could be to house any essential bathroom items that can't comfortably be contained in your bathroom.

> **Divine Guidance**
>
> The highest shelf of your linen closet is a good place to store extra rolls of toilet paper and tissues, since these are stackable and lightweight.

Since the bathroom-organizing angel is not coming, it's up to you to make sure this happens. Keep extras on a higher shelf since you won't be reaching for those every day.

Place a laundry basket in the bottom of your linen closet. This is a good way to keep dirty clothes where they're supposed to be instead of on the floor. Your family won't have to go far with their dirty clothes when they shower. Thereafter, carry the dirty clothes to the laundry room often. You don't want your clean towels to start smelling like dirty clothes.

Quick-Return Linen Systems

Getting housework done as quickly as possible will free you up to do other things that you enjoy, like work on hobbies or spend more time with your family or friends. To get

> **Divine Guidance**
>
> If you designate the same spot for certain items every time you put them away, finding these items will be easier and putting away clean linens will take less time.

highly organized, initiate a "linen system." Set aside a specific area for each type of item in your linen closet. One shelf could be allotted for sheet sets, one shelf may be for large bath towels, and so on. Avoid placing things "just anywhere."

Put every set of sheets for each bedroom together by room. This is because sheets that lay together should stay together. In addition, keep the pillowcases and flat sheet tucked inside the fitted sheet. Hence, you won't have to hunt for each separate piece—they will all be together. Do this for all your sheets in every room, and you won't have to worry about pulling one sheet from the bottom and having the whole pile fall down around you.

On wash day, strip your bed, wash the sheets, and return them directly to the same bed after drying. Bypass the linen closet altogether. This way, you'll save time by not having to get a clean pair of sheets out of the closet and not having to put the set that you recently washed back into the closet. The set will go straight to the bed.

A Prescription for Your Medicine Chest

The contents of your medicine chest are rather specialized, but a little organization will still be useful. Don't stack things on top of each other. They're going to fall over—and into the sink—as soon as you open the door. Keep similar items together: Store all your bandages together and all your cold medicines together.

Being organized entails having the essentials on hand. Be sure to keep the following handy:

- Pain/fever relievers, like aspirin or acetaminophen (with liquid versions for small children)
- Bandages, gauze, and adhesive tape, ideally in various sizes and widths
- Hydrogen peroxide for treating open wounds
- Antacids for heartburn and stomachaches
- Antidiarrhea medication
- Sodium bicarbonate for soaking and soothing
- Syrup of ipecac to induce vomiting

In addition to storing these items in your medicine chest, it is a good idea to maintain a first-aid kit for emergencies. Make sure you keep it out of the hands of curious youngsters, but do teach your older kids how to appropriately use its contents.

Rx Safety

Most chests contain medicines that can harm any family member, especially children, if taken in improper doses. There are also medicines that can be a year old or much older. This is dangerous because medicines can break down over time into substances that are *completely different* from the original substance.

When it comes to your medicine chest, "When in doubt throw it out." Never take an old prescription that's been lying around. If you have a prescription for a mystery illness you had last winter, chuck the leftover pills. Many people keep medicines on hand for use in a similar illness or in case someone else needs them, but this is a bad idea.

It's risky to take other people's medicines or give your medicine to someone else. The heat and dampness of the bathroom can make medicines age faster. You may want to store medicines someplace else, such as on a high shelf in your kitchen.

Caution Corner

Before you absentmindedly reach for another dose of medicine, consider another sort of prescription. Jeff Levin, research scientist and author of *Religion in Aging and Health*, explains, "Religious involvement deserves to be recognized as one of the most significant factors that promote health and well-being among many groups of people." He adds that published evidence overwhelmingly confirms that our spiritual life influences our health.

When you dispose of medicine, always flush it down the toilet—do not discard in a trash can. A curious child may decide that those pills should be in his mouth instead of in the trash. Also protect your pets. Some medicines may taste sweet to animals, so be cautious of what you throw in the trash can.

Make sure there is a childproof lock on your medicine chest. Children want to check everything out, especially brightly colored pills and liquids. An unfortunate side effect of better tasting liquid medicines is that, these days, kids *want* to take their medicine—more of it than is healthy, that is. Be careful that these medicines are out of the reach of children.

Bathroom Safety in General

By some estimates, more than 150,000 people are treated every year due to bathroom-related injuries. This is not surprising, with all the potential safety hazards in your bathroom, ranging from things like razor blades to wet floors. To safeguard yourself and your family against common accidents, prepare to make some changes in the bathroom.

Nearly everyone has slipped in the bathtub at some time. To prevent this from happening again, install nonslip flooring. If you have a new tub, it probably came with nonslip flooring. If not, you can purchase mats or floor decals to make the bottom of your tub less slippery.

Some people use a towel on the floor beside the shower or bathtub to step onto after they're finished bathing or showering. Instead of using a towel, use a bath mat with nonslip backing. When you step onto it, it doesn't slide out from under you as a towel might.

Any hotel worth its salt has a grab bar on the wall, within easy reach over the bathtub's soap dish, and this is a move worth imitating. Whether or not there is an elderly person in your home, grab bars are beneficial. If no one in your home ever has to use it, consider yourselves blessed.

> **Divine Guidance**
>
> A grab bar inside the tub can be used to help pull yourself up from the bathtub, pull yourself up if you fall, or help you to steady yourself to prevent a fall.

Chapter 7

In the Bedroom

The more elements of life you incorporate into your bedroom, the more disorganized your bedroom will become! You may be among those who use their bedroom as an entertainment center, a study, a storage area, or a dressing room. You may even use your bedroom as an office, especially if you have a small home. Invariably, you will have more things to organize, keep track of, and clean.

If your bedroom is disheveled and in disarray, with clothes lying in every corner and children running in and out like it's a playroom, you may need a complete organization overhaul.

Organizational issues aside, if you use your bedroom as a study or office, you may not be able to relax or sleep because you are constantly exposed to everything you have to do. Yet, this is the room you want and need to relax in.

If some identifiable item causes you worry or stress, remove that item from the bedroom. If something comforts you, leave it in the bedroom. Any way you slice it, protect this sacred turf!

The larger your family is, the greater the chance is that your bedroom is the only room in the house that is uniquely yours.

Shelves, Drawers, and Tables

Unfortunately, sometimes the bedroom is the dumping ground for trinkets in your house. They land in the bedroom because it's the least likely place that guests will see them or children will find them. To score an early organizational win, recognize that most of the trinkets and decorations need to go. Here are some ideas about what to do with those items that make the cut.

Knickknack City

Move all the knickknacks off the dresser so they won't be in your way. If you have decorative items or pictures that you want to display in your bedroom, hang some shelves and then park the items on the shelves. The items won't be in your way and you won't have them cluttering up the top of your dresser or chest of drawers.

Caution Corner

The more you display, the more you dust. Don't overload your shelves with too much.

Books can often be worse offenders than trinkets. If you do most of your reading in your bedroom and you have the space, install one or several bookcases in your bedroom. This will save you some time because all your books will be in one place and you won't have to hunt for them.

Diminish Dresser Drawer Drama

Cleaning out your drawers may seem scary—depending on how long it's been—but you can do it! What's the worst thing you could face in the process? Clothes may be wadded up and mashed in any space possible. If you have to share drawers with your spouse, it's possible that your T-shirts are mixed up with his or her underwear, or vice versa.

Divine Guidance

Decorate your bedroom before the rest of the house, advises Christian decorating expert and author Terry Willits. "It will provide a pleasant place to escape and bring patience to your partnership ...." She adds in an article on Christianity Today.com, "Most rooms in the house can be multipurpose, but not the bedroom. Make it a refuge for rest."

If your drawers are in tip-top shape, you'll save time getting ready and you won't have to rack your brain remembering where your favorite blue shirt is.

To achieve an acceptable level of organization, acquire a box and place in it all the old clothes you don't wear. Then either give these items to someone else or take them to your church to be passed on to the needy. If you find garments that have holes in them, throw them out or use them as dust rags. Whatever you do, remove them from your drawers.

Arrange all your like items together. Put your underwear in one drawer, put shorts or casual clothing in another, and so on. On a similar note, you may have items that you wear more often than others. In this case, keep these items near the top of the drawer so you can quickly grab your favorites.

To store more items in a single dresser drawer, roll your clothes instead of folding them (see the previous chapter for rolling towels). Rolling works best with T-shirts or knit items. Fold the sleeves of your T-shirts in and roll from the bottom. In addition to giving you more space, your knits won't wrinkle as badly. This also works well with bulky sweat suits.

Once you have all of your things sorted and separated, you might want to think about keeping them that way. Try to set aside the chest of drawers for your husband and the dresser for yourself, or vice versa. If this isn't practical for you because one person needs more drawers than the other, or if you have only one piece of furniture, designate specific drawers for each person. Stick to this so your clothes don't get mixed up.

Caution Corner

If you make a habit of piling things on top of others on your dresser, you eventually reach the point at which you can't use all of the mirror.

If you have a chest of drawers or a dresser/mirror combination in your bedroom, clear off the top surfaces. Many times pictures, jewelry, or knickknacks are placed on top of dressers.

Nip Nightstand Nightmares in the Bud

A nightstand is a near necessity in the bedroom. Where else are you going to put personal items that you may need throughout the night? And if you need an alarm clock to wake you in the morning, the nightstand is the most convenient place for it.

Make sure the nightstand beside your bed has at least one drawer. You'll need one drawer to put personal items that you may use in the middle of the night or for items that you don't want other members of your family to see. Drawers are also good hiding places for things you may enjoy before you go to bed, such as books or magazines.

Ideally, your nightstands should be no higher than the top of your bed. This makes it easier if you're trying to find something in the middle of the night while you're lying down. It may even be advantageous to use a nightstand that is a few inches shorter than the top of your mattress.

When You and Your Husband Work Different Hours

Here is the bedroom dilemma of our age: If people living in the same household work different hours, the schedule tends to get turned upside down and everything becomes more complicated, starting in the bedroom. It's difficult finding quality time to spend with your spouse when you both work the same hours, much less when you work different hours.

If you're in bed from 11:00 at night until 7:00 in the morning and your mate doesn't come in until 7:00 in the morning, private time for the two of you becomes an extinct entity. Several things can be done to alleviate the inconvenience of the situation:

- **Use different devices.** Perhaps you wake up at the same time every morning without needing an alarm clock, but your mate needs an earthquake to wake up. In this case, make sure an alarm clock is on his or her nightstand. If you don't need one, avoid cluttering your area. If your husband has the alarm clock on his side, it will be more accessible to him. Also, alarms don't necessarily need to make noise; some flash lights.

- **Shut off the light.** If your mate is a daytime sleeper, black-out shades or drapes are a must. How would you feel if you had to sleep with the sun shining in on you? Black-out shades and drapes may still let the light in around the edges and corners. If this happens, hang a blanket around the window to keep all the light out. That way, your spouse can go straight to bed when he or she comes in. Since you were nice enough to hang the blanket, ask him to remove the blanket after sleeping so you don't have to mess with it when you want to go to bed.

Divine Guidance

Depending on your needs, consider using a battery-powered alarm clock rather than an electric one. In the middle of the night, your alarm clock can fail for a variety of reasons. Small battery-powered timekeepers often run for a year or more before the battery needs replacement. Wake up on time. Don't be late getting the children to school!

That's the Spirit

The Bible reminds men to be respectful of their marriage partners: "Husbands, in the same way be considerate as you live with your wives, and treat them with respect as the weaker partner and as heirs with you of the gracious gift of life, so that nothing will hinder your prayers." (1 Peter 3:7)

- **Leave messages.** Create some type of message system. Leave a pad and pencil on each nightstand with things your mate needs to know. This is a better alternative than waking him or her up. If your mate needs to pick up the kids at school, or if the plumber is coming by at noon, it's better for him to know that before he goes to sleep than to be awakened by the phone or the door bell.

- **Occupy the kids.** If your mate works third shift and sleeps during the day, take the kids on an outing or to visit friends or relatives, or play quiet games with them after school.

When Your Spouse Travels Often

Your family's schedule will be as disrupted when your mate travels as it would if your mate were working different hours. When your mate gets home from a trip, the last thing either of you wants to do is to spend a lot of time unpacking and catching up on messages. Your mate will most likely want to relax and spend time with you and the family.

To shorten the amount of "work" time before and after a trip, set out two sets of key items. Your mate doesn't need two separate wardrobes, but having a few extras set aside for trips will help shorten the packing time so your mate can spend more quality time with you before leaving. Your spouse will also need an extra set of toiletries. If he or she can carry an extra set, these items won't need to be unpacked each time.

Also, try not to change your sleeping habits when your mate travels. Go to bed at the same time you normally would. Don't turn on the television or listen to the radio because the house is so "quiet." For example, if you have become accustomed to listening to the radio at night when you go to sleep, you may have trouble falling asleep without it, which could cause problems upon your mate's return.

Supporting Devices

Some ways of organizing your bedroom do not rely on shelves, drawers, and nightstands to store your "stuff." An integral part of organization involves arranging your bedroom so that it's easy for you to use it. If you have a mate with different views on what such improvements should be, that's fine. A little compromise rarely hurts.

Consider the virtues of installing a folding screen. Large decorative screens can be highly useful while adding a measure of decorative flair to your bedroom. You may use this area behind the screen as a dressing area. Also, you can hang your wardrobe for the next day on the back of the screen where it's hidden but can easily be retrieved.

Caution Corner

One device that you might choose to nix is the electric blanket. Many small appliances in your home produce a low-frequency electromagnetic field a few feet around them. Extended exposure to low-frequency fields has been linked to cancer. To protect yourself, use quilts or blankets instead of an electric blanket.

To maintain greater control of potential sound disturbances, check out the Sound Screen, a portable white-noise device developed by the Marpac Corporation. The Sound Screen emits different frequencies and amplitudes of a droning, nondisruptive blanket of sound (much like that of rushing water, a fan, or a distant motor). You can use this device to minimize the effects of startling or disruptive sounds outside your room.

Sound Screen and Sleep Mate
Marpac Corporation
P.O. Box 3098
Wilmington, NC 28406-0098
1-800-999-6962 (USA and Canada)
910-763-7861 (worldwide)
www.marpac.com

By placing the screen about 10 feet from your head in the direction of any disruptive noise, you can minimize its effects immediately. How important to you is good sleep?

Space-age earplugs called Noise Filters are available from the Aearo Company. They cost little per pair and weigh even less. Noise Filters are used by airline runway traffic crews (employees who guide planes to and from their gates). These plugs are the industrial-strength, heavy-duty variety that renders a near-silent world. Without getting into the specifics, the material in the plugs expands in your outer ear canal, blocking out sound in ways traditional earplugs cannot.

Noise Filter
Aearo Company
5457 West 79th St.
Indianapolis, IN 46268
317-692-6666
317-692-6772 (fax)
www.aearo.com

Closet Sharing, Closet Paring

Deep down, many people dislike sharing a closet with someone else, even if it's their spouse. You may be wondering how to share this area with your mate without fighting over which space belongs to whom. Your mate may be the type that throws clothes down on the floor that pile up until they drift over (or fall over) into your half of the closet. Instead of squabbling over a few feet, compromise and save space when necessary.

Do you have outdated or seldom-worn clothes in your closet? Perhaps you could have a yard sale and try to make some money off your junk. Or give the items to a friend, or to your church, or deliver them to Goodwill.

Also, you could store items that you hold dear in another location. Holding on to a pair of jeans that is two sizes too small is iffy, though. Perhaps, you know you'll get into them again after you lose that weight. Even though you probably don't need to keep them, if you can't bear to throw them away, don't. In situations like this, pack a box and store it somewhere else where conserving space and being organized is not so crucial.

That's the Spirit

All houses or apartments have conventional closets, tiny rooms, or spaces in which we store clothes (mostly) and other items. But we also have spiritual closets into which we sometimes try to segment faith—but not very effectively, according to the website Christianethics.com. "The gospel relates to all creatures and it applies in all situations," Dr. James A. Nash writes for the site. "The gospel ... insists that Christ cannot be compartmentalized, locked in some 'spiritual' closet." Christ is central in individuals' spiritual lives, Nash continues, and calls for proclamation of the good news.

Closet Encounters of the First Kind

A simple way to achieve organization in your closet is to put all your blouses or dress shirts together, hang all your dress pants together, and assemble all your jeans together. If you have similar items hanging near each other, you don't have to hunt for things when you're in a hurry. Do the same for your mate's clothes, and neither of you will have problems finding what you're looking for.

Divine Guidance

To give yourself a full-length view of your ensembles, hang a stylish mirror on your closet door. It will make your bedroom appear larger, and you will have a full-length view of your appearance. Perhaps you'll be able to catch yourself before you walk out of the house wearing one navy sock and one black sock.

If you prefer, you can hang entire outfits together instead of grouping similar items. This suggestion probably works better for men than for women because men generally don't have as many suits or complete outfits. This may end up being more time-consuming for a woman who tends to coordinate a piece from one suit with a piece from another.

If you're blessed with many outfits that you actually wear, consolidate these into summer and winter wardrobes. Then pack the wardrobe that you don't need into a cedar chest or box, and keep it in an area that isn't damp. This will give you lots more room in your closet, and your clothes won't wrinkle as much because they won't be so mashed together. Your mate, who is probably sharing the closet with you, will be grateful.

Common-Sense Solutions for the Clothes Horse

If you must share a closet, an easy way of finding what you're looking for is to put all the clothes on an electric (or manual) carousel, given that your closet is deep enough. When your mate is using the closet, he or she can flip a switch and have all the clothes in front without having to dig for them. Then when you come into the closet, flip the switch again to rotate your clothes in front of you.

For couples who have to share a closet, try using separate closet poles. Closet poles can hold clothes and other accessories and can keep items separated so you're not looking through your mate's side of the closet for a shirt you know you hung up last Thursday.

Box It Up

If you haven't worn something for at least a year, put it in a box so that you can at least free up your dresser drawers and closets. Close the box and label it as you see fit. You might write, "Check again next spring," "Open after I've dropped 10 pounds," or "Examine contents after January 1st." Don't forget to put the current date on the box.

Later, when you review the contents of the clothes you've boxed, you have several options, including these:

1. Reinsert them into your wardrobe lineup, and this time wear the darned things.
2. Continue to keep them boxed, which guarantees that you'll have to go through this process again.
3. Rip them to shreds and use them as rags.
4. Give them away (the preferred option).

The mere act of freeing up the space in your dresser drawers and closets yields a feeling of simplicity and enables you to more easily find and wear current clothing.

That's the Spirit

Doing something for someone else usually feels better than hoarding things you *think* you'll use again. Regular acts of giving will keep you from falling into a rut of selfishness, which the Bible reminds us isn't a good way to go: "Do nothing out of selfish ambition or vain conceit, but in humility consider others better than yourselves." (Philippians 2:3)

Organizing the Accessories

The job of organizing your closet doesn't end when you have organized your clothes. You also keep other items in your closet, including ties, belts, and shoes. One of the easiest ways to simplify your closet is to first get everything off the floor that's currently parked there. Then the question becomes, what do you do with these items?

If you live in an older home with little closet space, you may need more space even after arranging clothes together the way they're easiest for you to find. This is one of those times when it is sensible to make a purchase that supports your quest.

An organizer with wire shelves is best because it allows air to circulate among all your garments. Buy only the smallest one that you need; extra space will give you an excuse to fill up the shelves with junk.

If you don't have space for a folding screen in your room to house your next day's wardrobe, a less expensive alternative is to install a wall hook on the back of the closet door. The outfit will be at your fingertips, to save time if you're in a hurry.

Or instead of throwing your belts on the floor in your closet and stashing your ties in a drawer, screw a few cuphooks into the closet wall. Hang your belts and ties on cuphooks and you won't have to search through the tangled maze to find the right item.

It's a Shoe-In

If the floor of your closet looks like a shrine to Imelda Marcos, do something with the shoes. You can get creative on this one. Old wine racks can be used to hold shoes, for example. Or, you can buy ready-built shoe caddies at most discount stores or simply use a shoe bag.

You can hang the shoe bag on the wall in your closet or on the back of the door. If you choose a shoe bag made of a mesh material, you can see which shoes are in which compartment, and you don't have to bend over to find them.

Visit a store such as Bed, Bath and Beyond, Hold Your Own, or any of the home center stores populating upscale communities, and you'll find a variety of "shoe management" supporting devices. Take measurements of your closets in advance so that you can determine which of these devices might comfortably fit within the space you have.

One of the greatest shoe management techniques of all is giving away those that you don't use. If you own more than 10 pairs of shoes, realistically there are at least two or three pairs that you haven't worn within a year, if not much longer. Some shoes go out of style. Some no longer suit your fancy. Some are stiff or for whatever reason don't fit you as well as they did when you first bought them or during the time you were wearing them frequently.

Undoubtedly you have community groups that would gladly accept donations of shoes, including Goodwill, the Salvation Army, and of course your own church. Be honest with yourself in deciding what shoes you will actually wear, and what shoes can safely be given away. Otherwise, the seldom-worn shoe will populate your closet for the rest of your days. You will feel good about giving away the excess shoes, and if the spirit moves you, have more room available for acquiring new shoes!

Speedy Setups for the Bedroom

Whether you're cleaning your bedroom or getting dressed, you want to be able to do so quickly, especially if you're on your way out the door. If you have everything in your bedroom arranged, the amount of time that you spend on daily activities will decrease, giving you more time for yourself.

Instead of throwing your clothes on the dresser or on the closet floor when they're dirty, put them in their proper place. If an item was worn for only a few hours and can be worn again, hang it back up pronto. It goes without saying, but, hey, to be thorough … to quickly determine whether something can be worn again without washing, smell it. If the shirt is dirty, put it in the dirty clothes hamper. Strongly encourage your mate to do the same thing.

If you have children or guests staying with you, keep an extra hamper or small laundry basket in each bedroom, to encourage others in your family to put their dirty clothes in a hamper instead of on the floor. Have your children take all their clothes to the laundry room on wash day so that you don't have to pick up clothes from each bedroom. Thereafter, if they don't bring something to the laundry room, it doesn't get washed.

To take this technique a step further, use separate hampers for dirty clothes that can be washed and for dirty clothes that have to be dry-cleaned. This way, you won't make a mistake and ruin an item that wasn't supposed to be washed, and you can quickly pick up items that need to go to the cleaners without having to look through a pile of dirty clothes.

Save even more time, and take out tomorrow's clothes tonight. Always get your clothes ready for the next day the night before—you know, like you had to do when you were five. To this day, when you set out your clothes the night before, you gain a great advantage for starting the day.

Divine Guidance

No clothes on the floor is a beautiful thing. The room looks neater, there's nothing to pick up, and there's nothing to trip over. Moreover, you set a nice example for your children.

Chapter 8

The Kids' Rooms

In this chapter, we'll focus on one of your toughest organizing challenges: the kids' rooms. When organizing your own bedroom, you have a broad measure of control over what you do. It is entirely your responsibility, so essentially you can arrange things the best possible way for you.

You may be thinking that although it's your child's room, you should still have control over what goes on, and this is true—to a point. It's a delicate situation! You want your child to realize that this is his room and that he has the responsibility for taking care of it. Yet, your child needs to take responsibility and not do whatever he wants—or even do nothing, if he wants.

The majority of the advice in the rest of this chapter is focused on teaching younger children to grow into dependable older children. The earlier you teach your child responsibility, the better. If you wait until your child is a teenager to start making him accountable for keeping his room in order, you may have waited too long.

It's a Small, Fun World

Children think the world revolves around fun. If only it were true! Put yourself in your child's position. If you were five years old, would dirty dishes bother you? I would guess not. When you instruct your child to do something, explain to them why you want them to do it and why it's important to the family that it gets done. You'll probably get more cooperation this way.

Once your child is old enough to read, you can develop a chore chart that lists all the members of the family and all the days of the week. For each day of the week, write down the chores for which each family is responsible. After the child is finished with the chore and it meets your approval, he can erase that item.

To increase a child's responsibility around the house, let him choose the chores he wants to do. If he would prefer dusting to washing dishes, so be it. He will be more likely to stick with a chore that he would rather do than be forced to do something he hates. In any case, set up a system in which both of you agree ahead of time so that he will know what you expect of him.

Children learn by example. If you or your mate aren't doing your share of the chores around the house, you can't expect your child to do his. Be careful that other siblings are doing their fair share, too. They probably won't be doing the same chores, but an equivalent amount of responsibility based on age is necessary to be fair.

Caution Corner

Aside from the potential conflicts and arguments, your child may not feel that taking care of his room is his responsibility, regardless of whether he actually does the cleaning.

Don't forget to say thank you! This is a tip that many parents take for granted. When your child completes a task, show your appreciation. You don't need to bribe anyone with gifts or candy. Simply say, "Thank you, I appreciate your help." A little recognition will go a long way. Your child will feel that he has done well and will be encouraged to do more in an attempt to please Mom and Dad.

That's the Spirit

Setting a parental example isn't limited to chores, of course. In *Straight Talk to Men*, Dr. James Dobson offers a succinct explanation of what makes a parent successful—and this passage is for women, too. "After all, how else can we get a handle on the ephemeral qualities of character and strength in a man of God?" asks Dobson, well-known founder and leader of the Christian organization Focus on the Family. "It is understood most readily by observing a good *model*."

Tackling the Dresser Drawers

Tips in the previous chapter helped you get your dresser drawers organized. Now it's time to help your child get his dresser drawers organized. Your mission is to encourage your child to take responsibility and make sure that clean clothes are stored in his dresser. Here are some suggestions:

- When you leave it up to your kids to handle their own clothes, they're probably not going to be as neat as you want them to. That's okay! Don't arrange things for them! This convinces your child that "I can't do anything right" or "Mom and Dad are going to do it anyway, so why am I fussing with it?"

- You'd be amazed by how many people take for granted the fact that their children are small! Your small child probably can't reach most of the drawers in a standard-size dresser. Even if he can reach it, he probably is not strong enough to pull it out far enough, reach over, and get what he needs. Use "shorter" furniture and dressers if you expect your small children to pick up after themselves. If they can't reach the drawer, how are they supposed to put things up? Try to see things from your child's perspective.

Divine Guidance

Surely you're not concerned about wrinkles with socks and T-shirts. It will be easier and less frustrating for a kid to place socks together in piles or lay T-shirts in a drawer without folding them perfectly. However, if you want to encourage folding, start your child off with items that are easier to fold, such as shorts or jeans.

- It makes sense to implement a system that your child will be able to understand and maintain. You might put similar clothing items in the same drawers. This will make it easier when you put up the clean clothes and when your kids are old enough to do this for themselves; they will be less confused when determining where to put the items. If your child wants the blue pajamas in the bottom drawer, put all of the pajamas in the bottom drawer.

- Try to arrange your child's clothing in such a way that requires a small amount of folding. Folding clothes is a tedious job for anyone, but especially for a small child. A small child with even the best coordination may have problems folding socks or T-shirts. Then again, why would items like socks or T-shirts need to be folded in the first place?

Keeping a Child's Clothes off the Floor, Bed, Desk, Chair ...

If your child seems to think you're her personal maid service, whatever you're currently doing to persuade your child to pick up isn't working! This underscores the importance of starting young. Don't wait until your daughter is 12 and expect her to automatically start picking up after herself. It's most likely not going to happen.

"Inducing" a Child to Pick Up After Himself

Retire publicly and permanently as maid. If your child knows you're going to pick up the room anyway, there's no motivation for him to take care of it. If a teenager is looking for an outfit to wear to a party and realizes that it hasn't been washed because he left it on the floor, he will be more likely to put the dirty clothes in their proper place.

Whatever you do, treat your young child like a human being who deserves respect. You wouldn't tell an adult roommate to pick up his or her clothes "Because I said so!" You would most likely treat a contemporary with respect, so use the same approach with your child. Quoting the "Honor your father and your mother" commandment is equally uninspiring. Treating children with respect means focusing not on their behavior, but on their hearts, advises John MacArthur. "We cannot merely target behavior, or our parenting will be shallow and superficial, and we will raise our children to be spiritually shallow."

 Divine Guidance

When your child is older, let him listen to his songs (at a reasonable volume) if he wants to while cleaning. He can sing, dance, and even impersonate others. Let your child pretend to be Mom or Dad while cleaning, if it helps.

Make Straightening-Up Time Fun Time

Be creative when convincing your child to pick up after herself. If she thinks it's a bore (which, arguably, it is!), the clothes and toys will most likely stay on the floor, so seek to make it fun. Some parents try scavenger hunts. Hide a prize under something that has to be cleaned up. Picking up will go quickly this way. You must keep the prize well hidden until your child is almost done cleaning, of course, or else it defeats the purpose of the hunt.

Slide a Bit on Standards

Unfortunately, if you have an older child or teenager who is shirking responsibility, you may have to take a firmer position than discussed here. In any event, don't expect your child to do the job of an adult. When your child is doing a chore, don't expect the job to be the same quality as if you were doing it. This is especially true when your child is beginning to help out around the house.

Everyone, whether child or adult, has to learn the best way of doing things. Your child may have done his best, and you should reward him instead of criticizing because it's not up to adult standards.

That's the Spirit

When you participate in activities with your children, you're not just playing—you're coaching. According to the dictionary, a coach "instructs, directs, or prompts." There are no Bible verses for coaching, but there are about 140 verses for teaching: "[Jesus] said to them, 'Therefore every teacher of the law who has been instructed about the kingdom of heaven is like the owner of a house who brings out of his storeroom new treasures as well as old.'" (Matthew 13:52)

The Closet Experience

Your child's closet may be filled with an unorganized pile of toys and clothes. However, are you and the grandparents buying lots of things for your children that they don't necessarily want or need?

If you've retained toys that your eight-year-old played with when he was a baby, ask yourself, "Why are we keeping this?" When you think about all the wasted space and all the junk that is stored in your child's closet, there's no question why there's no room. Remember the principles encountered earlier in this book—pare down!

Closet Organization

From little mouths often springs fashion sense. Even young children know what they want to wear and what they don't like. Instead of buying your child something you know won't be worn, leave it in the store. "Mom, that's the ugliest thing I've ever seen" is a good hint that it won't be worn if you buy it. Not only do you save

 **Divine Guidance**

Once every six months (or more often, if needed) take the extras to Goodwill, hold a yard sale, or pass them on to a friend with a small child.

money, but you save space in the closet. In that sense, closet organization begins with what you *don't* put in the closet.

Beyond limiting new additions, be sure to remove your child's old and outgrown clothes. Your growing child goes through clothes at a rapid pace. Pack up the old in boxes or plastic containers. Put these on a high shelf in your child's closet.

Retain and Contain

Here are tips for storing and organizing what you do keep. Hang your children's shoes in a shoe bag, and hang the bag on the inside of the door at an appropriate height for your child to reach it. The child will be able to see exactly where each pair of shoes is, and the shoes won't be all over the floor. If your child outgrows the shoes, remove the shoes and put them in the same place as outgrown clothes. This will free up some space in the shoe bag for newer shoes.

Consider installing two clothes rods in your child's closet. The first rod should be standard height. The second rod, however, should be considerably lower so that your younger children can pick out their own clothes, with your supervision, and re-hang clean clothes. By hanging two rods, your child can get to her clothes and you double the space for hanging.

Divine Guidance

If you like to participate in sports activities with your child, keep the sports equipment in a central location that is convenient for everyone and easy for you. Store items in crates in a hall closet or possibly in a spare bedroom or laundry room. Make every attempt to ensure that equipment is put back in the proper place after each use.

The Electronic Jungle

Understandably, kids today have access to many more forms of communication than you did at their age. This is good and bad. Computers are wonderful learning tools, and if your child has one, he can be exposed to knowledge at the touch of a key.

However, overuse of a PC or the television can be hard for you to control. If your child has a television and video cassette recorder in her room, it's important that you have the means to keep track of what she's watching when she's in her room alone.

TVs and PCs

Going into your child's room to see what he or she is watching on TV, or visiting on the Internet, may not seem as if it is an organizing technique. Rest assured that organizing your child's viewing and surfing habits are as important as anything you might do in arranging the physical items and furniture within your child's room to ensure his health and well-being.

Parental control comes with most cable systems, but it's up to you to use it. Because a program is rated PG doesn't mean it's suitable for your child to watch. Spend a few minutes watching the start of your children's show. You'll have a sense of the tone and quality of the programming after only one minute.

The same goes for the Internet. If your home has access to the Internet, there are parental controls for your child's PC, but these controls can be circumvented. Your child can probably figure out how to bypass many of these controls in less than 30 minutes. Internet providers urge parents not to depend on parental controls. For example, America Online says, "It's important to note that no system of controls makes up for good old-fashioned parental supervision." Nonetheless, install the most secure filter to block pornography, gambling, and other objectionable content from their view. There's no substitution for you going into your child's room to see what he is up to.

Divine Guidance

As a parent, you want the best for your kids. Electronic equipment, including video games, walkmans, and stereos, are nice gifts, but insist that your kids spend some part of their day with you! If possible, try eating your evening meal together so that you can see your children and actually spend quality time with them. Talk is cheap. (This means no Walkman and no television—for you, too!)

Sound Off

If you can hear your kid's stereo two blocks away, it's past the time to turn down the volume. When children are home alone, they tend to turn up the volume to dangerous levels. If the stereo is too loud, the child is risking hearing loss, not to mention bothering the neighbors.

Don't take the walkman for granted, either. It actually can be worse than the stereo. With walkmans, the sound is being projected directly into the child's ears and can cause permanent damage more quickly than a loud stereo. If you've talked to your child about the dangers of hearing loss and they still resist, perhaps the only thing you can do is confiscate the stereo or walkman.

While on the topic of electronic gismos and gadgets, help your child organize the various tapes, CD's, cartridges, discs, and other "software" items that may be strewn about the bedroom. Stores such as Radio Shack, Best Buy, and home center outlets offer a variety of shelves, casings, and containers that will neatly house and keep organized a variety of tapes, discs, and other software that your child may currently be haphazardly distributing throughout the room.

Dolls, Toys, Sports Equipment, and Other Stuff

From the looks of your kids' rooms, Santa Claus has been good to your children over the years. There are tons of toys on the floor as well as throughout the house. You probably ask yourself, "Does my daughter need 15 Barbies?" and "Where did all these toy trucks come from?"

Sometimes it seems impossible to keep your children's toys in order. Do your children appreciate and take care of all the toys they have? Where do you keep them? And what do you do with all the old toys?

That's the Spirit

Unlike any toy or gift you buy, your love is everlasting. Sure, a little gift might show your child that you were thinking of her while you were apart. But so would some makeup time after your return. By telling your child what you saw and did on your trip, you can help her use her imagination to go there. "This is how we know that we love the children of God: by loving God and carrying out his commands." (1 John 5:2)

Regardless of whether you or the proud grandparents are doing the buying, your child doesn't need a new toy every time someone goes to the store or every time someone returns from a trip. Sometimes it seems that children come to expect gifts and don't appreciate them when they receive them. They may love a toy for a few days and then decide it's no fun anymore. If you give a gift after every trip, watch out. Less expense and less clutter yield less to do. Let being a great parent or grand-parent be your "gift" in itself.

Toy Story

If little Jake's room looks like the toy section in a major department store, it's probably time to clear some things out. Even the most motivated of children can't play with everything all the time. If your child has outgrown older items or doesn't play with some toys anymore, pass these toys down to someone who wants them. Make sure you let your child help pick out what goes and what stays.

Rotate toys if your child has many toys. Remove some of the items for several weeks or months; when you reintroduce them, remove other toys. Your child will look forward to playing with items that haven't been around for a while.

Toy Storing

Remember, your little one is … little! If there are tall shelves in his room, the child may not be able to reach what he wants to play with, which means you'll have to get it for him. Plastic storage containers are good for storing toys; they are durable and can hold virtually anything. Also, your child can see through the plastic and find exactly what he's looking for without having to dig through boxes of toys.

Or, try color coding, a popular method for keeping items straight in children's rooms. You can let your child know where to put his toys by color coding each item. You can purchase small, colored stickers to put on toys and buy plastic storage containers of different colors.

Caution Corner

The more toys a child has to deal with, the harder it is to decide what to play with, which is true for anyone! Worse, it's more difficult to induce your children to put their toys away when finished play-ing with them.

When a child sees a blue sticker on an item, the child knows that this item goes in the blue storage container. If you have more than one child sharing the room, color coding helps keep each child's toys separate and may cut down on the arguments.

Don Aslett, in *Make Your House Do the Housework*, presents a novel idea of what to do with all the sports equipment that may be lying around your child's room. "Mount their balls and bats and gloves right on the wall.

When not in use, they'll provide decoration your kids will love and that you won't have to dust or worry about. This way, the kids always know where the equipment belongs and might even put it back."

To save time picking up and cleaning up after your children, keep a toy box or large plastic container in various rooms in your home. Having different items in different rooms will keep your children happy because they will always have something to play with—and you won't have to run all over the house putting things back in their right spots.

Divine Guidance

Keep a few small items in your car so that your child will have something to occupy his time when you're driving. This will cut down on your child acting up out of boredom and will reduce incessant questioning about when you're going to "be there." By making these items toys for the car and not for use in the house, your child will look forward to playing with them and you will get some peace and quiet when you're driving.

Keeping your child's room and possessions organized is among your toughest household challenge, but with early training and a little ingenuity, the task is manageable!

Part 3

In and Around Your Home

In this part, the largest of the book, we explore other rooms inside your home, as well as vital spaces adjacent to it and outside. Beginning with the laundry room and moving on to the den, basement, garage, and other areas within the house, we offer a variety of ideas for effective organization and storage of your possessions. This part also includes recommendations for staying organized when guests arrive, when entertaining, when giving gifts, and even when managing a pet. Finally, since you're likely always on the go, we offer key tips for keeping your car organized.

Laundry Room Management

Sorting laundry—does it ever end? As soon as you get everything washed, it's all dirty again. It's bad enough with one person, but if you have a large family, you can get bogged down in the amount of laundry you have to do every week. Yet, there's no reason to get down in the dumps over your laundry chore. Don't get flustered, get organized. Enlist help from the family members. With a little bit of aid from this chapter, sorting laundry will be a piece of cake!

Everyone's Job

Give everyone in your home a hamper, clothes basket, or laundry bag of their own. Your children can keep a hamper in their room or closet, and you and your mate can do the same. Dirty clothes are more likely to end up where they're supposed to be if there's a convenient place, other than the floor, to put the clothes.

With the help of hampers, have your children sort their own laundry. You have enough to do without taking time out of your busy day for things that others are capable of doing. You may need to double-check the first few times, though, to make sure they didn't put any items in the wrong pile. If one of your daughter's favorite "dry-clean only" outfits is ruined from an accidental machine washing, she will probably be more careful the next time she separates clothes. You may lose money on a ruined outfit in the beginning, but the time you save by not double-checking everyone's laundry will be more than worth it in the long run. After that, they're on their own.

> **Divine Guidance**
>
> Place a box of baking soda in each hamper to absorb moisture and keep the smell down if it will be a few days before you wash. Arm and Hammer seems to have a lock on this product.

Persuade everyone in your family to check their pockets before sorting their laundry. This will prevent ink from leaking on the clothes and tissue pieces from being distributed all over everything. Also have them remove shoulder pads, turn down cuffs, and button all buttons. If these things are done, folding will be easier.

Add checking zippers to your pre-laundry routine. Open zippers, flung about at high speeds during the wash and spin cycles, can tear other clothes. Instruct your crew to close the zippers on their garments so that the zippers won't tear other garments.

Laundry Room Logic

After you and your children have separated your laundry, here's an easy way to stay organized and keep track of everything: Have separate hampers for white clothes, colored clothes, towels, and other clothing in the laundry room. Each person can place all his or her laundry in the appropriate hamper. This will cut your time dramatically when you're ready to start your washing.

You may have certain days set aside for doing laundry. However, if you're like most people, you do the washing when you have time or when something is dirty and you want to wear it the next day. If you're in the latter category, bypass the idea of a hamper for everyone and instruct family members to put their dirty laundry in the installed (family) hampers every day. Everything will be waiting for you on whichever day you decide to wash.

Designate a hamper or laundry bag for fabrics that can only be dry-cleaned. Keep this in your laundry room in an area where it won't be confused with machine-washable clothes. Granted, it won't be as convenient having to walk to the laundry room to drop off garments, but it will be less of a hassle for you when it's time to take them to the dry cleaners. Everything will be in one spot, ready to go.

Use a similar rationale for washing bed linens. It may be easier to wash all the sheets at once instead of washing a certain set one week and a different set the next. Chances are, they're all dirty anyway, especially in the summer. By washing everything at once, you won't forget which sets you've washed and which sets you haven't.

That's the Spirit

Where does Christianity fit in the laundry room? Ask Steven Curtis Chapman. A noted Christian singer, Chapman built a studio above his garage and called it "The Laundry Room." "That's part of what I think is unique about [the *Declaration* CD] musically—I had the freedom to try different things where normally in a regular studio situation I might feel pressured by time," he said in an interview with ChristianityToday.com. "With this home studio … If we got a wild idea, I felt free to just try it … to experiment. Because of that, creatively speaking, this record goes a little deeper for me." So don't leave God out of the laundry room!

Simple Solutions

There's no point in washing clothes any more than you have to. If you set aside one day of the week to wash your family's clothes, you'll be sure to have full loads and you won't waste time and water during the week washing half-loads of clothes. If you do one fewer load of clothes per week, you will save money on your electricity and prevent unnecessary wear and tear on your washer and dryer.

To accomplish your goal of doing less laundry, you might …

- Buy an item that is similar to your favorite, perhaps in a different color that will still go with the same clothes as the first one. You will have an extra and you won't have to wash it as often.

- Have enough towels and wash clothes for each member of your family to last a week. Also have a week's supply of socks and underwear for each family member.

- Buy common everyday items (like children's tees) in large quantities.

These suggestions might seem like they will make for more laundry—actually, you might have an additional load to do, but it will save time in everybody's day.

Here are some more solutions for simplifying your laundry days:

- Keep enough laundry detergent on hand. Detergent also is now available in premeasured packets; you simply open a packet and don't have to measure detergent. There's also less mess because less detergent is being spilled. Even older children can handle the detergent if you teach them how to do the laundry properly.

- Keep a trash can in your laundry room; it will be one of the handiest things you'll have. Whether you're disposing of lint, used dryer sheets, or empty detergent boxes, you'll find it much more convenient to have a can there instead of having to travel to another room to dispose of trash.

Caution Corner

Sometimes premeasured packets of laundry detergent can be more expensive. If you have hard water, you'll need more detergent than these packets provide. Keep an eye on this.

- Keep an ample supply of clothes hangers in the laundry room. There will always be a few items that you will hang instead of folding. Each member of the family can have his or her own hook, for simplicity's sake.

- Dress pants and jeans can be hung up and placed on hangers attached to the wall in the laundry room. If you have the space for a drying rack, then by all means install one for clothes you'd prefer not to put in the dryer.

Wash Your Clothes the "Right" Way!

Overloading is bad for many reasons. Your clothes can't circulate as well, which decreases cleaning. Decreased cleaning leads to washing extra loads, and this puts unnecessary stress on your washing machine. Your washer could break down, and then you're out a lot more money than it would have cost you to simply wash an extra load.

Fabric softeners are important because they reduce static and make your clothes softer. "Which are better, liquid or sheets?" Some say that dryer sheets work better because liquid softeners are diluted with water. This may be true, but there doesn't seem to be any firm evidence. Use the product that is more economical and convenient for you (or the one you think smells the best).

Bleach with the best of them. At some point in your life, you've probably ruined something by bleaching it incorrectly. Don't feel bad—most people have made the same mistake. The problem may have been the wrong type of bleach. Chlorine bleaches will destroy—or, at the least, spot—your colored clothing items. If you feel it necessary to bleach colored fabrics, use an oxygen-based bleach. These are safer for colors but aren't as effective in removing stains.

What should you do if you accidentally have a shirt that bleeds in your load or if you accidentally wash something in the wrong temperature and the colors fade or bleed? Try the new "no bleed" balls that are now for sale and use them in "all temperature" detergent. This doesn't work in every situation, but most of the time the results are acceptable.

That's the Spirit

Other people have wronged you—it's true for nearly everyone—and most likely you've wronged others, possibly without you even realizing it. The stain of unforgiveness remains. Unlike laundry, you can't just bleach out those inside stains. But God's detergent is guaranteed: "For if you forgive men when they sin against you, your heavenly Father will also forgive you. But if you do not forgive men their sins, your Father will not forgive your sins." (Matthew 6:14–15)

Choose to be delicate when washing. Hand washing is a good alternative to machine washing because it provides little agitation to damage delicate fabrics. However, when you do hand wash an item, gently move the fabric through the water so that the detergent can be dispersed well throughout the garment. Use a detergent that is made for delicate fabrics. Stronger detergents can fade or damage fragile clothing.

Leave large items to the Laundromat. Larger items such as comforters, quilts, and sleeping bags should be washed in large-capacity washers available at Laundromats. Standard-sized washing machines were not made for these products, and you will increase the chance of damaging your washing machine by continuously washing large items.

Some stores carry mesh bags in which you can put "delicates" (bras and panties). The hooks in bras won't snag on things. Other items in your wash, like buttons, won't ruin these delicates, which can represent the most expensive items in your wardrobe. The mesh lets the detergent and water through easily.

No Fold, No Guilt, No Problem

If you spend a large amount of time during your week folding clothes and want a way out of this predicament, pay attention! While this may go against everything you were ever taught, you don't need to fold all the clothing items in your home.

If you're going to wear certain clothes while lounging around the house (or working in the house), or if your kids are going to wear them while playing, who cares if there are some wrinkles? It's not necessary to fold them. Just put them in the drawer. The same goes for your children's clothes.

You also may be wasting your time folding household items from the wash. For instance, when you strip the linens off the beds in your home, wash the sheets and put them back on the bed immediately after drying. You have to deal with only one set of sheets, and since they're going back on the bed, you won't have to fold them. A similar principle applies with towels. Instead of folding towels after washing, hang them back up on the towel rack.

> **Divine Guidance**
> Everyday T-shirts and shorts can be placed in the drawer without folding, as can socks and underwear.

> **Divine Guidance**
> The rolling technique for shirts (the jellyroll) is to fold the arms in and roll from the bottom. Roll pants and shorts from cuff to waistband.

For clothes that do need folding, here's a suggestion that may work better for a larger or "busy" family. Whoever takes the clothes out of the dryer folds all the items and leaves them stacked by the dryer for the owner to pick up and put up. As long as the items were taken out of the dryer soon and folded, the wrinkling should be minimized. Alternatively, especially if you have older children or teenagers, you might instruct each person to take his clothes out of the dryer, fold them, and return them to the proper drawers or closets.

If you're fortunate to have space in the laundry room, install a small folding table so you can fold your clothes in the laundry room immediately after they come out of the dryer. Leave the folded clothes stored on the table so family members can come by and pick them up. You can place your hampers underneath the folding table to maximize the space in a small laundry room, or add a pull-out ironing board.

You can also minimize wrinkling by rolling clothes in the shape of a jellyroll instead of folding them before you put them away. This tip works best for knits and delicate fabrics.

Drying Tips to Protect Your Clothes

Years ago, people had no choice but to hang soaking wet clothes out to dry in the sun, if the sun happened to be shining at all. Today, many people still line-dry clothes, but most dry their clothes in an automatic dryer. Although line-drying is cheaper, you have to consider the amount of time you spend hanging clothes out and bringing dry clothes in. Also, clothes tend to be softer and more comfortable when dried in an automatic dryer.

In case you haven't noticed, there's probably more than one setting on your dryer. You can save time, save money on your electric bill, and decrease wrinkling by drying your clothes on the correct setting. Check your owner's manual for appropriate heat suggestions.

For example, permanent-press fabrics and delicate fabrics shouldn't be exposed to high heat.

When you remove items from your washing machine, shake them before you put them in the dryer. This may seem trivial, but it makes sense in many ways. Shaking untangles clothing and decreases drying time. It also protects clothing because a shirt that is tangled around a pant leg can become damaged or, at the least, highly wrinkled during the drying process.

Make haste once the clothes are dried. Taking clothes out of the dryer quickly has many benefits. First, the quicker you take items out of the dryer, the less wrinkling you'll have to deal with. Next, you won't put it off and risk forgetting about the clothes until you're getting dressed and need the, by now, very wrinkled item, which you don't have time to iron because you're late for work.

Also consider using clotheslines here and employ your kids. Kids get a kick out of helping to hang up things to dry outside if it's a warm summer day (and your home-owners association doesn't have a problem with it).

Take a big hint for small loads. Have you ever noticed that sometimes it takes longer to dry small loads than large ones? If you have small loads to dry, put a few pillow cases or a towel in with your clothes. With a few extra items in the dryer, drying time actually decreases and you save money. This is because small loads by themselves don't tumble as well as large loads, which can increase drying time and wrinkling.

Lay down the line on lint. Make sure you or someone in your family clears the filter after each load of clothes is dried. A clean lint filter helps air circulate more efficiently, so drying time is decreased. This saves you money and valuable time.

> **Divine Guidance**
>
> Cleaning the lint out of your dryer filter also puts less stress on the dryer, which may lead to a longer life for your dryer.

Old Machinery for New

When you consider that an average washing machine uses 15,597 gallons of water per year (Maytag's estimate), it's amazing that you don't have to replace washing machines more often. Washing machines and dryers are two of the most convenient appliances in your home.

Although washers and dryers are convenient and have long lives, there are ways of decreasing the everyday wear and tear on these appliances. The most common problem that shortens the life of the washer and dryer is loading with too many clothes. If you've overloaded too many times and are in the market for a new washer or dryer in the future, here are some things to consider:

> **Divine Guidance**
>
> Although front-loading washing machines originally cost more, sometimes they can end up saving you money in the long run in water and detergent, and get your clothes cleaner. Also, the more items you push into them, the better the clothes get cleaned (thus, fewer loads).

- A basic washer and dryer is all you need to clean and dry your clothes. The only options you need on washers are water-level selectors, temperature selectors, and normal, gentle, or permanent press cycle selectors. All you need on dryers are gentle, permanent press, and normal timers. Most of these options are standard on washers and dryers. More alternatives cost extra money and are more expensive to fix when they break down.

- Measure twice, buy once. This is more important if you live in an apartment and are unsure of the power connection and voltage. Most washers and dryers, whether separate or stackable, are 27 inches wide. So measure the area before you buy! Also, most units operate on 120 volts, but some need 220 volts. Verify your power source before you make an expensive purchase.

- If someone in your family is getting new appliances, perhaps you can get a good deal "borrowing" or purchasing a washer or dryer inexpensively. Granted, you won't have any type of warranty or guarantee, but paying next to nothing for a washer or dryer that's in reasonably good shape will more than offset the cost of small repairs.

- Install your dryer on a foot-high platform. This prevents you from having to bend over as far when putting clothes in the dryer and taking them out of the dryer. Make sure the platform is made out of some type of material other than wood. Wood is a fire hazard and shouldn't be used to house a dryer. A high-density plastic works better.

- When installing your new or used dryer, use the straightest and shortest line of venting duct possible. Straighter lines won't clog with lint as often and cut down on the fire hazard. Inspect the outside vent to make sure no small critters have crawled in and made themselves at home (yes, this has actually happened!).

With a little forethought and a little planning, using your washer and dryer to optimal effect can be a relative breeze.

Considering the bigger picture of laundry room management, the larger your family, the more time you spend traipsing in and out of the laundry room. Mastering the basics as addressed here will help you to stay organized and give you more time to tend to other things!

The Din In Your Den

If your home is large enough to have a den, well then, you're faced with another room to keep organized! In this chapter, we'll cover the basics of staying in control of your den, managing a home entertainment center, setting up a den office, and more.

For many families, the den provides a more comfortable environment than the traditional living room. Because this area is generally for family relaxation, it tends to become a popular dumping ground for things that are used and then not put back in their proper place. Therefore, your den can get disorganized quickly. You may find yourself cleaning and searching for lost items more often than necessary.

Den Basics

You may want to put a few pictures of your family in your den or keep your child's soccer trophy in there. Nothing says "I belong here" better than tangible evidence. Pictures convey pride and can help promote closeness in the family. Nevertheless, avoid leaving things lying around your living area that don't belong there. Get all your family members involved in this.

Don't let kids leave their toys or homework lying around when other places are designated for these things. If you have children, keep a basket or chest in your den to hold board games, toys, or other items that occupy a kid's interest. This way, you won't be carrying toys all over the house if and when your kids don't pick up after themselves. Also, if someone "drops in," you have a place to stash things so your den isn't cluttered.

> **Caution Corner**
>
> If tots have the habit of sticking gum, candy, or stickers on your wood furniture, there is an easy remedy (short of banning the children from stepping into the room again). Use a small amount of lemon oil to soften the gum or glue before rubbing it with a soft nylon sponge. Don't let the lemon oil stay on the wood for too long because it may damage the finish. Also, always scrub in the direction of the wood grain.

Publications Overflowing

If you have too many magazines in your house, start discarding a few, or even pitch the magazine rack. Magazine racks can proliferate unless you take steps to clear them out as you go. Unfortunately, many people don't do this. Old issues pile up. This means when you get around to cleaning, you've got a lot of outdated material issue to deal with.

If you've already looked through a magazine and found nothing of interest, dispose of it. Either throw it away, put it with the recyclables, or give it to a friend. If you stick to this habit, you won't have to go through stacks of magazines to figure out why you kept them and whether you still need them.

If you find an article in a magazine that you want to keep, one option is to cut it out and dispose of the rest of the magazine. If it's a recipe, put it in your recipe file or cookbook; if it's an article for your child, give it to your child.

> **That's the Spirit**
>
> As you look through your piles of magazines and files of clippings, do you find much of it related to your faith? If you believe that you need to get closer to God, check your local Christian bookstore to find what type of magazines or books will help you reach that end. Dr. Larry Crabb, founder of the Institute of Biblical Counseling and author of *Finding God*, states, "To find God, we have to make changes in how we live so we can seek him without thinking of what return that effort will bring."

Keep your articles in an organized folder in a desk drawer—that is, allocate them all to their end destination as soon as you comfortably can. This is a simple way to avoid a buildup of publications and clippings. If you clip many articles, go through your file once a month and discard articles that are no longer relevant.

When Collections Become Clutter

If you're collecting issues of a certain magazine, keep these issues where they will be safe. You may want to store them in a fireproof box in the closet or elsewhere in your home. Keeping them in the magazine rack only clutters your living room, and you risk the chance of damaging the magazines.

If you're drowning in clutter, check with your local library to see if they carry the magazines to which you subscribe. If so, cancel some of your common subscriptions. Plan an outing or reading day for you and your kids to go to the library to read magazines or books. This will be fun and will help you win back your living room or den.

Some of the items in your magazine rack are bound to be catalogs. To prevent these from being sent, call the vendor's customer service department (most have toll-free numbers) and have your name removed from the mailing list.

Your Entertainment Center

Your entertainment center probably has a variety of electronic equipment. In a typical home today, a television, DVD unit, cable or satellite box, stereo, and video games can all be stored together in one place. Some entertainment centers have enough shelves to hold each piece of equipment, while others come up short. Some also have small cabinets where you can store a few of your video cassette tapes or a video cassette recorder.

Although you may be short on room, don't pile things on top of each other. Electronic equipment often is not designed to have heavy items stacked on top of it. You may be able to get away with putting the cable box or DVD on top of the television, but limit your stacking to that.

By the way, it is okay to use the top of the entertainment center to display pictures of your family or friends.

Caution Corner

Electronic equipment builds up heat and needs enough space around it for the heat to dissipate. You can install a small organizer unit available in office supply stores, which enables you to place electronic equipment in cubbyholes and thus stack up more items without having them literally on top of the equipment.

Since your entertainment center is already "weighted down" with electronics, a few decorative items will suffice. Don't overcrowd the top of your entertainment center, though. Overcrowding increases the time it takes for you to dust.

Remote Control

Have you ever spent five minutes looking for the remote control instead of walking to the television to turn it on? Some people think there's a remote fairy that steals it while they're sleeping and stuffs it in between the sofa cushions. Rescue the remote from your ravenous couch. If you have three or four remotes in your den—one for the television, another for the CD player, another to operate the VCR, and so on— keep them together. They can be stored on a coffee table, entertainment center, end table, or wherever it's most convenient.

Divine Guidance

Consider getting a universal remote that takes the place of all of your others. It takes a while to learn, but the convenience of having all the controls in one device makes it all worthwhile. One innovative guy took a block of wood and used Velcro to keep each remote on one side of the block. Homemade, but effective for keeping them together.

Store Extra Tapes or Discs Elsewhere

Most of the shows people tape never get watched again! Even if this is only partially true, it's unlikely that you watch all your recordings often. Therefore, there is little need to store all your tapes or discs and shelves in your entertainment center. This makes your den look crowded and only gives you more things to keep labeled, organized, and dusted.

Store your tapes in a closet or in another area of the house. Try not to fall into the trap of buying a cabinet to hold all your tapes. This takes up more space in your living area and may not hold enough tapes anyway. Use the replacement principle discussed in Part 1 to keep your video or DVD collection to a manageable minimum.

Label Your Copies

This leads us to the obvious but often overlooked necessity of labeling television shows or movies that you've recorded. Having to look through 20 or more tapes to find where you put last Sunday's episode of *60 Minutes* is no picnic and can be quite frustrating.

In large families, it's sometimes a good idea to designate one or two tapes to each person with that person's name on the label. Then each person knows what's on his or her tape (or at least has the responsibility to know) and won't confuse it with another person's tape.

Maybe all your tapes and materials are spiritual, and you can divvy them up among family members. If they're not, you can still use those mainstream videos for Christian purposes.

That's the Spirit

InterVarsity Christian Fellowship reported on its website (www.ivcf.org) a fresh trend of using secular videos for ministry. Schools such as the University of Nevada–Las Vegas use the videos to explain spiritual matters. Steve Martin's movie *The Man with Two Brains*, for instance, was used to show how we ask God for something, but don't always listen for his answer. After his girlfriend dies, Martin's character asks her for a sign about their relationship. Suddenly, her picture spins as the wind blows and then everything stops. "Really, I'm just looking for some kind of sign," Martin says.

Window Treatments

Along the walls of your den or living room (or other rooms of your house), you likely have curtains and window coverings. These items are often designed for style and ease of hanging (engineered organization!). Many different types of window treatments on the market are designed to span the distance between causal and elegant.

Divine Guidance

Even if you don't have a den area, you easily can create the illusion of more space by using windows and window treatments or clever decorations.

To furnish a room, buy what appeals to you and looks good in your home. You can't go wrong with curtains, but there are other simple, decorative options:

- Valences can be used alone, with curtains, or to accent shades or blinds. These popular window dressings combine versatility with affordability. Also, it's easy enough to replace valences whenever the mood suits you.

- Are you tired of dusting miniblinds every other week and having the strings break when raising and lowering the blinds? Shades are a simple alternative. Shades are making a comeback in some circles, and for good reason: They keep the light out in varying degrees. You get to choose from little coverage to total blackout. Aside from the good ol' white plastic stand-bys, solid and printed decorative fabric shades are available in hundreds of patterns and designs. These shades are easy to hang, and most can be dry-cleaned.

- It used to be that when you bought curtains, hanging them was a major pain. New designs, such as the tabbed curtains, are now available. The tab slips over the curtain rod, and that's it. Your curtains are up in a flash. This is much easier than hanging traditional curtains, attempting to gauge the distance between clips so your curtains hang correctly.

- Salt your droopy sheers. If you've hung sheers underneath your curtains, don't go out and buy new ones as the old ones lose their shape. There's a relatively simple way to renew your old ones. The famed household advisor Heloise suggests literally salting your drapes. "After washing them, dip the sheers in a sink full of warm water in which you've dissolved a cup of Epson salts. Hang them on the shower-curtain rod to dry." After this, iron your sheers and hang them back up. They will have a firmer drape and look like new.

This list of window treatment is by no means exhaustive, but it will give you a good idea of the variety of options available. Perhaps you can donate whatever you discard to a charitable or service organization.

The Den Office

Some people use all or part of the den in their home as an office. If that includes you, you may be pleased to know that from an organizing standpoint, this arrangement has many advantages (and a few disadvantages).

That's the Spirit

What does your den office say about you? What about your faith? And does it inspire you and keep that faith in focus? Kathleen Hawkins, author of *Spirit Incorporated*, suggests developing a support system—which could include your office. "Build a library of inspirational books … listen to motivational tapes." The goal is to have spiritual growth resources handy so you'll use them more often.

Here is a list of the advantages of the den office:

- Proximity to the rest of the house
- Heating, cooling, and ventilation control
- Proximity to bathroom
- Proximity to front entrance

Here is a list of the disadvantages of the den office:

- May not offer desired level of privacy
- May not be soundproof
- May be too small or may lack sufficient storage space
- May lack desired electrical outlets

Even in a custom-designed home-based office, you need to control communications with the outside world. The telephone, fax, and e-mail create an enormous number of interruptions, perhaps as you would experience in a commercial office. A den office in a home with a mate or children may not give you the privacy and quiet that you need to do your best work. If this is the case, many ways are available to sound-proof and cordon off your office space.

Room dividers and sound barriers are available in a wide variety of shapes and sizes. Placed in front of your desk or outside the door to your office, they can improve on any existing sound barriers.

Divine Guidance

You'll know you have achieved the right balance when you can make or receive a phone call at any time without fear of distraction or disruption.

One work-at-home graphic artist turns on a small fan next to her office door. The gentle, rhythmic white noise of the fan's motor serves as a sound buffer, absorbing most of the sounds her husband makes in the rest of the apartment. Some people prefer soft classical music or non-intrusive Muzak-type backgrounds to serve as a buffer to other distracting sounds. Various white-noise and sound-dampening gadgets are also available (see Chapter 7 on bedroom sound screens). They mask sounds (such as noisy kids) and quickly pay for themselves.

An Organized Approach to the Phone

When using the phone, it makes sense to take an organized approach. Have you ever called someone and had to wait while he paused to get a pen or some paper? How could anyone proceed in this world without having a pen and paper by every phone in their house? If others in *your household* remove the pen or use up the supply of paper, consider attaching the pen on a wire or string. You can always tie a knot and secure the wire or string on the underside of the table using a thumbtack. Do this with the den phone as well as the other phones in your home.

Got Phone Books?

Not having a phone book nearby is also frustrating. Your phone company supplies you with the number of phone books equal to the number of phone lines in your household. In some areas, you may request additional phone books for no extra charge or for a nominal fee.

Get phone books of surrounding locales as well. If you live on the border of a phone exchange, it makes sense to get phone books for adjacent areas that may require you to dial a 1 or an area code if you frequently call to those areas. It can be cumbersome to have to rely on directory assistance and, in some areas, can be quite costly, not to mention time-consuming and downright aggravating.

Caution Corner

You don't have to go right to the White Pages or Yellow Pages when you need some help or service. Don't forget that Christian businesses and enterprises share your goals and beliefs. Those businesses aren't always easy to locate, but some areas have publishers that print such directories, as do churches. You can also go online to sites such as Christianusa.net, which lists businesses that identify themselves as Christian.

A Pad for Phone Messages

The least expensive notepaper of all comes from using recycled sheets. Suppose you have an 8.5 × 11–inch piece of paper that was used on one side and has one blank side ready for reuse. Using scissors or the straight edge of a ruler, reduce that piece of paper to six fairly equal smaller pieces of paper that serve as your makeshift notepad. Cut or tear the paper down the middle. Divide each half into thirds, and you've got six pieces.

Thereafter, when taking messages for others, decide in advance where you'll pass such messages so that everyone knows and agrees on where to retrieve them.

The Care and Feeding of Your Personal Computer

A personal computer, if you have one, is one of the most expensive items in your home. If you have a den, chances are that you keep it there. What happens when the computer malfunctions? Are you equipped to work without it? Do you have the money to replace a computer in the event of an accident? Computers don't require a lot of upkeep, and working in a clean, food-free environment is a good way to avoid an expensive repair bill for something that could have been prevented.

You never know when a natural or man-made disaster is going to destroy your computer or the information in it. To prevent losing all the precious information your business depends on, make tape backups of your information frequently. If you're not sure how to make a backup of your computer system, contact the manufacturer of your computer software or the manufacturer of your computer. Keep backup tapes in a fireproof cabinet, your car trunk, or some other secure place for safekeeping. Also, further protect your PC investment by investing in a good power surge protector. Not all surge protectors are made the same way, so ask around before you buy and always compare prices.

Treat your disks gingerly. Avoid leaving computer discs in direct sunlight or near direct heat. Disks are fragile and accidentally leaving one in your car on a hot summer's day can destroy all the information on it.

Purchase a picture-perfect monitor. If you'll be spending a lot of time at your computer, it pays to purchase a larger screen than most standard computer systems come equipped with. Buy a color monitor with a nonglare screen and low electromagnetic wave emissions. This will help your eyesight and prevent you from becoming fatigued after a few hours at the computer.

Cut down on background noise. In addition to extraneous noise in your home, office equipment gives off a fair amount of noise that can be distracting while you're trying to work. If you prefer not to listen to music when you work, consider placing a heat-resistant pad underneath the equipment to cut down on the noise and vibrations.

Eat at the table, not the computer. If you spend most of your time at your computer, chances are you've snacked while entering data. Perhaps you keep a cup of coffee beside the computer throughout the day. If you spill something on your computer, it is unsafe and the amount of money to replace damaged computer parts may be excessive. In a widely reported incident, a coffee spill onto a mainframe computer cost the *Los Angeles Times* $37,000 in repairs and considerable downtime!

All About Breaks

You know what they say about all work and no play! You'll be tired and stressed out, and start making careless mistakes in your work if you don't take a break. Get up and move around every once in a while. Go do some errands or pick up the kids. Take a productive break where you can get more than one thing done while resting your mind from the work piling up on your desk.

Consolidate your activities. When running errands, combine what you do so the amount of time you spend away from work decreases. When you pick up your dry cleaning, pick up a prescription from the druggist if you know you'll be needing it in a few days. You're already away from work and by getting this taken care of now, you won't waste more time or gas in the next few days.

Hire help for running errands. When you're busy running a business, it's difficult to handle personal and family errands. Check with your local high school guidance counselor or job placement center to hire a teenager to run errands such as dropping off and picking up dry cleaning. You'll be amazed at the amount of work you can get done while others handle errands for you.

Make the business a family affair. If you have a teenager who has his license, put him to work running errands for you. This will save time and money (since you probably won't pay your child as much as you would pay a stranger!). This is also a good way to monitor how much money your child is making and spending on a weekly basis.

Take a lunch break. You're allowed a lunch break like everyone else. Even if you don't leave home, move to another room, turn on the answering machine and take some time for yourself.

Take advantage of delivery services. If your budget allows, use delivery dry-cleaning services, grocers, and of course, lunch delivery from restaurants you enjoy. The cost may seem steep at first, but when you consider the time you spend away from your office, the gas you use in your car to make the trips, and the vital calls you miss, it may be well worth the price.

Down to the Basement

If you live in a newer home, you may have a full basement that provides a complete lower level. Conversely, an older house may have a smaller area or little more than a crawl space. This chapter examines some easy organization and storage possibilities for your basement, as well as some helpful hints on what goes into remodeling and finishing your basement.

On the downside, a basement that's in bad condition can give the homeowner or buyer serious problems. If you're in the market for a new home with a basement, carefully examine the basement for evidence of moisture problems or existing water damage. If you find a home you like, have a professional (of your choosing) check it out so you don't buy your way into a problem of someone else's doing.

Should It Stay or Should It Go?

If you're not otherwise using your basement, it could be the perfect place for storing the things you don't have room for upstairs. In fact, the reason many people purchase homes with basements is for extra storage space. It's a good idea to keep all your basement items organized so you can find what you need as desired.

As you would for other areas of your home, go through everything in your basement once or twice a year to see if there are old things you can throw out, sell, or give to other people. There's no need to keep something if you're not going to use it.

How much junk is in the basement that has not been used in a long time? Cleaning up the basement, like the attic or any part of the house, might seem like a pointless task—or, at least, one without gain. At best, the place looks like it did when you moved in. The bad news, fellows, is that men are usually the culprits behind basement accumulations, according to Jim Killam, journalism professor at Northern Illinois University. "I've determined this is a process most men go through: We grow up, we get married and we gradually begin stocking our basements with miscellaneous bits and pieces of every house we've ever lived in." He added a laundry list of items stored in his basement, including random screws, useless lumber scraps, rubber gaskets, and leftover wire.

> **Caution Corner**
>
> There's no point in letting things pile up year after year. When you finally do get around to cleaning the basement, it will take a considerable amount of time and be much more difficult than if you had gone through things a few times each year.

Many of the following recommendations are predicated on your having a *dry* basement. Organize these items room by room so that all kitchen items are together, all bathroom items are together, and so on. For example:

- If you catch some good bulk-shopping deals on toilet paper, cereal, or other non-perishable items, keep the extras downstairs in a clean, dry area of the basement.

- Basements are generally cooler in temperature (unless directly heated), which makes them ideal for keeping your canned goods or perishable items like fruits and vegetables. Make sure the basement has good air circulation, and check frequently for spoilage so your basement—and subsequently, the whole house—doesn't start smelling like rotten tomatoes.

- Perhaps your kitchen freezer is overflowing. In this case, consider putting another freezer in your basement. This is a good tip for people who buy meat in bulk. The basement is generally cooler than the upstairs, so if the power goes off, there is less chance of food spoilage.

> **Caution Corner**
>
> Make sure there are no moisture problems in your basement before putting a freezer down there. To be on the safe side, put your freezer on a platform so there won't be an electrical hazard if pipes burst or the basement floods.

- If you have old furniture that's in good condition, cover the items with plastic and store them downstairs. Be sure to keep them stored in an area that isn't damp.

After you've organized and stored extra items in your basement, make a location list and hang it on the back of the basement door. This list will tell you where you've stored all the extras. You can make the list detailed in the form of a grid or map so that others can find what you've stored. If it's only you, jot down the general location so you can find the extra dishes three years from now when you're looking for them.

Storage Options

To keep your basement storage organized, you will need to add some shelves (yes, shelves help in virtually every room) or storage containers. If you pile everything on the floor, there soon will be no floor space, and if pipes burst or the basement floods, most of what is kept on the floor will be ruined. You can hang shelves or buy ready-made accessories at discount retailers. Keep in mind that these usually have to be assembled, so it may be easier and less expensive to hang shelves yourself.

If you have a relative who owes you a favor and has experience with woodworking, try to get him to build you a storage cabinet. There's a good chance that it will be more durable than one you have to put together from a retailer or home improvement store.

When you or your mate is hanging shelves, hang them on a stud that is an accessible height for the person who will be using them the most. This benefits tall people also. Instead of having to reach for an item, they can see over the contents, which makes it easier to spot the item that is stuck in the back.

Instead of using cardboard boxes to store items, use plastic crates and containers. Plastic crates come in the see-through variety and are more durable. You don't have to open anything to see what's in the crate, and they are extremely difficult to break. If you already have many empty cardboard boxes, go ahead and use them, but label everything that goes into the box so you don't have to search when you're looking for something.

Caution Corner

Plastic is better because termites, if they are prevalent in your area, love cardboard boxes and can work right through cracks in your basement or garage.

Whether there's one person or many in your family, finding things in the basement will be easier by color coding plastic containers or crates for each person. All individual items that are kept in the basement can be easily identified by putting them in the appropriately colored containers. Assign a color to each child, and stay with it.

Converting Your Basement into Something Else

Some people use their basement as their children's play area. This can be a good idea for many reasons. The upstairs won't get as cluttered with toys and books. This means you won't spend as much time picking up after the kids. Also, with the play area being downstairs, the mess will be hidden from neighbors and other guests, so if the kids don't pick up their toys, you don't have to worry about your house looking messy. After all, this is your children's area. If they don't mind the mess, you shouldn't.

Since your children won't be children forever, the basement can be easily switched to a family recreation room as they get older. Some people put in a pool table, entertainment center, or other items that are used for hobbies. This way, you and your mate can enjoy the basement as much as your children did when they were young.

That's the Spirit

A little library, a small spot to pray and listen for God's voice, might be the best use of all for the extra basement space. Hobbies are nice, of course, but faith lasts more than a lifetime. Such a space requires little decoration, too. The point of being there is to focus on the silence, waiting to learn God's will. Psalm 42:1–2 expresses the need to get away and be with God: "As the deer pants for streams of water, so I long for you, O God. I thirst for God, the living God. When can I come and stand before him?"

If you are considering converting your basement into a place to enjoy your hobbies, here are some great suggestions:

- **Dream shop.** Perhaps you are considering adding a workshop or woodworking haven to your basement. This can be a great idea, as long as you keep a couple things in mind: First, make sure all the power tools have double insulation or grounded plugs. (This also goes for small appliances you may have stored in your basement.) Second, consider installing additional ventilation so your basement doesn't become a greasy or dusty mess.

Caution Corner

Keep all power tools and hobby equipment locked up when you're not using them. This will keep them away from children and also out of sight of potential burglars, who may look through basement windows to check out the loot.

- **Shutterbug.** Amateur photographers (and professionals, for that matter) need a dark room for developing photographs. Your basement may be a good place for this because it's cool and dark. Also, since the basement is more private, there is less chance that someone will walk in on you while you're developing pictures and subsequently ruin them.

- **Laundry revisited.** You might even put a laundry room in your basement (see Chapter 9). If you put your washer and dryer downstairs, this frees upstairs space for a large closet or perhaps a second bathroom. When you decide to turn your basement into a laundry room, put your washer and dryer on an elevated riser so they will be protected in case your pipes burst or the basement floods. Keep in mind that having a laundry room downstairs isn't as convenient because you have to run up and down the stairs constantly.

- **Book worm.** If there are no moisture problems in your basement, consider turning it into a small library or study. This is especially cozy if there's a fireplace in your basement. You can escape the television and other distractions and retreat into a book, with less chance for interruptions. You can also have bookcases built into the walls or buy ready-made bookcases for convenience.

- **Fire bug.** If you have a fireplace upstairs, there's a good chance that one can be installed downstairs. If you already have a fireplace downstairs and seldom use it, *Interior Remodeling* magazine suggests that you have it cleaned and checked every year, as you would with the upstairs fireplace. Creosote can build up and create a substantial fire hazard. In addition, if it's been a long time since you've used your basement fireplace, have a professional check it before you use it.

If you have toddlers, consider installing gates and putting childproof locks on your basement door. Locks are available that mount high where your children can't reach them. This will prevent your child from opening the basement door and falling down the steps. You may also want to install gates in the basement to keep children out of certain areas.

Unsacred Burial Grounds

If your basement is turning into a dumping ground for items that you have no other place for, you may be creating a safety hazard right under you and your family. Strong solvents and cleaners are sometimes kept in the basement in close contact with combustible materials. Not only is this a fire hazard, but if the solvent containers aren't tightly secured, fumes can seep into your upstairs living area. Be careful when storing items in your basement. If you consider the product a hazard in another area in your home, it's most likely a hazard in your basement as well.

Most homes have flammable liquids (gasoline, paint thinner, and so on) stored in the basement or garage. Although neither place is favorable, it's better to keep them in the garage because these products are fire hazards and should not be kept directly in your house. If you have no choice but to keep them in the basement, keep flammables away from heat sources. Never store gasoline in the house because the fumes can escape, and your house can literally explode if there is a spark and the fume concentration is high enough.

If you've ever seen the basement of a pack rat, you have probably seen stacks of newspapers and magazines in cardboard boxes. These products, in addition to old wooden furniture, are combustible and present a fire hazard if a small fire ever starts in the basement. Once these items ignite, the fire will spread quickly, and there may be little you can do other than get out.

Caution Corner

Paint-stained or oil-stained rags are a fire hazard if left unattended. Either store these items in metal containers or, better yet, get rid of them. Keep the containers away from heat sources. If possible, keep containers outside or in an outbuilding.

Whatever purpose you decide to put your basement to, consider your cleaning options. Carrying around a vacuum cleaner and cleaning supplies is aggravating for the one doing the cleaning. To alleviate the cleaning problem in your new den, install a small closet where you can keep extra cleaning supplies and an extra vacuum cleaner. You will save time, and your back will thank you for not having to carry a vacuum cleaner up and down steps.

That's the Spirit

The sermon illustration is often used of Jesus as a house cleaner. You invite him into your living room to take over, and pretty soon he wants to take over the kitchen and even the attic—places where your little sins and weaknesses are hidden. As your Savior and Lord, let him in! In Revelation 3:20, Jesus says, "Here I stand at the door and knock. If you hear me calling and open the door, I will come in, and we will share a meal as friends."

To Remodel or Not to Remodel? That Is the Question

Finishing or remodeling the basement is a goal of many homeowners. There are important aspects to consider, however, before spending any money on remodeling. Think of the practicalities of remodeling your basement.

Often people get excited with the prospect, remodel the basement, and then seldom spend any time in their new room. The amount of expense you incur should be directly proportional to the amount of time you'll spend in your newly finished basement. If you're not going to spend a lot of time down there, don't spend a lot of money.

Space limitations are usually the first problem that homeowners run into when remodeling. Building codes require about 7.5 feet of headroom, but check your local building codes before you do anything! Set up a budget before you get started, and then stick to it. Here are some things to consider before you begin remodeling:

- **Lighting and ventilation.** Are there adequate light sources in the basement without having to rewire the basement for electricity? Is there a window for light and ventilation? Ventilation is important when remodeling, especially if electrical equipment or musical instruments will be kept in the basement. You may want an outside entrance if you're planning to start a small business out of your basement.

- **Noise busters.** Excessive sound or echoes in the basement may put a halt to your remodeling. Installing carpet and office petitions will absorb some of the sound. Suspended ceilings may also help curb noise. Unless you live in an ultrabusy household, these tips should take care of any excessive noise from upstairs.

Divine Guidance

Make sure the heating system you choose is efficient, so you won't be throwing away money when you pay your electric bill each month.

- **Heating and air conditioning.** If you're remodeling the basement to be used for a family room or office where you and your family will be spending a lot of time, you will need an adequate heating and air conditioning system. There is a good chance that the heating system you have will be sufficient for heating your basement. If not, you may have to run ducts to each room that will be heated.

Dealing with Damp Basements

If there are structural problems or, more common, water damage in your basement, you'll spend a chunk of change unless you catch the problem when it first starts. Moisture damage is the biggest problem with basements, especially in older homes. The National Association of Home Builders estimates that 95 percent of wet basements can be dried up inexpensively. Especially if you're going to resell, your home will lose value if moisture problems haven't been taken care of.

Troubleshooting 101

To determine the source of any dampness in your basement, hang a mirror on a wall as you normally would. Check it the next morning. If the mirror is moist or fogged over, your problem is condensation, and this can be remedied with a dehumidifier. If the mirror is dry and the wall is damp, the problem is seepage, so you're back to looking for cracks. Also, be sure to close and securely latch all windows.

When the roof sheathing in your attic gets frosted over in the winter or it mildews, the cause is probably dampness in your basement. A vapor barrier under the attic insulation will help reduce frost, although it won't eliminate the moisture problem in the basement. Check to see if the ground around your home slopes away from the house; surface water during a rain or snow melt will likely accumulate around the foundation. If you continue to have a moisture problem, coat the interior portions of the foundation wall with a cement-based sealer, such as Thoroseal.

Rising damp lines (dark, wavy lines on the concrete walls above your basement floor) are due to the capillary action of moisture rising up from below. The lines are a cause for concern only if you seek to cover the walls. If your basement is relatively dry, some basic maintenance will ensure that it stays that way. Keep your outside gutters clean so that they don't overflow, and ensure that down spouts lead a good distance away from the house or empty into dry wells.

Hungry Pests

Termites and carpenter ants can wreak havoc on your basement as well as other areas in your house. Termites eat the wood, while carpenter ants tunnel into wood and make their nests. Small piles of sawdust will tip you off that carpenter ants are present. Blowing insecticide dust or boric acid into the nest will help, but may not be enough. You will most likely need to consult an exterminator.

Cockroaches can usually be handled by installing "roach hotels," commercially available products that safely lure and then poison the roaches. Obviously, you want to eliminate tempting roaches with food, crumbs, and the various glues associated with bag and box assembly.

Rats will love to make your warm, damp basement their home, so set rat traps or have an exterminator take care of that problem as well.

Caution Corner

Insects, vermin—throw in a plague or two, and you have some serious signs of the world ending. It's unlikely that such an event will originate in your basement, but you have to take steps to remove the little troublemakers. The fable—not much more than that—says that St. Patrick drove the snakes from Ireland. A few prayers on your part wouldn't hurt, but in the long run, someone is going to have to give the pests a decent Christian burial.

Musty Smells, or Worse ...

If you don't have a moisture problem in your basement, you may still have a musty smell if the basement isn't used often or if there's a ventilation problem. One of the easiest ways to get rid of this odor is to put activated charcoal in basement areas. If the odor persists, there is probably a larger moisture problem that should be taken care of by the previously mentioned tips or by a professional.

If there is a sewage smell in your basement, check for backed-up sewage. If this isn't the problem, check the plumbing fixtures or unused toilets or sinks in your basement. If they haven't been used in a while, the water usually in the trap (which provides a barrier to sewer gas) has probably evaporated. The problem can be alleviated by pouring water down the drain to fill the trap.

You may have radon gas from the ground seeping through cracks in your basement. Radon gas is colorless and odorless, and according to the Environmental Protection Agency (EPA), radon exposure may be responsible for as many as 100 lung cancer deaths per day. Testing kits are available at nominal prices at home improvement stores. If it turns out that you do have radon gas, get a contractor to seal all the cracks and waterproof your basement.

Other Storage Areas

If you don't have a full or partial basement, but have a tiny cellar, big enough, perhaps, to only accommodate one person in it at a time, organization techniques in this space will also serve you well.

- Ensure that the small cellar is easily accessible, whether from inside your home or from an exterior entrance.

- Install a light nearby. If not feasible, use a dependable flashlight or suitable substitute.

- Don't keep anything on the steps, as these are invitations to having someone trip and fall.

- If floor space is limited use the walls to secure supplies, tools, and whatever you may choose to keep.

- Keep the area clean, as such cellars often accumulate dust and dirt in a hurry.

Freestanding storage units of varying sizes are available from hardware and home center stores at a surprisingly affordable price. Storage units may come preassembled or in modular form that you can assemble on your own. Most often they are not heated. However, they enable you to maintain a fine level of organization because you can store things in them that otherwise clutter your garage or other attached storage areas to your home.

As with the small cellar, or garage for that matter, keep the storage area clean, use wall space to maximum advantage, and allow yourself the ability to easily maneuver within the storage unit. You don't want to be bumping into things or falling over things.

Keep the center of the storage unit clear and arrange your possessions to wrap around the facility in a U-type configuration. As such, you'll have access to everything and won't have to reach over something to get to something else.

If you have a barn or facility for animals such as horses, goats, pigs, or chickens, you know that cleanliness is the watchword. Your best configuration for organization usually is to maintain at least a clear center aisle with equipment or animals, if that be the case, berthed to the left and right. Never store anything where an animal can run into it, and knock it over, or otherwise be injured by it.

Don't fall into the trap that too many people fall into who happen to have cellars, storage units, barns, or other storage facilities in and around their homes. They load them up with too many items. It starts off harmless enough, and for the first few months or even years everything seems fine.

Lo and behold, you take a look at these facilities and they are jam-packed with stuff. They haven't been cleaned in the longest time and they represent hazards to those who dare to venture in. Some of these storage areas are firetraps containing flammable materials. Others represent accidents waiting to happen, such as in the case where tools with sharp points might injure unsuspecting patrons. Better to be safe than sorry. Take control of these spaces now before anyone gets hurt. In such cases, a little organization goes a long, long way!

Chapter 12

Pet Management 101

Scientists are finding proof of what was once only suspected: that contact with animals has specific and measurable beneficial effects on both body and mind. According to an article in *Newsweek*, "The mere presence of animals can increase a sick person's chances of survival and has been shown to lower heart rate, calm disturbed children, and get incommunicative people to initiate conversation."

The article reports that the exact mechanisms by which animals exert their effects upon health and well-being are still largely mysterious. The mounting evidence that pets do make a difference has spawned a variety of organizations eager to further research and create service programs involving animals.

Why do animals exert effects upon the health and well-being of humans? Nobody knows! Scientists now suspect that animal companionship is beneficial because, unlike human interaction, it is uncomplicated! Unlike humans, pets are nonjudgmental, accepting, and attentive; they don't talk back, criticize, or give orders. They give people something to be responsible for and offer a viable outlet for physical contact. But animals also have a unique capacity to draw people out.

"Buy Me" "... No, Me"

Nearly three out of five households in America have at least one dog, not to mention a possible second dog and other pets. Nevertheless, having a dog may serve many purposes—safety and security, companionship, and even less stress.

Picking the ideal puppy or kitty is fun, but don't be taken in by those big droopy eyes and wagging tail. Before you shop, decide what type of dog or cat you want—not necessarily what *breed*, but rather, what *type of personality*. A fun-loving, hyper dog is best for outside, whereas a fat, declawed cat should be kept indoors.

Paul Donovan, veterinarian and director of Alburtis Animal Hospital in Alburtis, Pennsylvania, recommends a belly test when picking a pet. "Pick a dog who appears healthy, roll him over on his back, and hold him there. If he's a submissive dog, you should be able to hold him in that position without much struggle. A dog who's aggressive will probably fight to get out of that position."

> ### That's the Spirit
>
> If you have a well-behaved pet, you may see some of the Christian virtues mirrored that you need to possess: faithfulness, obedience, humility, peace, and courage, to name a few. The fruit of the Spirit demands more of us humans in Galatians 5:22–23: "love, joy, peace, patience, kindness, goodness, faithfulness, gentleness, and self-control."

You may have your heart set on a certain breed of dog when you're looking for a new pet. That's fine, but be aware that certain breeds are prone to specific health problems. This means you may spend a large amount of money on veterinary bills in the future. Before getting a new pet, call your local humane society to get specific information on breeds you might be interested in.

Unless you absolutely must have a specific breed of dog, save yourself a lot of expense and buy a pound mutt. When your pet is from a pound, not only are you getting a new friend, but you're possibly saving a life. Mutts (mixed-breed dogs) are less likely to have health problems, although large dogs are prone to hip and joint problems.

Canine Training

You may prefer to let your dog be who he is and not worry about training. ("I've got to be me ....") This is fine if your dog is well behaved to begin with. However, if you have a wild mutt who thinks everyone who comes in your yard should be jumped on and slobbered over, a little training may be in order. Many professional agencies will train your dog for you, but if you find that impersonal or expensive, there are a few things you can do to calm a wild dog.

Be predictable with your training. Consistency is the key to training your pooch. Using commands consistently can keep your dog from getting confused. It's also important to stay on a training schedule. For example, if you work with your pet every day and then skip a week, don't expect the pet to readily remember or pick up new concepts.

Ply Them with Milkbones

Bribery works as well with dogs as it does with some people. Your dog won't be easily trained if he's not having any fun. Many dog trainers keep treats on hand, such as dog biscuits and snacks, while teaching dogs new tricks.

Most likely, your dog won't understand what you're saying to him. He will, however, understand your tone of voice. The tone of your voice is important when training your dog. When your dog does something good, encourage and reward him with a nicer, softer voice. When he does something bad, scold with a lower-pitched, louder voice. Your dog will learn to differentiate between the two, which will make training easier.

Divine Guidance

For all the joy a new pet can bring into a home, it can also bring some stress. Once again, look upon the stressful moments as opportunities to pray and get closer to God. Call it spiritual self-improvement. It's similar to having patience with a toddler. Eventually your dog will grow up and treat your home right. But in the meantime ....

"Accident" Avoidance

When it comes to dogs, housebreaking is easy. It's difficult for the dog who simply wants to go to the bathroom, and it's difficult for you when you have to clean up accidents on your new carpet. The easiest way to solve this problem is to put the animal on a schedule. Take him out after he wakes up from a nap, after he eats, or anytime he's too quiet or starts sniffing around excessively. When outside, talk to the pet only after he goes to the bathroom. Then praise him in a high-pitched voice.

Every once in a while, your pet will have an accident on the floor. Whether it is on purpose or by accident, it's important that you clean the spot immediately to prevent permanent stains. For carpets, mix a paste of laundry detergent and work into the stain. Blot dry and flush with water. Dry and vacuum the area.

Canine Mental and Physical Health

Be on guard to alleviate your dog's stress. Certain breeds of dogs are sensitive to loud noises such as sirens, thunder, and even loud yells. Helping your dog break his fear of loud noises should be done gradually.

Veterinarian Linda King suggests a process called desensitization. "A pet is introduced to a low-volume recording of the fear-inducing sound and rewarded for relaxed behavior with praise and treats. The noise is gradually increased until the pet shows no signs of fear even at loud levels. If a pet does show signs of fright, it's not rewarded by treats or attention, as this encourages fearful behavior."

> **Divine Guidance**
>
> If you can't take your pet for a walk, at least engage in some play activity. Throw a ball or Frisbee up and down the steps, or play another game in which your pet can get some exercise.

Exercise is good for your body as well as your pet's body. Most pets need to be walked or played with at least once a day. Larger animals need more exercise, whereas smaller pets don't need as much. Generally, if a dog doesn't calm down right after going for its daily walk, he hasn't walked long enough.

Shoo Flea, Don't Bother Me

Fleas are a big problem for pets and, by association, pet owners. Fleas put undue stress on your animal and invade your home. The best advice for getting rid of fleas comes from your veterinarian. He knows your pet's history and can determine the best medicine for him. Never give your pet pills or spray anything on him unless you know it's safe for your pet. Over-the-counter store items can be dangerous to an animal with allergies.

In the overall battle against fleas, getting fleas literally off your pet's body isn't the only problem you face. You also have to get rid of the fleas around the pet's bedding and inside the house (if it's an inside pet). This is no easy job. Sprays and powders don't work well because most of the fleas "flee" the area while it's being treated and then return when the potency diminishes. You'll need to thoroughly bomb the inside of your home while your pet is being treated at the same time so that the pet won't bring in new fleas to infest the house.

Fleas prefer humid areas, so if there are areas of thick grass around your home, or if trash or wood is stacked, these areas probably harbor fleas. Clean out any junk piles and keep the yard cut as close to the ground as possible.

Bright sunlight kills fleas, so keep your yard mowed, especially around shaded areas. Some sprays on the market are environmentally friendly, and you may consider purchasing one of these products for your yard.

> **Divine Guidance**
>
> Sacrifice is the offering or giving something of value. No, not the biblical sacrifice on an altar, but the more contemporary version. When men and women make sacrifices, we do it out of love. We do it for each other, and we do it for pets. Putting up with fleas because you have a pet is a sacrifice. Hopefully, the return in the form of the pet's love and affection and the joy it brings to a household will be worth the sacrifice you make for it. It's another opportunity to behave in a godly way.

Puppies Galore

Owning a pet is a major responsibility. Usually you acquire pets when they are small. In the case of dogs, training your puppy early means that you have a grown, trained dog later.

When it comes to pet toys, keep all of your puppy's toys in one area within one room. Put them in a basket or box so the puppy always knows exactly where they are. Keep the number of actual toys to some sane, manageable level. Chances are your puppy will be pulling out toys and playing with them all over the room or house, so the fewer you have to begin with, the fewer you will have to put back. If you buy too many toys, most puppies will be resistant to you taking any of them away. The trick is to stay in control from the outset!

While some dog owners maintain that you can train your dog to pick up after himself, for most dog owners that an iffy proposition at best. Better to organize your home around the fact that your dog is going to remain a dog for the rest of his life.

Chances are the puppy will gnaw at the basket or box, so get a plastic one. The puppy may leave little plastic scraps around, but that is preferable to having the puppy gnaw at wood, or worse, try to gnaw at some metal. Always keep the basket in one special room, hopefully a room that is bereft of other possessions.

Dogs love to chew! For some reason known only to shoe manufacturers, dogs love to chew on shoes ... especially high heels or flip-flops. If you wish to keep your shoe collection intact, either mount them higher up than your dog can reach, cordon off your shoe closet, or keep your bedroom door perpetually closed. Otherwise, you can expect that one or more pairs of your shoes are going to get the "treatment."

Organizing Dog Food Purchase and Storage

Dogs don't tire of the same food over and over, unless they have been spoiled by getting table scraps from your meals. If your dog still thinks that dog food is the cat's pajamas, buy in bulk. A 50-pound bag is not too big, presuming that you can maneuver it.

- Store your food in a new, clean trashcan or large plastic container that seals tightly. This will keep odor down, and mice, ants, and bugs out of it. Such a container will keep the food fresher and dryer longer.

- Leave a cup equal to your dog's typical serving in the container so that meal-time is a breeze. You merely have to scoop out a cup's worth and that is dinner!

You can store the dog food container in your pantry or in a closet if the odor is not offensive. Pantries that have a completely close-able door are preferable. Otherwise, you run the risk of having your dog mull around inside the pantry where trouble is predictable.

If space is a problem in storing the dog food, or if there are odor issues, perhaps you can store it in the laundry room or utility room away from the kitchen. Keep the area in and around the canister clean. Use disinfectant on a periodic basis.

Love your dog, feed your dog, and stay organized.

Cat Crazy

Cats are much more independent and, in many cases, more self-sufficient than dogs. If you're a cat person, you know that despite the ease of care, there are also problems when sharing your life and home with a cat. Cats love to scratch. They'll scratch you, the furniture, and whatever else is convenient. There's also a litter box to deal with. That thing will start to reek if it's not handled promptly. Despite the problems, if you can stay in control, cats make good pets.

Scratch Management

Your cat will undoubtedly prefer to scratch your furniture or drapes instead of a toy or scratching post you buy for him. Aside from keeping cats out of the house or room, the most effective way of training them is the same as training dogs—positive reinforcement. Talk to Tabby with a stern voice when he's scratching something he's not supposed to; praise him in a soothing voice and pet him when he's in the right place.

One option for controlling cat scratching is declawing. This should be done only after a careful consultation with a vet because it limits much of a cat's behavior. Careful trimming is also an option, but most cats don't allow people to mess with their paws.

Caution Corner

When your cats get into a "catfight," it's usually over territory or a mate. The easiest way to stop a fight is to douse both participants with water.

A product called Soft Paws offers small pieces of rubberized plastic that fit over the claws on each toe. This prevents scratching from damaging furniture and carpet. Consult your vet to see if this product is right for your pet.

Cats absolutely hate getting wet. One way to curb unwanted behavior is to keep a filled water gun to squirt at the cat when he's scratching or otherwise doing something he's not supposed to do.

Feline Grooming and Health

Being the groomers that they are, cats tend to get hairballs, especially when they're shedding. The best protection against hairballs is constant grooming by you. Brush your cat at least once a day to remove loose hair. Glycerine-based products on the market are formulated to lubricate hair so that it passes through the digestive tract if your cat is still having a problem.

Cats are susceptible to urinary tract infections and disorders, many of which are due to an increased amount of magnesium in the diet. Urinary tract problems can be serious health problems: If left untreated, your cat may die. Fish is the culprit in some of these cases. Seafood-type cat foods are also problematic. Try to get your cat to eat other types of cat foods, possibly the ones on the market that are specially formulated for urinary tract health.

> **Divine Guidance**
>
> Since treating animals humanely is a godly way to behave, you should consider spaying or neutering pets. Unless you plan to breed whatever pet or pets you own, there's little reason to not spay or neuter a dog or cat. Such a procedure helps both the pet and the animal population, and it is supported by the SPCA and several humane societies. Need more proof? The SPCA explains that in six years, one unspayed female dog, her offspring, and their puppies—if none get spayed or neutered—can produce up to 67,000 dogs. In the same six years, one unspayed female cat, her kittens, and their kittens can add up to 73,000 cats. Suppose they were all in your backyard ....

Lost and Found

Pet owners routinely form strong attachments with the pets, especially the larger mammals, so for many people, losing a pet is no small issue. It's easier to recover a lost animal who's licensed and wearing a tag—but a second tag with your name and phone number can help even more.

Pets are licensed in many parts of the country, but the nametag is an equally good idea for them. Other ideas for permanent ID include microchips that contain the licensee or animal owner's address, phone number, and other useful information. The devices, which cost about $50 (and are merely the size of a grain of rice), are implanted under the skin in the scruff of the neck and read by scanners that are often standard equipment in animal shelters and veterinary hospitals.

> **Divine Guidance**
>
> One option for pet identification is to tattoo your Social Security number or other identification number on the pet's inner right thigh. It costs about $25 and is not painful!

The American Kennel Club's Companion Animal Recovery maintains nationwide records of registered animals with microchips or tattoos. If the animal is found and identified, the owner is contacted. You can enroll by calling 1-800-252-7894 for a one-time nominal fee per animal. Assistance dogs, such as Seeing Eye dogs, are eligible for free lifetime enrollment. The American Kennel Club's website, www.akc.org/car.htm, helps all members list lost pets—even pets without identification.

The American Pet Registry searches local agencies as well as a large database to help find members' lost pets. The Pet Registry also provides an owner's kit with posters and other finding aids. The annual fee is about $25 for the first pet and only $1 for each additional pet. For more information, call toll-free 1-888-APR-FIND.

You can also list your dog or other pet with the National Dog Registry (it graciously lists pets other than dogs). The Dog Registry refers members to local authorized tattoo services. A one-time $38 registration fee also covers an owner's subsequent pets. For more information, call toll-free 1-800-NDR-DOGS.

Chapter 13

House Guests

It's one thing to stay organized when the number of people under your roof stays constant; it's quite another thing when kids, guests, or other strangers come and go. Routines are disrupted and contingencies are invoked. In this chapter, we'll take a wide-ranging look at such topics as dealing with "weekend children," accommodating house guests, organizing a guest bedroom and guest bathroom, and more.

Organizing Your "Weekend Children"

Suppose you see your kids only on the weekends—you know how precious this time together is. A custody agreement is difficult for all parties involved, especially the children. If your part of the agreement is having the children on the weekends, you may have problems adjusting to caring for them on your own. From major things like keeping your home allergen-free, to the little things like what kind of snacks they like, organizing your weekend children can be a difficult job.

Safe Home and Safe Kids

It is important that you make your home safe for your children. I'll give only some quick tips here since we've covered much of it before: Tie up loose phone cords, put plastic covers in sockets, and keep household chemicals out of reach. Leave everything like this throughout the week so that you don't have to worry about it Friday evening before you pick them up.

No one wants to think that an emergency may happen to a child. Unfortunately, accidents occur and it's important to be prepared. Do you know what your children are allergic to? Do you know the name of the pediatrician? What's the insurance policy number? Do you know the number for the poison control center? Always keep a list of emergency numbers nearby.

> ### That's the Spirit
>
> Weekends are short, and sometimes church and faith are put aside. But they shouldn't be. John MacArthur reminds parents of their spiritual jobs. "You have a better opportunity than anyone else to help frame what they know about Christ," MacArthur writes in *What the Bible Says About Parenting*. "Every moment of their lives is a teaching opportunity ...."

Their Home Away from Home

If your child enjoys certain snacks or chips, keep these on hand. Make a habit of purchasing your child's favorite snack foods when you go on your weekly grocery shopping trip. This will make it easier on you so you don't spend your weekend at convenience stores picking up soda because you bought the wrong kind or don't keep soda in the house for just you.

Make things easy for your children by buying some extra clothes, bathroom necessities, and toys, and keep them at your house. That way, cumbersome suitcases will be unnecessary. In addition, this makes your child feel like she's at home instead of at a hotel where she has to spend two or three weekends a month.

Out of Sight but in Touch

Be sure to make yourself available to your child when he needs you. Regardless of what your living agreement is, call your child frequently during the week and keep track of what's going on in school and how he's doing. Just because you (legally) see your child only on the weekend doesn't mean you have to feel like a second-class parent.

If you see your children only on the weekends, don't try to make up for lost time by buying presents. Kids are smart. Even though they may enjoy getting presents at the time, they can see right through it. You may mean well, but the best thing you can give your child is your time.

Also, try not to rely excessively on baby sitters. Schedule business dinners and dates during the week so the weekend is free for your son or daughter. If you're spending only a few weekends a month with your child, focus on your child for the time you have together. It's okay to leave him with a sitter every now and then, but you're losing quality time when you do this.

A Work-Free Zone

It's understandable that occasionally you may need to bring some work home, but try working an extra hour a few days a week so you'll have time with your kids.

Write down important events and birthdays in the calendar you use the most. Nothing is worse than forgetting a birthday or what day your daughter gets her report card. Write down events as soon as you learn of them so you don't forget. You can color code and use a specific color of pen so you can find activities at a glance.

Gracefully Negotiate Redefined Relationships

Regardless of whether you're an "old" parent or a "new" stepparent, your relationship with your child will be tested at times. Whether through problems with a mate or an ex, or an outside occurrence that has nothing to do with your child, sometimes parents will take shortcuts or try to mold their children into who they want them to be. There is no perfect plan for parenting, but it's important to realize that your child is an individual with feelings and abilities separate from yours. Be aware of these feelings, and don't take them for granted.

Try to coordinate rules and discipline for your children with your ex, especially if there's a new stepparent involved. If one of you is stricter on the child than the other, the child might begin to listen to one parent and not take the other parent seriously, or the child may come to resent the stricter parent.

In any event, sit down together and talk about rules and discipline. Even if you no longer get along, it's worth the effort.

Organizing Your Guest Bedroom and Bathroom

A perfect guest never wears out his welcome, or so they say. Perhaps you've been lucky. Whether you love your guests or they leave something to be desired, it's your responsibility as a host to make them as comfortable as possible. This includes providing them with a comfortable atmosphere to sleep and a clean area to call home, at least for a few days.

> **That's the Spirit**
>
> Whether guest or host, there is a spiritual protocol to follow. Jesus taught his disciples to not seek the best room or the best seat at a table: "But when you are invited, take the lowest place so that when your host comes, he will say to you, 'Friend, move up to a better place.' Then you will be honored in the presence of all your fellow guests. For everyone who exalts himself will be humbled, and he who humbles himself will be exalted." (Luke 14:10–11)

Those Little Extras

While the guest room is vacant, take full advantage of the extra space. The guest bedroom is the perfect place to store extra blankets and pillows. One reason is so these items won't be cluttering up your bedroom closet; second, it's because your guests will need them.

If you have a treadmill or small weight machine (that's in good condition), you may want to store it in the guest bedroom. It won't be cluttering up your bedroom, and your guests may enjoy using it while they're staying with you. Make sure it's in good condition so your guests won't hurt themselves.

Although your guests won't be staying long enough to hang too many clothes in the spare closet, ensure that there are plenty of hangers in the closet and little dust. Keep the closet in the guest room as organized as you would your own (refer to Chapter 7).

Install a mirror in the guest bedroom to prevent your guests from traveling to your room to use yours after they're dressed. This way they won't be in your way or your family's way when you're all getting ready to go out.

Avoid the Bathroom Blues

Add a small cabinet over the toilet to provide extra space for you to hold items that you don't want others to see. Extra rolls of toilet paper, personal hygiene products, or other small items can be put in this cabinet instead of under the sink (where you may need to keep towels or washcloths if you don't have a linen closet). If you don't have space under the sink, then look all around your bathroom for available wall space that might accommodate a small cabinet.

If you prefer not to hang a cabinet, perhaps you could purchase a bathroom accessory that rests on the floor but reaches up to several feet over the toilet. These tall shelving accessories usually have a small cabinet area along with one or two shelves. Many varieties are available in department stores. One caveat: Don't store anything on top of these. Items that may fall from this height can hurt someone, and it's too difficult trying to reach what you need.

> **Divine Guidance**
>
> Since shelves are visible to everyone, don't overcrowd them. Put small items on the shelves that you won't mind others seeing.

If you have cabinets only under your sink, consider installing permanent shelves over your commode. These shelves may look more stylish and take up less space than a stand-up unit over the commode. This is a good place for colorful items such as plants or bubble bath.

May You Never Run Out

It's a sign of disorganization, let alone just plain gauche, to run out of toilet paper at an inopportune moment. And it's the height of inhospitality to run out of toilet paper when a guest comes over! Store a second roll in the bathroom in or under a decorative container. Keep it stocked continuously so that you always have an extra roll and so that no guest ever, ever is concerned about running out at a critical moment. Also, keep many extras stocked in a linen closet or nearby storage room (refer to the section that follows).

Save yourself some time and effort by avoiding cleaning a room that's not used much. That's not to say it should be ignored, but since there probably won't be as many furnishings or decorative items in the guest bedroom, there's not as much to catch the dust. Clean your guest bedroom once a month or, of course, right before guests arrive. And always wash and replace the sheets right after your guests leave.

Accommodating Guests

Many of your overnight guests may be your children's playmates, but every once in a while, you might like to invite a grown-up over. Whether it is a relative or a friend from out of town, have a few things prepared before your guest's arrival, if possible. A one-night stay is usually relatively simple, but if your guests decide to stay a few days or a week, this may cause a problem for your family. Here are a few basic tips to ensure that your guests will be comfortable:

- If you have overnight guests, ask them about their food preferences and what they like to drink. Chances are, you'll like some of the same things, so cooking for guests may not be such a chore. If you have guests who are picky, consider buying food ready-made at a deli, to save you some time and effort.

Caution Corner

If you have company coming, keep the pets in a separate room and clean thoroughly the day before their arrival. You want your guests to be comfortable, not sneezing their collective heads off.

That's the Spirit

Don't discount the possibility that a guest's problem or prolonged stay could have an unseen purpose. It might at least offer an opportunity to show your faith in an inconvenient moment. "Whenever we have the opportunity, we should do good to everyone, especially to our Christian brothers and sisters." (Galatians 6:10)

- You may take it for granted that you don't have allergies. Some people are sensitive to allergens in your home, including pet dander or dust. Poll your potential guests beforehand.

- Keep extras such as shampoo, combs, and an extra toothbrush on hand for guests. Invariably, someone will forget something; try to provide small items for them. However, if someone forgets clothing or something expensive, don't feel obligated to provide something valuable that may get dirty or damaged. Offer alternatives.

Longer Stays

Sometimes problems arise with a relative or friend and you offer a special dose of hospitality to that person—like having them move in with you. Having someone live with you who's not part of the immediate family, however, puts stress on everyone in the household. Sharing facilities and finding private time alone can become difficult.

Be gracious about the situation. It won't be permanent (unless you let it), and remember that this is your home and you're in charge. In cases when an elderly parent or grandparent will move in permanently, ensure that you make proper arrangements before this happens.

Prepare a Schedule

Unless you have an older parent living with you, prepare a time frame for friends and in-laws who are staying with you. Agree to the length of stay before the person arrives. If you've agreed to two months, hold firm to your decision. Mark it on a highly visible calendar.

If someone is coming to stay with you for an extended period, other rules need to be devised. For example, younger guests should help with the cleaning chores or should pay some part of the rent or grocery bills. Older guests, such as parents, call for a different arrangement. In this case, you're much more of a host, requiring them only to make their own beds, keep their bathrooms relatively clean, and help out wherever they volunteer to do so. Most older guests, by the third or fourth day, will likely suggest to you some ways that they could be supportive.

Divine Guidance

Make it politely and poignantly clear to the parent staying with you that although he is welcome in your home, this is your home and it will be run the way you see fit, not the way his home was run.

Don't let conflicts arise between you and your mate regarding guests (especially relatives) who are staying with you. This is your home, and you are allowing someone else to stay with you (presumably) out of the goodness of your heart. If the guest is wearing out his welcome or causing problems, talk with your mate about it and try to come to a mutual agreement.

Additional Ground Rules for House Guests

What about the situation when one of your house guests who is slated to stay for a few days or weeks seeks to stay for much longer? In that case, have a heart-to-heart discussion about the ramifications of a longer stay. Don't risk incurring a heated misunderstanding because a house guest has a completely different notion than you about his length of stay.

The time to discuss this issue is on a bright and cheery day, perhaps in the morning, at or after breakfast, perhaps on a Saturday or Sunday, when you are not necessarily rushed. While you may want to be as accommodating as possible and work to achieve an effective solution, you must be master of your domain. If you are not, nothing else in this book about getting organized will quite seem the same.

When your visitor turns out to be someone with a huge appetite, watch out! If he frequently gobbles the goodies in the kitchen, and doesn't replace them, volunteer to go shopping, or donate a compensatory sum, chances are you've got a house guest "issue." Don't laugh, this can cause more upset than you might expect.

A household guest does represent an additional mouth to feed. While a guest may go out to restaurants and other food establishments and you may be taking your guest to such establishments, many meals will be consumed right in your home. If you are away for much of the day, and your guest is not, it is logical to assume that your guest will be doing some eating.

As with the length of stay, discussion as to how the food situation should be worked out needs to be addressed sooner rather than later. So, too, are topics such as household responsibilities, handling the mail, receiving visitors, and so on. You can't assume things are going to run smoothly.

Your guest might expect you to be a chauffeur of sorts, taking him or her to leisure events, retail stores, doctor's visits, and so on. You, on the other hand, may have thought that the local bus, which runs right in front of your house, is more than sufficient. Iron all of this out in the first couple days when things are at their friendliest.

Your guest, especially if it is a close relative, may want to use your automobile. How do you feel about lending out your car, even to dear old Mom or Dad? Do you wish them to replace the consumed gas? What are your expectations about car cleanliness, and perhaps most important, when it ought to be returned?

If you work from home, then you have additional organizational challenges when entertaining a long-term guest. You may need to inform your guest of the hours during which you don't wish to be disturbed. When you are working, you are working, and everyone in the household needs to know it, even a guest. Explain the phone system to the guest, if you have more than one line.

- What line should the guest never touch?
- What line can the guest use freely?
- How would you like the guest to help you with or refrain from handling phone calls?

The larger your home, potentially, the less of an issue your working from home may be. In a smaller house, you have a greater chance of bumping into one another. Regardless of the size of your household, important parameters need to be defined. In this case, rather than waiting a few days, you need to discuss these things at the outset. If your livelihood is dependent upon what you do from home and that rent or mortgage bill is due, you have got to get to work!

Adding someone to your household is an organizational challenge in and of itself. As reticent as you may be to discuss tender topics, you will find the going much easier discussing these topics early on than waiting until misunderstandings and hurt feelings arise.

Entertaining and Gift Giving

If you've ever planned a gathering, you know how much work is involved. Even a get-together as simple as a baby shower can be arduous if you're not prepared. It takes only one minor disaster, like running out of drinks, or a major disaster such as forgetting to pick up the champagne for the wedding reception, to make you swear you'll never plan another party.

Most of the time, being prepared is the difference between a good party and a bad party. Hopefully, the hints in this chapter will help you tie up the loose ends before your guests arrive.

Throwing a Party Requires Details

Depending on what type of party you're having, you'll need to decide some general details one month to two months in advance. The first thing you need to do is set a firm budget and stick to it. Next, you need to decide on a date, time, and place for the party. Will the party be formal or informal? Will it be indoors or outdoors? After you decide on these items, set up a calendar and circle important dates for things that need to be done ahead of time.

Caution Corner

If you're reserving a caterer for an event such as a wedding reception, you may need to reserve the same caterer for the rehearsal dinner the night before. Many people forget this until close to the wedding, when the date has long been taken.

If you'll need a caterer or photographer, call them as soon as you decide on a firm date for the party. Due to weddings and other events, it may be difficult to find a reputable caterer and photographer for when you need them. This is why reserving your date ahead of time is so important.

Approximately one month before the party, you may need to arrange for extra help. For example, if you have children who won't be attending the party, you'll need to find a baby sitter and arrange to have the children picked up a few hours before the party begins. Perhaps you could section off a part of your house to offer baby-sitting to your guests. Many people have children, too, so this can be a great option.

If you need a bartender or entertainer, it's best to book a month ahead of time. Recruit someone to help you address invitations so they'll be ready when you need to send them out. Don't try to do everything yourself.

If you plan on fixing the meal or hors d'oeuvres yourself, instead of spending the money on a caterer, practice cooking each new item you plan to serve ahead of time so that you are sure you can make it and it's appropriate for the party. If an item is too difficult or expensive, nix it and make something else. If what you're cooking is freezable, another option is to freeze it ahead of time so you'll have less to do the day of the party.

Caution Corner

Wedding? Hired a caterer, got the rings, bought champagne, bought flowers, registered for place settings … seems like you've got it all … hmmmm …. Everything is accounted for … except the church! Never forget the purpose of the celebration. And don't expect the church to have a weekend free for you just because you need it. The wedding planner advice to help would-be brides make arrangements applies to churches, too: "First the room, then the groom."

As Party Day Approaches

If you've planned sufficiently, everything should be lined up and ready. Since you can't remember everything, recruit someone to go behind you and double-check everything. If you're on your own, think positively and take some advice from the following hints:

- If the party is at your home, bring out all the china, silverware, or crystal that you will need to use a day before the party. Polish the silverware and make sure everything is washed and that no pieces are being used that have knicks or cracks. Then keep all items in a safe place where they won't get broken. If you're allowing smoking at the party, set out enough ashtrays ahead of time so that you don't forget.

- Imagine your dining room or living room filled with people. If you anticipate a large crowd, you probably need to move some furniture around. You may even want to move some furniture out. If so, enlist some help from your husband or neighbor, and temporarily move the furniture to an area where your guests won't see it.

- About one week before the party, call everyone whose services you've retained and ask about everything you've ordered, to ensure that all is going according to schedule. Double-checking reservations (especially with baby sitters or bartenders) is always a good idea because someone may have forgotten or overbooked the day of your event. If this disaster happens, you still have one week to find someone else.

- You'll definitely need to clean your house either the day before the party or the morning of the party. Do a good cleaning job, not merely a wipe down. Make sure you clean the entire house, not simply the living and dining rooms. People will need to use the bathroom, and getting to the bathroom may mean walking past other rooms.

- Invariably, there will be an emergency: You'll run out of something, or something will break and need to be replaced before the party. Be prepared for this and have some cash available the day before the party. You'll also need it to tip people you've hired to help. Not everyone accepts credit cards, so be on the safe side and have an ample amount of cash stored in a safe place.

A party is supposed to be fun for everyone, right? Keep it that way by not losing your composure the day of a big party.

Crowd Control

Be careful when letting friends bring guests you don't know or don't like. This is your party, so keep it under control. Make it clear to everyone ahead of time what type of party it is (for example, beer and wine vs. hard liquor) and who you don't want there.

> **That's the Spirit**
>
> Uh oh. Wine and hard liquor. Drinking vs. teetotaling. The presence of alcohol (or its absence) can be a touchy subject for Christians. You'll have Christian friends who drink and some who don't, just as you'll have friends who are not as overt in their faith who drink and some who don't. The decision is yours, of course, but hospitality and moderation should be your guide. "Continue to show deep love for each other, for love covers a multitude of sins. Cheerfully share your home with those who need a meal or a place to stay." (1 Peter 4:8–9)

If your next party is in honor of a specific person, design the guest list for that person. Invite people the guest of honor will be comfortable with. If the person is shy, stick to inviting people you both know. If the person is more outgoing, invite a few of your acquaintances whom you think the guest of honor will feel comfortable around.

When arranging guest seating, place the furniture at an angle instead of head on. This is less confrontational and will make your guests feel more comfortable. Taking it a step further, when arranging dining room seating, put those with common interests near each other but not necessarily next to each other. You want the conversation to be complementary but not one-sided.

Plan Some Surprises, Forbid Others

If you're holding a small party for a new neighbor or co-worker, invite people you think will have something in common, as well as those with different interests. The idea is to invite those with something in common so that the guest of honor will get to know new people easily. Those with different interests may be equally fascinating but a bit harder to get to know. Therefore, blending the two types should expose your guest of honor to many different personality types and, hopefully, future friends.

> **Divine Guidance**
>
> If you're holding a party and prefer to have children stay with a baby sitter, let your guests know that and be firm with your decision.

Having two of your acquaintances become friends is a good surprise. Having a toddler throw a tantrum is not. Most parties you have in your home are probably suitable for children of guests to attend, but the kids should stay at home for some events. If you cave in and let one couple bring a child, other guests may be offended or upset that they weren't allowed to bring their kids.

Holiday Party Planning

The Christmas season is one of the most hectic times in your year. Every year people say that they'll start shopping early and finish everything before Thanksgiving. Not a bad idea. However, if you typically let December creep up on you without buying the first present, fear not—holiday survival hints are here, from cooking to buying the right gift.

With attending worship services at church, preparing meals for your family, and making sure that Santa Claus is good to everyone, you probably don't have much time left for yourself. Preparing the food is difficult if everyone likes something different or if you feel obligated to make certain traditional foods.

Cook in Advance

No one wants to spend Christmas Day in the kitchen. It's supposed to be, first and foremost, a time of fellowship and a moment to be thankful for the birth of the Messiah. It's a fun time, too, for opening gifts and spending time with your family. Make large batches of beef stew, chicken soup, or other soup in late November and early December, and freeze the leftovers.

When time is scarce close to Christmas and you're busy shopping and wrapping gifts, you can defrost the stew or soup and feed your family a healthful meal.

That's the Spirit

How do you balance the faithful and the worldly sides of Christmas? The commercial side of the holiday seems to overshadow the religious significance for many people. J. Hampton Keathley III, minister and writer for the Biblical Studies Foundation (www.Bible.org), said, "Parents can explain the traditions and have fun with them, but make sure your children understand the historical roots and use these things to teach the truth behind the traditions."

Plan family dinners and parties the day before Christmas, and do leftovers Christmas Day. Before or after church, you will probably have somewhere to visit on Christmas Day that will provide you with a meal anyway. Take the stress off and enjoy the day.

Get Some Help

If the holiday season is too hectic and you're running out of time and patience, buy the family dinner instead of slaving over a hot stove for a day and a half. In addition, buy as much food as you can ahead of time. There are two reasons for this. First, many stores run out of holiday-related items the closer it gets to the holiday. Second, you can bet that the baker's chocolate and fresh coconut will increase in price as Christmas approaches. If it doesn't spoil and you have the space, start buying what you need a month ahead of time.

If you opt not to cook, many supermarkets and delis cook turkeys, hams, and all the trimmings for your intended feast. Also, if you have relatives who are excellent cooks, see if you can talk them into fixing a few things for you. This is especially nice if you have an aunt who makes a fresh coconut cake to die for. As long as you pay for the ingredients and compensate (in a nice way) for their time, you may have a feast fit for a king with little effort on your part.

> **That's the Spirit**
>
> Christmas is based on an exchange of gifts: the gift of God to man—his Son; and the gift of man to God—when we first give ourselves to God.
>
> —Vance Havner, minister and evangelist

To further simplify your Christmas cooking, team up with neighbors and relatives on your dessert specialties. If you make the best chocolate pies around, bake several pies to share with your team. Another member of the team can make her specialty, while another member can make something else. Everyone can split up the goods so all team members have delicious desserts for the holidays.

Organize Your Gift Shopping

It's difficult to buy presents for some people—and you know who they are! Instead of feeling flustered the next time the look on a recipient's face betrays his true feelings about the gift, rethink how you shop.

Adjusting how you shop and when you shop can make buying easier for you, and you'll be more likely to buy a gift that's appreciated. For example, carefully pick the days you shop. Mondays and Tuesdays are much less crowded than the weekends. You may have to shop in the evenings if you work away from home. Since you'll be tired by this point, buy smaller gifts, such as CDs, gift certificates, and jewelry, so you're not stuck carrying around large packages. Also, have the presents wrapped there in the store. Paying an extra dollar will save you the headache of wrapping at home.

If you're a stickler for doing things yourself, decorative bags are an easy (and pretty) way of wrapping gifts. Gift bags can be expensive, but many discount retailers and dollar stores offer inexpensive lines of gift bags, tissue paper, and accessories (also refer to the section "Double Payoff"). Keep all the bags you receive, too, so that you can reuse them.

One of the most difficult chores at Christmas time is finding the right gift for friends and family. Some people are easy to buy for, but there are those who are picky or those you don't know that well. To help make this easier, create a year-round Christmas list. Whenever you hear a friend comment on something he or she likes, make note of it so that your Christmas shopping will be easier.

> **Divine Guidance**
>
> Many people buy a few extra gifts at Christmas, in case they receive an unexpected gift from someone for whom they have purchased nothing. Buying one or two gifts is fine. Any more is excess.

Gift Shopping Smarts

Invariably you'll forget to shop for someone until the last minute. When this happens, go with the trusty gift certificate. Some malls offer mall-wide gift certificates so that the recipient can get whatever is desired at any mall store.

If your friend has a special hobby, buy a gift certificate from the store that caters to this hobby. Note that some people feel more loved when thought apparently goes into their present instead of getting the quick-fix gift certificate. Some are ecstatic that they can get want they actually want.

To make it easy on yourself, order as many gifts as you can online or through the mail. As long as you order the products a few weeks before Christmas, there should be no problem with them getting there on time. Be careful when you order. Get a delivery date, and call the day before to make sure it was sent. Make sure you know correct sizes before you order so that you don't spend the week after Christmas sending everything back.

> **That's the Spirit**
>
> If you need a simple reminder of the meaning of Christmas, one verse says a lot: "For God so loved the world that he gave his one and only Son, that whoever believes in him shall not perish but have eternal life." (John 3:16)

Christians should know that the purpose of life is to grow closer to God—and that it's important to share that belief (sometimes gently). Evangelism isn't always the most admired trait, though. So instead of doing a Bible-thumping sermon on the nearest street corner, maybe giving some Christian-themed presents will show your love to people around you. A book that touches needs from a Christian perspective or a new CD by a contemporary Christian singer can be a nice way of offering a little of your faith to others. It's not as intimidating as an impersonation of Elmer Gantry, and it helps diminish the commercial aspect of gift giving.

Double Payoff

While shopping for Christmas gifts, pick up a few birthday items for friends and family whose special day is a month or two ahead. Although you don't want to think about another holiday, at least you won't have to go shopping a month after Christmas.

> **Divine Guidance**
>
> Once you get all your gifts home, keep all tags and receipts in one place so that they're convenient to find in case you need to take a gift back.

You already know that most stores hold great sales on Christmas items a few days after the holiday. This is a good time to buy wrapping paper, Christmas cards, bows, boxes, and the like. It's also a good time to buy Christmas crafts and art supplies. You'll have everything you need when you start on next year's crafts and ornaments.

Other Present Ideas

If you have access to a video camera, make a few tapes of yourself to send to friends you don't see often. It can be more fun than talking on the phone and much more memorable. You can catch them up on new happenings in your life, and it's an inexpensive gift that's more special than many of the expensive ones.

Sometimes it's difficult to decide what to buy for people—say, those you work with. It's also difficult to afford if you work with many folks. A week or two before the holidays, plan an evening out to a restaurant or club of everyone's choice. The only thing it costs is what you pay for dinner, and you get to spend a fun night out with your friends.

Organizing Your Car

Whether you're a busy parent, a salesperson, or both, you're probably always on the go in your car. It's important to keep your car organized and neat. Organization doesn't have to be difficult; in fact, disorganization proves to be *more* difficult. For example, if you take a shortcut to your child's soccer practice or business meeting and happen to get lost, having a map, street finder, or built-in PC locator would be a lifesaver at the time. Along the same lines, what happens if you get up to the toll booth only to realize that you've forgotten your money? Thinking ahead of time will save you headaches, which is the topic of this chapter.

Map Your Course

When traveling, unless you have a snazzy late-model vehicle with a built-in street finder based on a global-positioning satellite, always keep a supply of maps for cities and towns that you frequent.

If you carry a notebook computer with you, consider purchasing street-finder software so you can plan your way when you're in the car or hotel room. If you choose to do this, keep maps in the car as back-ups and for toting into gas stations, hotels, and other places where you may find yourself asking people questions. Keep a car-size version of the phone book (if your city has them); this saves time, and even has maps.

Spare Change and Keys

If you have a long commute or you drive frequently, have a roll of quarters and dimes under the seat or in a place where you can quickly put your hands on them. It's easy to forget about the occasional toll road you might encounter—or not even know they're there, if you're in unfamiliar territory. You also may get lost or be out longer than you expected and get very hungry. With a roll of quarters stashed in your car, you can always afford a snack on the road.

Divine Guidance

If you travel across the country, invest in a wire-bound map of the United States that has every state with main roads and side roads.

It is also a good idea to stash a set of your house keys in the car and to have a set of car keys hidden in or around your house. If you ever lock yourself out of your house, there's an extra set of keys in your car. You can keep an extra car key hidden in a magnetic case somewhere under your car. If you feel uneasy doing this, keep an extra car key in your purse or wallet, or hide one somewhere in your yard. This may be under a designated rock, attached to the inside of the doghouse, or wherever is best for you.

If you lock yourself out of your car and house, you can still get into one of them—and hence, the other—without breaking a window or calling a locksmith.

A Well-Stocked Car

Suppose it's late at night. You're on an unfamiliar country road. It's cold and rainy, and your car has committed the ultimate betrayal: It has broken down. You're 20 miles from home, and you don't know anyone who lives in the area. You left your cell phone at home (or it just went dead, and the battery charger is in the other car), and no one knows your whereabouts. The temperature outside is plummeting. What will you do? What *will* you do?

Caution Corner

You probably don't think about keeping certain emergency items in your car or even consider that you may be involved in an accident or other predicament. The only way to ensure that this won't happen to you is to prepare yourself and your car for any emergency.

Hopefully this situation will never happen to you. If it already has, you know the fear of being stuck with no help to rely on. You start wishing you had taken the car in for servicing when it was making that clicking noise. You promise yourself that when you get out of this situation, it will *never* happen again.

You never know when your car is going to break down, but if you keep your car serviced and well maintained, you're less likely to get stuck in the middle of nowhere. Preparation is a key component of organization that has been emphasized throughout the book, and this chapter is no different. Having a few necessities in your car can make all the difference.

That's the Spirit

Not many people think of faith as a vehicle, but what's going to take you to salvation? In *Prayer and the Art of Volkswagen Maintenance*, author Donald Miller is out to repair a faith—his—in need of overhaul. "Church doesn't stimulate me the way it used to. It is most often the same as the week before. The worship lyrics are presented on a screen that has all but the little bouncing ball over the words, then the pastor gets up for a ten-minute sermon that could be understood by a group of third graders." On his van trip from Texas to Oregon, Miller finds that the New Testament itself is the manual for fixing the soul.

A Well-Stocked Glove Compartment

Some glove compartments are small, some big. Most of them share one thing in common—a lot of clutter and junk. Actually, only a few things *need* to be in your glove compartment: car registration, insurance card, safety inspection and emission test information, and the like.

Since most newer-model cars have consoles for storing extra items, other stuff can go elsewhere. In a tidy glove compartment, you'll have room for a few other items, but pick and choose those carefully.

Put your garbage in a trash receptacle, not the glove compartment. If the door to your glove compartment is getting harder to close, it's time to clean it out. The glove compartment is not a trash can or semipermanent home of unnecessary papers and receipts. If the items are important, take them inside and put them in a folder where you can maintain them. In addition to the already mentioned items, your glove compartment need contain only the car manual, a small flashlight, and perhaps recent service records.

Extras for the Well Organized

If you've done a good job thus far of keeping your glove compartment free and clear, you can keep a few extra items there on a temporary basis. An extra pair of sunglasses (in a case) will usually fit perfectly in the glove compartment of your car. This way, any time you get into your car, you'll always have sunglasses even if you leave the pair you normally wear at home.

Divine Guidance

Keep a few small items in your car so that your child will have something to occupy his time when you're driving. This will cut down on your child acting up out of boredom and will reduce incessant questioning about when you're going to "be there." By making these items toys for the car and not for use in the house, your child will look forward to playing with them and you will get some peace and quiet when you're driving.

One sure sign of disorganization is looking into your car and seeing 25 CDs lying on the seats. If you have a stereo player and often opt for listening to your favorite group, educational material, or relaxation tapes instead of the radio, keep but a few tapes or CDs on hand at a time. If you prefer, you can buy a cassette or CD holder. However, if you have only two or three favorites, you can put these in your glove compartment so they won't be in direct sunlight or sliding around in a seat.

If you're in a hurry when you leave your house, it's easy to leave your gloves lying on your table or in the pockets of another coat. Even though the pair in the car will be a little chilly on a cold morning, they'll warm up and you'll be glad you have them.

Caution Corner

If you live in a cold climate, make sure you keep an extra pair of gloves in your glove compartment. You never know when your car might break down or you need to walk a long distance in the cold.

Whether you're a busy parent or a businessperson, chances are good that you have many small items to keep up with in your car. Pens, coins, cassettes, and other items can be difficult to find when they're thrown in a glove compartment, purse, or briefcase. To make common small items easier to find, put them in a clear plastic bag so you can see through to the contents and find what you're looking for easily.

The Grand Old Trunk

How you use your trunk space is important. You can hide many things in the trunk. Be careful and don't leave valuable items in sight, and be cautious about where and when you hide things in the trunk. If someone watches you place your purse or briefcase in the trunk, it can pique his curiosity and tempt him to want to break into your vehicle.

You never know when an accident can happen and you'll be stuck by the side of the road in unfamiliar territory. To prepare for an incident like this, keep the following supplies stashed in your trunk:

- Tissues
- A flashlight
- An umbrella
- Jumper cables
- A warm, thick blanket
- Flares
- A first-aid kit

You may even consider keeping some type of nonperishable food in your trunk, in case you're stuck somewhere overnight. Remember to replace the food every now and then. Even raisins won't last forever.

If you're a person on the go, you may opt to carry a gym bag in your trunk with a clean T-shirt, a fresh pair of socks and underwear, clean exercise clothing, and a toothbrush. Although you may usually carry these items with you, sometimes you're in a hurry and forget. With these extras in the car, you won't have to drive back home to pick up exercise clothing.

Caution Corner

Most people leave home without it. Not the American Express card, the Bible. Why keep the Good Book in your vehicle? What if you could bring only one item onto a desert island? Would you pick the Bible? Dirk Been did in summer 2000, when he was a castaway on the original "Survivor" reality show, which deposited people on a South China Sea island off the coast of Borneo. The group of castaways ate rats and faced tropical heat and serious illnesses such as malaria to compete for $1 million. Contestants could bring one "luxury" item on the island. Been chose his Bible—and didn't regret it for one second.

Back Seat Potential

As your family gets larger, you'll obviously need more back seat space. After all, the compact car you drove in high school may have become crowded with only two or three passengers stuffed in the car. If you're single or without a family, you may still need more space for business purposes.

Similar to the trunk, the back seat can be another place to store items, but do so carefully. Avoid leaving your purse, cellular phone, or other expensive items sitting in the back seat. This makes it too easy for a crook who may be snooping around your car. If you have no choice but to keep an item in the back seat, cover it up before you get out of your car.

If a thief can see your valuables, all he has to do is break the window, reach in, and grab them. Even if you have a car alarm, he'll pick a time when no one is around so he can be off before anyone notices. Park at a shopping center with highly visible security guards making the rounds, and there is less need for concern.

Tips to Keep You Rolling

Like you, your car needs periodic checkups. Even if your vehicle is new, that doesn't mean you can skip preventative maintenance. It's true that you shouldn't have big problems with a new car or truck, but regular servicing is especially important with new vehicles so that they'll run smoother for a longer period of time.

Caution Corner

When you hear strange noises coming from your car, it's vital to give them immediate attention. Ignoring the problem will only make it worse and probably cost you more in the long run. Find a mechanic you can trust to fix the problems so that you can be confident your car will take you places where and when you need to go.

Fluids and Your Car

For the average driver, it's about time to change the oil every 3,000 miles. However you don't need additives that are mainly stop-gap measures for cars that actually need mechanical attention. Most oil additives only mask a serious mechanical problem—and usually for a short time.

Smell your transmission fluid to see if you're having a problem! The experts say that when an automatic vehicle is having problems, the transmission fluid develops a certain odor. Pull out the transmission dipstick and have a sniff. If it smells burned, it's time to see a mechanic. So take a sniff when it's running fine. When you sniff later, you'll have some scent to compare it to.

The octane rating of the gas you use matters, but not for the reason that most people presume. Dennis Simanaitis, *Road and Track* magazine's engineering editor, says, "There is no more energy in a gallon of premium gas than there is in a gallon of regular. The main difference between the grades is octane—the resistance to ping. If your car engine pings, you'll hear a rattling metallic sound when you accelerate. Ping can damage an engine if it's allowed to go on too long, and a higher-octane gasoline might solve the problem."

Steer clear of shabby stations that look like they don't sell much gasoline. When gas station storage tanks sit almost empty for extended periods, water can condense inside, fouling the gasoline. Pumping that mixture of water and gasoline into your car will not help its performance and may hamper it.

Tune-Up Time?

Some signs that your car's engine may be malfunctioning are subtle because modern computerized controls, designed to keep the engine running efficiently, mask the beginning symptoms of trouble. Early indicators signaling that a tune-up is in order are as follows:

- Difficulty starting
- Frequent stalling
- Poor gas mileage
- An odd exhaust odor

When you do deliver your car to the shop, make sure that it's seen by someone with at least 10 years of experience in auto repair and who has a reputation for dependable workmanship on car models like the one you drive.

That's the Spirit

If faith is a vehicle, what fuels it? Belief. How do you get refills on belief? Go to church, read the Bible, listen to God. That last part is the most mysterious. Charles Stanley writes in *How to Listen to God* that "whatever God speaks to us will stimulate our spiritual growth. That means that God will never tell us to do anything or think of anything that will set us back spiritually."

Cell Phones

In the past you might have been able to leave home without worrying about the telephone, but in today's society, you take your phone with you. Because you never know when an accident will happen, keep a cell phone (that you know how to operate) with you. For example, a college woman slid on a patch of ice, wrecked her car, and broke her back. She quite candidly reports that if she didn't have a phone with her and if it hadn't been for a nice man who happened to see her down the embankment, she may have been stuck there for hours.

Most cellular phones for the car come equipped with a speaker device attached above the driver's side window. Automatic dialing is available for your frequently called numbers. This is beneficial because you can simply push a button and talk hands-free.

Caution Corner

To be completely safe, use your phone *only* when parked or in a very congested traffic jam. If your car is rolling at all, it is dangerous to divert your attention to a cell phone.

Your Portable Office

If you're a career professional and travel often by car, you may find it vital to have your car serve as a mobile office. Even if you work in the home, sometimes you need to get in touch with someone while you're on the road. A car with a speaker phone and list of important numbers will help immensely by saving the time it would take you to drive home and get the number or stop at a pay phone (perhaps in a rough neighborhood).

If you have a computer at home, type a list of important phone numbers and addresses, and save these to a disk. Keep a copy of these numbers and addresses in your car. Put them where they're convenient for you. If it's easier to keep the list tucked away under the seat or in the console, this is fine. Or, you might attach the list to the top side of your sun visor.

You can also add credit card or personal identification numbers to the list. In this case, make doubly sure you keep the list in a safe place. If you're worried about the list getting stolen, change a few numbers around in a pattern that you've made up and can remember. For example, increase or decrease the last digit of your credit card number by one. A thief probably won't be able to figure out your pattern.

Divine Guidance

If you never update the numbers list you keep in your car, after a few months you'll be stuck with archaic numbers of people you no longer have contact or business with. On the other hand, if you update and never delete any numbers, your list may soon be as long as your car. Once a month, review the list and make any additions or deletions that are necessary. This takes only a few minutes a month, and you'll always be prepared if you need to call someone while on the road.

Keep a folder in your car that zips closed for items such as envelopes, stamps, pads, and a few pencils or pens. You never know when you'll walk out of the house with an item to mail but forget to put a stamp on it. If you have stamps in the car, you can still mail your item without having to drive to the post office.

You might also want to keep some deposit slips or ATM deposit envelopes so you can fill them out in the car and not while you're in front of the ATM machine. The less time you spend in front of an ATM machine with money in your hand, the safer you'll be.

Back-Ups in Place

Make photocopies of important maintenance records or credit card and insurance information to keep hidden in your car. If someone steals your wallet or purse, or if someone breaks into your home and steals your credit cards, you'll have a copy of all your numbers and can quickly contact the credit card companies to cancel your cards.

Also, if your home is damaged by fire or natural disaster, such as a flood or tornado, having copies of important items in your car or safe-deposit box will help you stay in control when a crisis occurs.

You'll never be perfectly organized while living on this earth, but take heart in what Saint Augustine says: "Heaven is the perfectly ordered and harmonious enjoyment of God and of one another in God."

Chapter 16

Garages and Other Storage Areas

The inside of your garage may be the first thing you see when you come home from work or from picking the kids up from soccer practice. Have you ever thought of your garage as a hazardous area? It's important to keep your garage area organized and safe. According to the National Safety Council, "Garages and carports are among the most hazardous rooms in a typical home, and the primary hazard may be absent-mindedness."

Don't cram your garage with stuff as if it's some kind of catch-all room. Store things with care, and keep dangerous items out of the reach of children. A little organization can go a long way. Heck, you might even be able to get your car back inside. Fortunately, organizing your garage doesn't have to be as painful as, say, having a root canal. The key, as this chapter points out, is to break the work down into manageable parts and enlist help from those around you.

Clean Your Garage Like a Pro

Cleaning a garage, ideally, should be a breeze. After all, it's merely a large room with a concrete or asphalt floor. However, when you add the "stuff" that you have acquired over the years, plus one or two vehicles, you find a lot to clean and to clean around. A careless mate, mischievous children, and vandals can add to your cleaning woes and cause you to spend more time than necessary cleaning your garage. The following are some solid garage-cleaning tips.

If there's any type of spill on the garage floor or carport, be on the safe side and clean it immediately so there are no accidents. Along with being bad for the environment, antifreeze can injure or kill your pets. Antifreeze tastes sweet (don't try a taste test at home or anywhere else), and even a small amount can be enough to kill an animal. Keep all containers of antifreeze tightly sealed, and clean up any spills.

Many environmentally friendly solvents and cleaners have been on the market for years. There is also a new type of antifreeze that is less toxic than the traditional ethylene glycol. If you haven't already, switch to one of these so if there is an accidental spill, your yard won't pay the price and your pets will be protected.

Removing oil stains from concrete or asphalt can be difficult. Even if you've tried water and detergent, you may have a residual stain. The next time you're faced with this problem use paint thinner or mineral spirits. Pour a small amount on the stain, scrub it in, and absorb it with cat litter. Let it sit for 30 minutes and sweep it up.

That's the Spirit

The days in which people dumped their used oil and cleaners out in the woods or down the drain, one hopes, are gone. The article "The Household Side of Hazardous Waste," by Sharon Rehder (*Conservationist,* February 1995, pages 10–13) indicates that, "at any given time, the average home contains more than 100 pounds of hazardous products and household hazardous waste. The materials are often stored under kitchen sinks, in basements, garages, or elsewhere." Always dispose of chemicals properly. If you're unsure about the proper disposal method, call your local waste-management department or local office of the Environmental Protection Agency (www.epa.gov).

Reclaiming Your Garage

What happens when you look for something you stored in your garage and can't find it? It's nearly impossible to clean and organize when items are stacked five-high in your garage. Recruit your kids and actually take *everything* out of the garage. Once you have everything out of the garage, have each family member sort the items and pick out what can be thrown out or given away. Then have them pick only what they want to retain, meaning that what's left can be tossed.

Three Basic Options

A simple three-pile system of sorting works best. Separate everything into three piles. Identify items as …

1. Will go.

2. Will stay.

3. Are "too good" to toss (and are likely salable).

Round up and cart away all those items in the "go" pile. Give them away if they're reusable. Then separate all the items that will stay in your garage into categories. Sports equipment should go in one category, while tools go in another. If you have hazardous products, especially flammables, purchase a small fireproof cabinet from a home-improvement store.

Figure out how to position those items that you want to keep in your garage space. This is the difficult part and will require compromise. Mom might want her items near the garage door, where they will be accessible to her, while Dad wants his tools and workbench in the same area. Approach the situation rationally. Should certain items be near the door to the house because they're used more often? Are some things too bulky to be kept near the door because they block access?

Divine Guidance

You can save time by storing things where you can get your hands on them, and you can make money by selling home-made crafts or doing service work in your garage.

Now, if you have many items in the "too good to throw away" pile, plan a garage sale as soon as possible. If you put it off, those things will likely find their way back into the garage, which defeats the purpose of removing them to begin with!

Be a Wall Wizard

If you've always dreamed of opening a woodworking shop and you have space in the garage, use wall mounts and shelving to support your quest. Perhaps you simply want to be able to walk to your car without stepping over a pile of junk. Either way, using the garage to its fullest potential will make your life easier.

If you choose to store all your items on the floor, by the time you get everything in the garage, there will be little place to park the family vehicles and to walk around. If this is the case, purchase some ready-made cabinets and shelves to hang in the garage. This is a good idea because you can lock the cabinets to keep things away from children; also, if a thief snoops around your garage, he can't see all the goods.

You don't necessarily need to hang shelves on the walls to hold extra items in the garage. Since the garage doesn't need to be kept "pretty," hang empty coffee cans or soup cans on the wall to hold small items such as nails, screws, and the like. You can hang these directly on the wall over a workbench or on a pegboard. Make sure to attach them above the reach of children.

> ### That's the Spirit
>
> Bent nails, rusty screws, nuts and bolts that don't match (and no longer seem to be needed) …. Do you ever wonder why you hang on to some things and what you're going to do with them? Spiritually speaking, you might be hanging on to a hope that God can make your world of the present better, says Dr. Larry Crabb. "We naturally turn to God only to use him to improve our present lives. All our troublesome passions spring from this core passion to make our present lives better …."

Creative Containers

Whether you're a seamstress or a mechanic, plastic storage containers from manufacturers such as Tupperware or Rubbermaid will help you keep small items organized. Storage containers with small compartments can be used to house anything from buttons to washers. This is convenient because if you drop the container, it won't break and small items won't spill all over creation.

Hang on to any baby food jars you encounter. If you have a table or workbench with drawers in the garage, keep small items stored in baby food jars in those drawers. You can keep different sizes of nails in different jars, as long as each bottle is labeled clearly. If you don't have any drawers, nail or glue the cap to the underside of a shelf and unscrew the bottom when you need an item from the jar.

> ### Divine Guidance
>
> Avoid drowning in a sea of cords. It seems inevitable that once you use a drop cord for the first time, you can never wind it back up as tightly as it was to begin with. To keep your drop cords in order, wind these as tightly as possible and secure them with thick rubber bands. For smaller drop cords, wind them up and stick them inside empty cardboard tubes. You can keep everything together in one drawer, and cords won't be tangled up with each other.

Garden Tools in a Barrel

Use a heavy-duty plastic garbage can on wheels for storing long-handled yard and garden tools, such as rakes and hoes. Glue or drill hooks into the side of the garbage can and attach smaller tools to the hooks. Prevent the can from tipping over by balancing tools carefully and avoiding overload. With your implements correctly stored, all you have to do is drag the garbage can with you around the yard or garden.

If gardening happens to be your forte, or if you have more supplies than you know what to do with, consider building a permanent storage unit in the garage or adjacent to the garage. Many home center stores have permanent storage unit models that you can buy or copy.

Other Hangups

Let's say your children constantly leave their bicycles in the middle of the garage or driveway, and you don't feel that running over the bikes with your car will be a good learning experience. Instead install heavy-duty rods or hooks on your garage wall for hanging the bicycles. It's best to hang the bicycles upside down and low to the ground so that your children can reach them. Even if the bike is heavy, your child can lift one wheel at a time and hook it onto the wall, out of the way. If it's still too heavy, he can enlist the help of older brothers or sisters. Make it a family chore and responsibility.

If you have an old hammock lying around your garage, hang it up and use it to store sports equipment. Soccer balls, basketballs, footballs, and other sports equipment will fit nicely in one secure bundle. If you don't have a hammock, most hardware stores carry mesh material that can serve the same purpose. Hang it across a corner at a height low enough to be available to anyone who needs to reach something.

Divine Guidance

Pegboards offer versatility when hanging things because you can quickly rearrange what to hang and where to hang it.

Corkboard is useful for the garage because it's so versatile. You can stick many things on corkboard, from blueprints to instructions for making that birdhouse you've been wanting to find time to work on. All the paperwork will be out of your way but accessible. Corkboard can be purchased from any home-improvement or discount-retail store.

Safety First, Always

For your safety and the safety of your family, always test your garage door. Every few months is fine for newer garage doors, but if your garage door is older (especially older than 1982), be on the safe side and check it every month.

The Consumer Products Safety Commission (CPSC) reports that every year, regrettably a few children are trapped and killed under automatic garage doors that failed to stop and reverse after contact. Inspect your garage door by performing this little test that the CPSC recommends: "Place a 2-inch block of wood on the ground under the door. Close the door, and if it doesn't reverse upon striking the wood, disconnect the opener. Have the opener serviced or replaced with a new unit that complies with new safety standards."

When it comes to safeguarding your garage from theft, recognize that professional thieves can devise many ways of unlocking your automatic or manual garage door. A combination lock and chain will make thieves work double-duty. If the intruder breaks a panel and unlocks the door, he will have to break a large enough panel to squeeze through because the chain and combination lock will prevent the door from being lifted.

> **That's the Spirit**
>
> If you can safeguard a garage, you should be able to keep your soul safe, too. Thieves trying to steal your soul? "Satan's regular way of working is to deceive," J. I. Packer writes in *Knowing and Doing the Will of God*, "and thereby get people to err without any suspicion that what they are thinking and doing is not right." Knowing that the devil is at work is the first step to safety. The next is to acknowledge the presence of God in all you do.

Attacking the Attic

As you did with the basement (see Chapter 11), you want to exploit your attic for storing items you don't use every day. Whether you need an extra bedroom or study, the attic may be a viable option in your home. If you don't have a basement, converting the attic may be your only option, especially if you don't have the money to build an addition onto your home.

Some issues, however, need to be addressed before you store anything in your attic. Always check for structural problems and take care of those first. For example, is the attic floor sturdy enough to hold the extra weight? Also, will rodents ruin valuable items that you keep in the attic? The following sections contain some hints to maximize the storage in your attic.

Divine Guidance

If you use your attic strictly for storage, similar to the recommendation for the basement, keep an inventory list posted somewhere in the attic. This will make it easier for anyone to locate the Christmas decorations or some other item that you packed away. The list doesn't have to be detailed; as long as it tells the basic location, people should have few problems finding what they need.

Exterminate and Air Out First

Hire an exterminator before you store anything in your attic, especially clothing. It's best to start with a professional and follow his tips on keeping pests out of your home. You may need to keep some rat poison in the attic and enlist a brave person to go in the attic occasionally to see if there are any rat corpses lying around (preferably before it starts to smell). If you think you have a vermin problem, you may want to store your valuables in a safe-deposit box.

Moisture problems in the attic can be as serious as in the basement and can make things smell (though probably not as bad as a rat corpse). Some of your moisture problems in the attic may be due to moisture problems in your basement, so start there. If you're having trouble after the basement has been taken care of, take steps to increase the air flow in your attic. You can set a 20-inch electric fan at the entrance, to draw air from inside the house. If the attic is still damp or musty, have a professional check it out.

Install skylights in attics that need more illumination. This will also help heat the attic and make it appear more spacious. "Manufacturers make skylights to fit common rafter spacings," says one expert. "By buying units that fit neatly within two or three rafter bays, you can minimize the number of rafters that need to be cut. You can choose from fixed skylights or ventilated skylights that can be opened."

Box It Up and Roll It

Plastic crates and reinforced cardboard boxes are useful for organizing your home and also are effective for attic storage. Cedar chests are commonly employed, but some of these can be exceedingly heavy. Label all crates and boxes with the contents, or consider color coding your storage containers. For example, put all your Christmas decorations in red crates, all your off-season clothes in blue crates, and so on.

If you tend to put volumes of items into your crates, you may find it difficult to lift them. It's easier to roll storage containers than to carry them. Acquire crates that are on wheels, or attach rollers yourself. Rollers and superglue can be purchased at most hardware and home-improvement stores, and are easily attached.

Once you get the crate out of the attic, you can roll it into your room, take out next season's clothes, and replace them with soon to be out-of-season clothes. The only lifting involved will be getting it up and down the attic stairs.

That's the Spirit

Attics don't have to be just for storage. If you have an attic where you can safely sit—without the floor breaking or heat boiling your brain—use it as a sanctuary. If you don't have such an attic, find a quiet spot on the floor, close your eyes, and imagine that you're sitting there in that Spartan space. Pray just for peace. "Pursue righteousness, faith, love, and peace, along with those who call on the Lord out of a pure heart." (2 Timothy 2:22)

Hang 'Em High

Instead of boxing up your clothes, hang them in your attic. You can easily install a wooden or metal rod across rafters to create a makeshift closet rod. If you hang out-of-season clothing in the attic, make sure you keep your clothes in some type of plastic cover. This will prevent your clothes from smelling like a musty attic and will keep the rats away.

If you've used all your floor space and the space underneath the eaves, you have another option for storing extra small items: Hang adjustable shelves from the rafters and ceiling. You can also hang plastic-covered wire baskets, which are available from home-improvement stores or discount retailers.

Novel Storage Areas

Storing objects in your home isn't a crime, but not taking advantage of viable storage area in your home is a waste of space. Also, when you find a hidden storage area in your home, you don't have to tell family members about it (let them buy this book on their own).

For example, most of the staircase undersides in your home are sealed off and unused. Yet you can easily use this sealed-off space for storage by installing a door underneath the staircase. The newfound space can be converted into a storage closet. Alternatively, you can employ the space for storing canned vegetables or fruit, or even for bookshelves.

Divine Guidance

Hidden areas are good for storing birthday and Christmas presents so that no one will know what they're getting before they're supposed to.

If your kitchen cabinets are attached to your ceiling by beams, you can use the space available for storing bulky pots and pans or china you seldom use. However, before you do this, be sure your cabinets are strong enough to hold the extra weight. You can enclose the soffit with regular cabinet doors or leave it open. If you have decorative pots and pans, this is a good place to store them, where everyone can see them.

Part 4

Organizing Your Vital Documents

Have you ever noticed that documents seem to pile up quickly?
The three chapters in this part all focus on the vital skill of managing vital papers and documents so that you can retrieve them
as necessary. After all, keeping files and piles organized goes a
long way toward keeping your home and home life in general
organized.

Chapter 17

The Files and Piles of Life

Into every life some piles will accumulate! A couple issues of a magazine, some coupons you clipped from the newspaper, a single day's worth of mail, some fliers left by your door, the electric bill that came in a couple of days ago, and bingo, you've got a pile! A basic step to making your life more organized is confronting the piles head-on.

By their nature, piles tend to correlate with disorganization. The higher the stack is and the more diverse the elements are that comprise it, the more disorganization the pile represents. Piles represent unfinished business and, therefore, a lack of completion of one's affairs. Yet there are ways to handle the piles that materialize a little too often in your life. And such is the subject of this chapter.

Filing: A Great Notion

In every family, key papers such as school, medical, and work-related documents can quickly become overwhelming. The not-so-closely guarded secret to managing the vital papers and documents in your life is ... filing!

Do you look upon filing papers as drudgery? If so, you're not alone! You don't see people shooting movies, writing Broadway plays, or producing hard rock albums on the topic. It's rather mundane, even pedestrian. Yet it's an unparalleled key to becoming organized. I file for several hours once a week. You need only time and energy—there's no magic to organizing.

The goal of filing is to gain the capacity to withdraw what you need when you need it. Everything you've ever filed or will file, presumably, has future value, if only enabling you to cover your derriere. People often avoid filing because they don't see the connection between filing and its future impact on their family or their careers.

You file items because you believe that they will come in handy. You also file because there are consequences for not retaining important documents. You save receipts from business expenses so you can be reimbursed by your organization and comply with IRS regulations.

Keeping in mind the importance of filing, also recognize that most of what confronts you will have exceedingly little impact on your career or your life. Your quest includes avoiding filing items that don't have future value.

> **Caution Corner**
>
> Filing is not glamorous, and it's not likely to ever be glamorous, but it is important. If you get too far behind in your filing, documents can get lost, thrown away, or even put in the wrong location. This can make you take extra steps to find the document or have a replacement sent to you.

Tools to Organize Your Files

Filing requires some basic tools and the proper mind-set. The tools include the following:

- **A chair.** You can file while standing if you have a four-drawer filing cabinet and you're dealing with the top drawer. At home, you're not likely to have such office furniture. Usually your filing activity is easier if you're in a chair, particularly a swivel chair. If you're way be-hind in your filing, you won't want to be on your feet.

- **A desk or flat surface.** This comes in handy when you staple or unstaple, paper clip or unpaper clip. Often you'll have to mark the folders you insert in your file cabinet, making notes on what you're filing, folding, ripping, or taping together.

- **File folders.** File folders are essential. Rather than the standard two-cut or three-cut manila folders, buy

> **Divine Guidance**
>
> You can set up a system similar to what you would see in a dentist's office, with visible, color-coded files. You could have everything related to taxes in red files, everything related to school in blue, and so on.

folders in blue, green, brown, red, pink, or black—any color you want. They can be letter size, legal size, or ones with a protruding label area.

- **File folder labels.** File folder labels can be color-coded as well. You don't have to order the same old white labels. You can easily have subsections within your green file folders by using labels of different colors. Color-coded dots enhance your ability to stay organized. These help you find files quickly, even if you're already using color-coded files and labels. You could put a small red dot on files you anticipate using in the next week or two. However, the real value of the dots and labels is that you can leave the files in the file drawer instead of on your shelf or desk.

- **Fasteners.** Keep staplers, paper clips, and other fasteners on hand; you never know when you'll need to fasten or unfasten items before you file them (see the section that follows for more information).

- **Filing cabinet.** Keep your file folders organized alphabetically and review them periodically to make sure they don't get out of order. If you find that another organizaional method works better, for example, filing folders by months and years, then do what works best for you.

What you file is not etched in stone. You can move things around, chuck them, or add or delete files. Your goal for now is to get things into their best apparent home.

Divine Guidance

Since you're organizing files for everything important, you have to include church- and faith-related materials, too. You have tax-deductible contributions to church, for starters. Keep your favorite faith-related magazine articles in another file. If you're involved in the business operations of the church, you'd better keep files. And if you take notes during sermons or prepare Bible studies, file them in the "God" files as well.

More on Fasteners

When it comes to organizing such files, the popular choice to park them in is a filing cabinet—preferably one with doors that swing open and closed rather easily. Since most of the files that you maintain at home are not legal size, the standard width filing cabinet should do fine. There are many varieties at the office supply stores including one-drawer, two-drawer, and three-drawer files.

Start with a two-drawer file cabinet, which might extend to 18–24 inches. Probably 24 inches will suffice. Use colored file folders to help separate items and give you visual control of your drawer. For example, anything related to money could be in green file folders, and anything related to health could be in a red file folder.

Desk drawers can also serve as filing cabinets although the space is limited and unless the desk is especially well designed, it is often difficult to easily open and close the drawer. For the types of information that you file and extract on a regular basis, having them nearby, such as in the lower left or right desk drawer, that can accommodate standard size files, is convenient.

If you find that the files are becoming voluminous, with little slack in the drawers, first prune what you can. Chuck the old and obsolete, duplicates, and anything else you feel that you don't need to retain. That exercise alone may enable you to avoid needing to buy a one- or two-drawer filing cabinet. As long as you have about 20 percent of your desk drawer vacant you're in decent shape.

> **Caution Corner**
>
> The moment you have to stuff files to force them into the drawer, and pull with considerable tug to extract them, it's a reasonable bet that there will be a filing cabinet in your future.

The Battle That Never Subsides

Even with PCs, fax/modems, e-mail, and the Internet, paper will continue to be the dominant means of communication and the scourge of your battle to stay organized. In many respects, at home and at work, to stay organized is to win the battle with paper.

Swift Resolution

The common denominator for addressing paper intrusions is to reduce the energy necessary for their swift resolution. Any time you face a pile or general clutter, or feel disorganized, keep in mind the following:

- Identifying items for recycling (chucking) is usually easiest. You want to get your accumulation to a lean and mean state by chucking things at high speed. This is your best chance to avoid getting bogged down in the irrelevancies.

- Frequently downgrade the status of items as you see fit. If you have too many items in your important file, you are stuck with the same problem you had before you dealt with the accumulation. Everything seems to be competing for your time and attention with equal fervor. If you can deftly downgrade the status of an item, perhaps from important and urgent to simply important or simply urgent, or to something that someone else can handle, then you have reduced the immediate burden that you face.

- Continue to look for what can be combined, automated, systemized, delegated, delayed, ignored, or otherwise used for fireplace kindling.

- When you have pared down piles or accumulations to the least possible volume, use whatever tools you have available to keep them neat and orderly. This could include a stapler, a rubber band, paper clips, file folders—all the things mentioned at the start of this chapter.

When you receive a catalog, a magazine, or some other thick packet in the mail, strip it down to its essence. What few articles, pages, or items of interest do you want to retain? Once you identify those, recycle the rest and reduce the potential for glut.

Your goal: Retain the few pages that seem important, and recycle the larger document.

Divine Guidance

The more like things that you can group together, the easier it will be to deal with them—and the easier it will be to recycle or discard duplicates.

Can you freely use the copier at work? If so, when new items arrive at home, consider the creative ways you can strip them down to their essence, particularly using the copier. Can you create a single sheet, perhaps front and back, that represents the key information of the larger document? Can you compile several small scraps or tidbits you want to retain?

The "C" Drawer

Alan Lakein, a management specialist of yesteryear, had an idea about what to do with the mounting piles of stuff you can't deal with right now but that you want to review when you have a chance. He suggested putting such items in what he calls a "C" drawer, meaning that it's not an "A" or "B" item. You can't chuck it entirely, but you certainly can't deal with it at the moment, either.

In this drawer, you temporarily house what you want out of sight and out of mind. Go back to your "C" drawer when you have the time (and mental and emotional strength!) to take out the items and see what needs to go into your file system (probably not much), what you can immediately chuck or recycle, and what goes back into the "C" drawer.

Larger but Fewer Files

The more files you have, the more difficult it is to find any particular file. You are better off with a handful of large files than many small ones; you have a much greater chance of choosing the right file. Hereafter, sort through your files, look for unnecessary items, and chuck them. Make it fun. Eliminate excess files until you have only the essential ones.

Even after you've pared down a particular pile to a smaller, more concise pile, ask yourself, "What am I continuing to retain that adds to unnecessary disorganization?" Perhaps you are already familiar with the issue an item represents and don't need to retain printed information relating to it. With this in mind, you may be able to chuck at least one third or more of the documents remaining in your already stripped-down pile.

> **Divine Guidance**
>
> All the folders that you use to file papers are potentially reusable. Label them over and give them new life. Reusing folders, as well as single sheets of paper with one blank side, gives you a quick and socially acceptable means of dealing with much of the paper that arrives during the day.

Lean and Mean

When you've pared down your piles to the lowest possible volume and gotten them into mean, lean, slim, trim shape, keep like items together using a stapler, paper clip, rubber band, or other organizational tool. A paper clip assembling a packet of papers works best if the assemblage is temporary. In general, the more like items you can fasten together, the easier it will be for you to find any particular item that you need.

If you have slimmed down several piles, you may arrange the piles in a cascading or stair-step manner down one side of your desk or table. In other words, if you had five slim piles, each would have the top 1 inch visible before being covered by the next, with the top page of the last pile entirely visible. This spatial arrangement allows you to draw upon any one of the five piles while keeping the other four in order.

> **That's the Spirit**
>
> When it comes to the order of things, change can be drastic. The way you order life around you is important, but remember that God has a new order: "And I heard a loud voice from the throne saying, 'Now the dwelling of God is with men, and he will live with them. They will be his people, and God himself will be with them and be their God. He will wipe every tear from their eyes. There will be no more death or mourning or crying or pain, for the old order of things has passed away.'" (Revelation 21:3–5)

Clarifying Questions

When you're confronted by yet another catalog, flyer, or document, ask yourself these key questions: What is the issue behind this document? What does the paper represent? Is it important to my family? Is it merely an information crutch (data that you already know)? If so, chuck it. Does it represent something you think might be important in the future? If so, put it in the "C" drawer. Here are some other questions to keep in mind:

- Are these papers irrelevant to your life? Often the underlying issue behind the paper flood is, in retrospect, too minor to merit your attention. Sure, it looms large at times, but what doesn't seem important when it arrives in screaming headlines? For years, newspapers have been able to sell their wares simply with clever use of language and font size. The issues addressed often have precious little to do with the typical reader.

- Did I need to receive this at all? This can be an insightful question to ask yourself. In many cases, the answer is no; that means you don't have to spend another second on the item. Now and then, something you didn't need to receive comes your way and looks semi-interesting. (Rare, but possible.) You can chuck most of these items immediately.

Divine Guidance

If you don't participate in the office pool, don't make an extra copy of that recipe, or don't learn about that software game, your life will not change. Keep focused on the papers you will realistically get to and deal with.

- How else can this be handled? Can someone else in your cosmos handle this for you and free up your time for more important things? If no one else but you will do, how else can you handle it? Can you pay by check instead of in person? Can you pay by credit card by fax instead of by check?

- Will it matter if I don't handle it at all? This is a critical question. Much of what confronts you requires no action on your part. For example, these are announcements regarding upcoming publications, ads that tout prices or services, and anything addressed to "Current Resident."

If you question whether to file an item, put it aside for a day or two and look at it again. Often the answer will present itself. Ask yourself, "What will happen if I pitch this?" If there's no notable downside, chuck it gleefully. Your house and your family will thank you.

Reclaim Your Home

Suppose you face a glut of documents on the table. How will you tackle it? Wade through everything rapidly and determine what can be tossed, and identify any duplicate or outdated items you don't need. Without hesitation, round up any suspects that fit these categories and trash or recycle them:

- Back issues of magazines you haven't touched in ages.
- All scraps and tidbits of information and used stick-em notes that have accumulated around your desk, in your wallet, and elsewhere. Get them on a single sheet or log them into a file on your computer.
- Excess catalogs.
- Outdated catalogs, flyers, brochures, and promotional materials.
- The hoard of thumbtacks, push pins, pennies, and paper clips that gather in the corners of your desk drawers.
- Take-out/delivery menus from restaurants you never visit (or visit so frequently that you've memorized the bill of fare).
- Lingering stacks of irrelevant documents and extra copies of relevant documents. Retain what you need. Toss the rest.

Divine Guidance

Throwing something out can be a drastic act—the last destination for something you once valued. Even if you find later that you miss something that you've thrown away, remember that God provides us with what we need.

"When in doubt, throw it out." These immortal words, uttered two decades ago by efficiency expert Edwin Bliss, are still true. If you're not sure about keeping something, in most cases you've already answered the question: No. If you're like most people, you have a tendency to over-collect, which contributes to obscuring anything you need to find. If you ever file too much stuff, use the "C" drawer discussed previously as a pit stop for potential file items.

Face Piles with Smiles

Here's a bold and effective way to tackle the piles of files that you face right now. First make sure you have a pen, some blank file folders, paper clips, rubber bands, and a stapler available. Now you're ready to collect everything that you suspect may need attention.

Step 1: Stack and pile. Stack up all the items in front of you in a temporary pile. In 30 minutes or less, you're going to dismantle and reallocate this simplicity-threatening pile. Assign each item to one of four locations: an Important pile, an Urgent pile, an Interesting pile, or the recycling bin, where most items will go.

Step 2: Assess and allocate. Allocate items to the best of your knowledge. If an item is urgent *and* important, place it in the Important pile near the top. If it's simply urgent, place it in the appropriate pile. If you are unsure about any particular item, you may place it at the bottom of the large stack, but do so only once for each item.

On the second encounter with the item, you have to classify an item. In 30 minutes or less, the voluminous pile should be gone and you'll be left with three neat or tiny piles. Rank the items and then rearrange them in each pile. Downgrade or toss anything you can. You're left with three smaller, more precisely arranged piles: Important, Urgent, and Interesting.

Step 3: How much work? Determine the work hours required to handle the tasks that the piles represent. Starting with the important pile, estimate how long it will take to complete each item. Add all your estimates and multiply that number by 1.5. Do the same with the other piles.

Step 4: Marshal your resources. Realistically, what will it take to accomplish all that you have laid out before you as important and urgent, important, and so on?

Caution Corner

Find the balance. Just as those words apply to life in general, they also certainly apply to stacking, allocating, and organizing. Remember to keep the end result in mind: getting closer to God. Sometimes we forget that all our great little organizing ideas can come from the Holy Spirit, especially when we pray.

As you approach the most important and urgent item, keep in mind that sometimes you can't take it all the way to completion. Maybe it requires help from others. Maybe you need someone else to approve certain steps. Take it as far as you can go and then consult with others, but during the interim, start on the next project. Similarly, take that as far as you can go—to completion, if you can.

Step 5: Scouting for the chuckable. Keep looking for what else you can chuck. What can be combined, ignored, or delayed? What can be delegated, automated, or systemized? The more items you can downgrade to the Interesting pile, the farther ahead you'll be because you can deal with these items when you feel like it.

This five-step procedure can be employed in tandem with organizing techniques that you already use, such as a to-do list, because you may need to look at the roster of tasks facing you with one glance. Stacking up and allocating your pile is so immediate and responsive to the tasks you face, especially for tasks of shorter duration, that you may find yourself abandoning other methods of organizing. You'll also find yourself dropping tasks that are not important or urgent.

Ready, Set, Tackle

After you've identified the most important project or task (the one at the top of the important folder), begin working on it to its completion. If you can't complete it because it requires help from others or for some other reason, proceed with it as far as you can go. Then place it back in the folder, either on top or where you determine that it now belongs. Now begin on the next most important items and proceed as far as you can go.

As time passes, you'll find that you need a break from working on the important tasks that you have so carefully arranged. Again, this happens to everyone. You can give your rapt attention and earnest efforts to the primo projects only for so long before your mind starts to wander. You need a mental break.

At this point, feel free to turn to items farther down in the pile that still require your attention but that don't require so much mental effort. Give yourself a 10-, 15-, or 20-minute run on lower-level items that are less mentally taxing. When you feel ready, turn back to the most important items, which, to your utter convenience, await you on the top of the pile.

> **Divine Guidance**
>
> When you need a change of pace, flip to the Urgent pile. The Interesting pile can be reviewed intermittently, perhaps every couple of days or weeks. It's okay if it grows exceedingly thick. Eventually, you'll reclassify or chuck its contents.

Chapter 18

Advance File and Pile Management

Have you ever considered that what you file and how you file is largely governed by the file headings you employ? These are the labels you place on the tab section of each file folder. It is easy enough to label one file folder Office Supplies and another Insurance and another New Technology. However, you probably want to be more creative than that to accommodate the gaggle of stuff that comes your way. Some of it appears worth retaining, at least in the short run, but doesn't seemingly have a proper home.

In this chapter, we'll take a look at how to set up file headings, create files in advance of their need, shelve items effectively, and in general, control files and piles.

File Headings Are the Key

Who is to say that you cannot label your file folders with the following headings:

- Review This After the First of the Year
- Hold Until After the Merger
- Check in One Month
- Check Next Spring
- Don't Know Where to File

Divine Guidance

If you are worried that a file labeled Don't Know Where to File may grow too large too rapidly, fear not. You always have the opportunity to open that file quickly, review its contents, and act on what you see, delegate, refile, or toss it. Ideally, what you review a second or third time can now be tossed.

By having a file labeled Don't Know Where to File, you automatically create a home for the handful of things that your instincts tell you to retain but that simply don't fit anything else that you're doing. Now at least you have a fair chance of getting your hands back on such items when, lo and behold, the time might be right to reread the items closely.

By using customized file headings, you can devise compartments that enable you to give the materials that cross your desk a good home, while you remain anxiety-free, guilt-free, and fat-free. If you often don't know where to file items, you can create a file called, Where to File This? (I use one called Check in One Month.)

Other handy file names that you could use include these:

- Read or Chuck
- Read When I Can
- Review for Possible Link to ABC Project

Creating Files in Advance

Suppose your son is planning to go to graduate school for a Master's degree. One way to accommodate the growing body of literature you'll be assembling is to create a file folder in advance of having anything to file. When stuff comes in that appears worth saving, it'll have a home.

Divine Guidance

While you're creating folders for the future, add one that has nothing to do with worldly goods or needs. Label it Heaven and put things in it that you think will help you make it through the Pearly Gates. Pay more attention to this file than any of the others. After all, what's most important?

Suppose you come across a brilliant article on how to finance his degree in a way that considerably reduces your burden. Where are you going to put that article? Park it on top of something else, where it will sit for weeks or months? You still won't know what to do with it, but you'll want to hang on to it, right?

What are some files you can create in advance of having anything to put in them? Will it make sense, based on where you're heading in life? Here are some suggestions:

- Your child's higher education fund
- Your retirement home
- Your vacation next year to Aruba
- Assistance for your aging parents
- Evolving technology that interests you
- A new medical operation that might affect you

At least 50 percent of dealing with all the piles of paper you confront is simply making room for them.

Sort for Similarity

In that great mass of stuff before you, if eight items refer to your son's school affairs, that's a clue to start a file folder labeled Matt's School Affairs. Do the same with other groups of similar items.

Plow through the entire pile; toss what you can and group like items until everything is tossed or grouped. Yes, some items will stand alone. Not to worry.

When approaching each of your mini-piles, ask yourself these questions:

- Can I consolidate each pile by using the back sides of documents, single-page copies, and shorter notes?
- Can I consolidate scraps and tidbits by using the copier to create a dossier page or stapling them into a packet?
- For piles that have only one or two items each, is there a way to group them?

Go through the materials you've put in mini-piles; see if any of them should go into all-encompassing files, such as Health Insurance.

Some efficiency experts suggest putting a date stamp on every item you file. If you've been holding onto an item for months on end and haven't used it, maybe it's time to chuck it. Although an item's future relevance isn't always linked to how long you've had it, generally, the longer you've held on to an item without using it, the smaller the chance is that it will be of future importance.

A Four-Pronged Variation

Here is an effective file/pile management variation. With this system, you can do only one of four things with the stuff that confronts you. You can …

1. Act on it.
2. Delegate it.
3. File it.
4. Recycle it.

Of any given pile of stuff on your desk, chances are good that most of it can be recycled. You don't need to be hanging on to it. A lesser portion can probably be filed; a slightly lesser portion of that can probably be delegated. That leaves you with a thin file of things to act on.

Getting back to the pile in question, don't spend too much time deciding which pile to place each item in. Simply make a quick assessment and go on to the next item. Once your four piles are complete, you will undoubtedly notice that the Recycle pile is the largest. The File pile, hopefully, is much smaller. The pile of stuff to delegate to other people is smaller still, and the file of things you need to act on should be the smallest of all.

Now go through the things that you need to act on and rank them according to what is most important.

> **Divine Guidance**
>
> As an organizing principle, whenever you stop and assess a pile or accumulation, categorizing the various items vastly increases your chances of whittling out the unnecessary. Dealing with the remaining papers usually represents a manageable task.

> **That's the Spirit**
>
> What's important? It's great to be organized, but that's a worldly objective. In the greater scheme of things, however, the Bible is clear on what's important: "Jesus said, 'Hear, O Israel, the Lord our God, the Lord is one. Love the Lord your God with all your heart and with all your soul and with all your mind and with all your strength. The second is this: Love your neighbor as yourself. There is no commandment greater than these.'" (Mark 12:28–31)

Rotating Tickler Files

Great benefits come from setting up a daily and monthly rotating tickler file. Here is how it works. Suppose something crosses your desk in March and looks interesting, but you don't have to act on it until April 25. If you have one file folder for each month of the year, January to December, for a total of 12, you can park the item in the April folder.

Going further, you set up an additional 31 file folders, marked 1, 2, and so on, all the way up to 31. Now, when April approaches, you open the April file folder, take out all the contents and allocate contents to file folders 1 through 31 as appropriate. You stick the April file folder at the end of the pack so that the month of May is now in front, preceded by file folders number 1 through 31.

If you receive something on the third day of the month but don't have to deal with it until the eighteenth, put it in the folder marked 18. Better yet, to give yourself some slack, put it in a folder two or three days before the eighteenth.

These 43 file folders, 1 through 31 and January through December, allow you to park anything in the appropriate place when the item doesn't have to be dealt with too soon.

> **Divine Guidance**
>
> With tickler files, immediately much of the clutter and stuff on your desk and around your office now has a home because you've determined a date when you're going to review the materials.

The materials in your tickler files are off your desk, off your counters, and off your mind. Yet you haven't lost them; you have simply parked them in a location where you'll be able to retrieve them close to the time that it makes the most sense to deal with them.

You can use a tickler file to write out your checks and pay your bills, and then store the envelopes in the appropriate folder before sending them. Write the checks in advance, sign them, seal them, stamp them, and put the envelope in the appropriate folder of your 31-day rotating tickler file.

Review Often

Many people who use tickler files find it convenient to review them at the start of each week and perhaps one or two more times during that week. The result is less clutter, greater organization, and greater focus and direction on the pressing tasks that you face.

> **Divine Guidance**
>
> Reducing clutter among your files can offer peace of mind, but so can using the materials you file. If you file away a plan to read the Bible each morning, start following the advice. Soon it will become a habit; the hard copy won't be necessary, and you'll have found two ways to gain peace of mind.

Tickler files automatically remind you of when you need to deal with a particular task. When the request for the task hits your desk, you can place it in the tickler file for the appropriate future date. Every day of the month, check your tickler file for that day to identify tasks to take on for the day.

The monthly files and 31-day tickler files will help you reduce clutter while offering you peace of mind. It's remarkably efficient. When you view something several days, weeks, or months after first filing it, you often have greater objectivity and a new chance to act on it, delegate it, or toss it. If a lot of stuff gets tossed, fine; at least you have those things out of your way.

Maintaining Perspective

You already know that smaller piles or smaller accumulations are easier to manage than larger ones. Hence, your goal is to continue to keep your piles as slim and trim as humanly possible (although there are exceptions, which will be discussed shortly). You want to reduce the weight and volume of each pile by retaining only the highly relevant information and nothing more. For example, rather than retaining a 10-page report, hang on to only the single page that you actually need.

Taking that principle further, rather than hanging on to a single page, if you need only one paragraph, phone number or address, or website, clip that actual portion and recycle the rest of the page. Attach the small clipping that you have retained to a sheet that contains other small relevant tidbits. Then put the whole thing down on the copier machine to create a dossier page that fully supports what you are working on while not taking up much space, physically or psychologically.

Remember, if you have several piles confronting you—and by now hopefully they are all slimmed down—arrange them in a stair-step or cascading fashion down one side of your desk or table. This enables you to have the top 1 inch or so visible for a file that is covered by the next file. Such an arrangement allows you to maintain visual control of what you have been accumulating and allows you to quickly withdraw any particular pile in the arrangement while keeping the others in order.

Shelve It

Some of the files and piles, and documents and publications you encounter may need to be shelved. These include …

- **Items you're bound to use within the next two weeks.** These include reference books, directories, phone books, manuals, instruction guides, books, and magazines (especially large ones, like annual directories and theme issues).

- **Items too large for a filing cabinet (or collections of such items).** Some thick items such as books (and some magazines) are better stored on a shelf. Any oversized item that simply won't fit in a file cabinet (and any item that is part of a continuing series) is probably best housed on your shelves.

  If you receive a key publication and it makes sense for you to hang on to back issues, these also belong on your shelves. In this case, you could acquire magazine holders; these are essentially precut or preassembled boxes that hold about 24 issues of a monthly magazine. The box itself enables you to stay in control. It's visual; you can stick a face-up label on it. It's easy to grab one issue from among the many you're retaining and it's easy to replace the issue. Cardboard magazine holders help you stay in control of incoming items.

- **Current affairs.** If you're examining a variety of items relating to some family or personal issue, the magazine boxes work well. If you keep your shelves behind your seat at your desk, keep one shelf compartment clear so you can lay incoming file folders flat on it. You'll have a place for new stuff while keeping your desk relatively clear. If you face many issues competing for your attention, it makes sense to have a single flat surface (even among your shelving units) readily available to accommodate active files.

- **Supplies that can go in supply cabinets.** Most people have little difficulty filling up their shelves. Understandably, your inclination might be to get more shelves, but it's best to avoid that. Your goal is to keep your home organized by using the furniture, shelving, and space that you already have. Keep supplies in a closet or, if you have one, a supply cabinet (isn't logic beautiful?) because you can store them in bulk. Stack them horizontally or vertically. Treat your shelves as somewhat sacred; align them so you can pull out key items at will.

If it takes you longer than 30 seconds to find something on your shelves, refine your system.

> **That's the Spirit**
>
> "Efficiency is enhanced not by what we accomplish, but more often by what we relinquish," says Charles Swindoll. Life is a constant process of giving things up. Jesus said in Mark 8:35, "If you try to keep your life for yourself, you will lose it. But if you give up your life for my sake and for the sake of the Good News, you will find true life."

Nearby or Away

In housing your files, your goal is to keep closest to you the items you use frequently; keep rarely used items farthest from you. Much of what you file won't be used often. (Whatever you have to hang on to can be stored away from your immediate workspace.)

Holding Bins

One way to stem the tide of the ever-burgeoning number of files and piles accumulating in your life is to adopt the principle of using holding bins.

What is a holding bin? In its simplest form, it can be a file that is simply labeled Review These Items on January 1. Or, a holding bin can be a shoebox, a polyethylene bag, a packing box, or a shipping crate. Whether large or small, or thin or voluminous, holding bins afford you the opportunity to park items for later review. This can dramatically help to simplify your life.

> **Divine Guidance**
>
> Recognize the value and power of using creatively labeled file folders to house materials that you would otherwise not know what to do with but that you sense you cannot chuck.

Any time you receive printed information that you suspect may be worth retaining but you cannot determine where it ought to go, the answer is evident—put it in a holding bin. In this case, the holding bin could literally be a file folder with a creative label such as Check Again Next Month, Review After Tom Graduates, Read Before Leaving for Trip to the Mountains, and so on.

Alternatives, Just in Case

After all the recommendations in this chapter, if you still find yourself hanging on to all kinds of stuff because you cannot bear to pitch it, here's a plan of attack:

1. Group like items, put them in a box or storage container, and mark the box with something descriptive, such as Check Again Next April or Review After the Recital.

2. Before storing a container, quickly plow through it once more to see what can be removed. This will simplify your task, and you'll thank yourself later.

3. Once the box is out of sight, build a safeguard into your system. Put a note in your April file that says to review the contents of the box located at XYZ. Sometimes, instead of storing vast volumes of material, you can simply scan it and keep it on disk.

These three steps will ensure that you remove from your immediate area that which you don't need, thereby freeing up space that could be put to better use, or simply left vacant!

Caution Corner

Safeguarding your system is wise. Of course, you can protect your spiritual files as well. If you subscribe to Christian magazines, for example, go to their websites—most do have one by now—and save an Internet version of an article you like. You've backed up your hard copy and also enabled an easier decision when it comes time to weed out the old copies in the files. Just double-check to ensure that you have the digital file before tossing any hard copy that you'll want to see later.

Paid Storage Space

If the papers you've boxed are valuable and compact, maybe it makes sense to put them in a safety-deposit box in a bank. If they're voluminous, you might consider putting them in a commercial self-storage unit (available in most metro areas).

When you rent a self-storage unit, you get a garage-like space that you can cram full of anything you don't need on a daily basis. See Storage in the Yellow Pages to learn what storage options are available in your area.

Paying to store materials brings up the issue of what you're retaining. Is it worth it to pay a bank or a company to save the stuff? If it is, then you'll feel all right about forking over the dough. If it doesn't seem worth the cash, you have a viable indicator that you can chuck the stuff.

You Control the Files and Piles

If you don't take control, you're setting yourself up for glutted files, a glutted home, and a glutted life. Rather than becoming organized, you'll be experiencing greater chaos. So do yourself and your family a favor by removing from your immediate environment the reams of paper and piles that you don't need to re-encounter for weeks or months, or ever again.

Chapter
19

Life Is a Desk, So Keep Yours Organized

Getting organized in your personal life supports your efforts in your professional life. The more organized you are at home, in your car, and in the other places in your life, the greater the probability is that you will have more energy, focus, and direction when you head into work. You will be more efficient and perhaps have greater peace of mind.

For more people today, the workplace has moved from a high-rise office building in the city to the comfort of home. Whether you work in a traditional office, at home, or someplace in between, your desk is among the most important areas of your life and of your family. In the last chapter, you learned the necessity of filing and keeping the paper in your life under control. Here we'll discuss taking charge of your desk and, by extension, your home, office, and life.

A Shipshape Desk

In the movie *Top Gun*, Tom Cruise plays a Navy fighter pilot. Among his many responsibilities is flying some of the nation's most expensive aircrafts. He has to land these Navy jets safely on aircraft carrier decks.

A few months after seeing the movie, I read an article in *Smithsonian* magazine describing how aircraft carrier decks have to be completely clean and clear before a plane can land. "All hands on deck" on an aircraft carrier deck traditionally meant that everyone, including senior officers, picked up a push broom and swept the deck completely clear when a plane was due to land.

Today they have giant blowers and vacuums to do the job. The goal is the same—to leave nothing on the surface of the deck, not even a paper clip. This ensures the highest probability of a successful landing. What happens if there is debris on the deck as a plane approaches? What if an earlier plane has not left the landing strip? The approaching plane is likely to crash and burn.

Your desktop is like the deck of an aircraft carrier. If you take the next pile of stuff you get and simply park it in the corner of your desk, good luck when another thing lands.

Nobody is coming to help you manage your desk; each new item you pile on will (figuratively) crash and burn into smoldering ruins as your work accumulates, unless you take charge of the situation.

> **Caution Corner**
>
> Even with the popularity of the Internet and e-mail, when we talk about information overload, paper is the largest culprit.

All other things being equal, if you have one project and one piece of paper in front of you, and the rest of your desk is clear, you're bound to have more energy, focus, and direction.

If all manner of distractions such as piles of reports, memos, and faxes compete for you attention, how can you have the same energy, focus, and direction for the task at hand?

Paper Is Still the Culprit

Stay in control of the paper that comes your way. Get off extraneous mailing lists. Develop a form letter, sticker, or stamper that you mail back to senders saying, "Please take me off your list." It's a wonderful morning when you open up your mailbox and see only 6 pieces of mail instead of 18, 12 of which are junk.

If you keep the spaces of your life clear, especially flat spaces like the top of your desk, the corners, and windowsills, control of your time and your life tends to follow.

Strip arriving mail down immediately—discover what parts are vital and what can be tossed or recycled. When I receive a large packet of information, I immediately go through with the edge of a ruler and rip out the paragraphs, addresses, phone numbers, and key data. I lay these down on the copier and create one single sheet from the package I received.

That's the Spirit

Is your spiritual life like your desk? Can you focus on God when you need him? Or is he hidden in your organizer that is parked there with 10 other things to do first? Many, if not most, people compartmentalize life into distinct areas—secular and spiritual—and the two never mix. But that's not how it has to be. Os Hillman writes in *Today God Is First* that God needs to be in your work life: "God wants us to perform miracles through each of our vocations." That's much harder to do with a messy desk that hides or forsakes any sign of faith.

When a response doesn't require formal business protocol, there are many ways to handle it quickly. I clip return address labels when they're provided on envelopes. I routinely use those labels to send something back. Not many people find this objectionable. Of course, don't do this for first-time contacts. However, you'll have a sense of when you can do so—for personal correspondence and people with whom you have long-term relationships, who know you well, or who see you often.

You can buy a rubber stamp that says Speed Reply—I have a big red one. I use the stamp on the letters I receive and handwrite my response on the actual letter. Then I fax it back or copy the letter and mail it. The letter is off my desk, and I have a written record of our correspondence.

A Workable Desk Arrangement

You don't have to be an interior decorator to create a comfortable and workable desk arrangement. The only requirement is that you make logical decisions concerning the arrangement of items around it. Positioning your desk and furniture in the most comfortable way will help you get your work done in a shorter amount of time.

Anything that's used at least twice a day should be within arm's reach or in a drawer that is close by. Other items that you use less frequently may be stored in a drawer, filing cabinet, or desk so they're still close but not in the way when you're working.

With a little discipline, anyone can have a well-organized desk. A trick that works for some people is to use priority boxes. More important papers go in one box, and less important items go in another. Although the boxes take up space, at least papers won't be piled up all over the desk. When you start looking for an important paper, you'll know which box it's in and you won't have to waste time scouring the place.

Elbow Room

To work most efficiently, give yourself plenty of room around your desk to move. Don't place file cabinets or shelves so close that you keep bumping into them. Invest in a desk chair with rollers so that you can move from one place to another and turn more easily.

Some people organize their space into small work centers. For example, you could keep all communication equipment, such as the phone, fax, computer, and printer, in one area. Another section could be a mail center where you take care of all the day's incoming mail and apply postage to outgoing mail.

> **Caution Corner**
>
> Leave excessive decorations off your desk. Your desk will crowd quickly enough without additional odds and ends cluttering the area. Clear out the unnecessary items and start enjoying a new, more efficient work life.

Assess and Reassess

Today you can find exactly the item you need or want to make you feel more comfortable and to be more productive at your desk. Whatever the item is, as you begin reaping the benefits, you will quickly forget the cost.

Periodically consider different devices that could support your desktop arrangement, such as computer trays, hanging lamps, and swivel mechanisms to conveniently move equipment as needed.

To create more surface space, you could use a mechanical arm that hoists your PC monitor over the desk. It swings forward and back, and left and right. Now that I have one, I don't know how I lived without it.

Newsflash: Your Desktop Is Not a Filing Cabinet

What to keep on top of your desk is uniquely individual. As a general rule, anything you use on a daily basis, such as a stapler, a roll of tape, or a pen, gets to stay on top of your desk. Remove anything that you can safely eliminate from your desktop. The fewer things you have in these vital places, the greater the sense of control you have over your immediate environment.

Inside your desk, retain items you use at least weekly, but don't start storing supplies there. Those belong farther away from you, in other storage areas. Your goal is to maintain the optimal number of items on and in your desk; enough so you work efficiently while there, but not enough to clutter up the works. Recognize that your desk drawers are not for storing supplies, per se. You may store a pad of paper, but not *pads* of paper.

You need only one pad at a time, and the general principle is to have the least amount of an item that you need, and then no more.

If you choose to use one of your desk drawers to contain file folders, then obviously, these will be file folders of pressing family matters. These files should be as thin and potent as you could make them.

Your goal is to have in front of you what you need and not much more. Oddly enough, once these flat surfaces are under control, you also gain a heightened sense of control over your time. Such a deal!

> ### That's the Spirit
>
> A messy desk curtails productivity and leads to loss of profit in the long run. "Hard workers have plenty of food; playing around brings poverty." (Proverbs 28:19)

The following items can help you keep your desk in shape:

- Color-coded file folders, tabs, labels, and long-life stampers. Long-life stampers can cut down on the time you spend handwriting or organizing material.
- A few three-ring notebooks for storing and maintaining similar items.
- A large wastebasket.
- Magazine holders for your shelves.

The following are useful tools for your desk and surrounding areas:

- Paper
- Letterhead
- Business envelopes
- Mailing supplies
- Overnight mail packets
- A letter opener
- A ruler
- Stamps
- A stapler and a staple remover
- Scissors
- Business cards
- Batteries
- Tape, packing tape, glue, a glue stick
- Bulletin board, thumb tacks, push pins, Post-It pads
- Pens, pencils, markers, and permanent markers
- File folders, file labels, label paper
- Postcards, note cards, greeting notes, scratch paper
- Paper clips, dove clips, fasteners

Near your desk, but not on it, go the loving and familiar items, such as pictures, plants, and motivators. Also, if an item supports your productivity, efficiency, and creativity (from full-spectrum lights to ocean-wave music, or whatever) install it near, but not on, your desk.

Hereafter, manage your desktop as if it's one of the most important elements to staying organized—because it is.

Planning at Your Desk

Correct use of calendars and computers can keep you rolling on the right track. Use one and only one calendar. The reasoning behind this is simple. If you document appointments in one place, you'll have to keep up with only one calendar. Some

Divine Guidance

Even though your calendar is primarily for business, add personal appointments to it as well. There's no point in sticking a card for a doctor's appointment on the refrigerator if you have one calendar that you look at every day.

Divine Guidance

Novelist Samuel Butler said that life is one long process of getting tired. It's a constant battle to keep little things from wearing us out and chipping away at our success. Organization is one way to beat those little things.

people have separate personal and professional calendars, but this is not necessary. Keep one calendar that you browse through daily, and jot down important items in it.

It may be best to stick to a simple planner. Unless you travel often, you probably don't need an elaborate day planner. Look around office supply stores to compare prices and contents of many different planners. If you're the only one seeing the planner, there's no point in buying an expensive one. If customers will see you using it, then invest a little more money. Don't spend a lot of money on a planner that provides more than you need.

How organized are you? Are you as organized as you think you are?

- Can you retrieve any paper from your desk files within a minute?
- Are your file headings all labeled?
- Do you keep marginally useful and outdated papers for longer than two months?
- Have you compactly stored backup materials for a report in a few folders?
- Can you file everything on your desk within 30 minutes?

Top Achievers Agree

I've discussed the issue of keeping one's desk organized with top achievers in many different professions. They all agree that when their desks and personal surroundings are in order, they feel far more energized at the start of the day. Conversely, when these top achievers start their day and see a huge mess, they feel somewhat defeated.

From the standpoint of staying organized, as well as feeling energized, clear your desk and surroundings each evening as you end work for the day so that the next day you can be at your best.

Clear Your Desk

In his book *Success Forces,* Joe Sugarman explains that by clearing your desk every evening, you automatically have to *choose* what to work on the next day. Though such reasoning is contrary to the advice of "time management" experts, I whole-heartedly endorse it. It is a discipline that yields a marvelous sense of order with which to start each day.

Clearing your desk and surroundings each evening is a discipline. Most people don't want to do it. It is easier simply to take off for the day. However, when you arrange your materials the evening before for higher productivity the next morning, a whole host of beneficial effects come into play.

Divine Guidance

Every evening after you've cleared your desk, congratulate yourself for what you accomplished that day.

When you leave with a clear desk, you give yourself a sense of closure or completion to your day. This ends up affording you a greater chance to enjoy the rest of your evening.

Boost in the Morning

When you arrive in the morning and are greeted by clear, clean surroundings, you gain a psychological boost much as the high achievers did. What is more, you get to make a fresh decision about what materials to extract from your desk, filing cabinet, or shelves based on what you want to accomplish that morning. This is a far different situation than merely dealing with what you left on the desk the night before.

Some projects span several days; in that sense, it can be prudent occasionally to simply leave a file folder open on your desk so that it will greet you the next morning. However, you don't want to fall into a situation in which you are always being greeted by stuff you left on the desk the night before.

When you begin each morning with a clear, clean desk and clear, clean surroundings, you can concentrate on what you deem most important and urgent.

Your PC, Your Friend

Spending all day in front of a computer can take a toll on your health. Here are tips to relieve fatigue while working, from Dr. Ronald Harwin and Colin Haynes, authors of *Healthy Computing:*

- Slight headaches and backaches often signal poor posture. Have someone check yours.

- Check the position of your wrists and arms when working at the keyboard. If your fingers are higher than your wrists, you're asking for painful trouble.

- Keep your workplace uncluttered so that you can use the keyboard and the mouse comfortably.

- Organize your work so that you have to stand up occasionally.

- Take a short break from keyboarding at least once every two hours; however, as often as every 20 minutes is preferable.

- Clean a dusty monitor screen.

- At least once an hour, drop your hands down to your sides. Gently shake your hands and fingers.

- If your shoulders feel tense, rotate them forward in a full circle four times. Then rotate each shoulder separately four times.

If you experience more severe problems than these, contact a doctor.

That's the Spirit

Where do you find energy after another long day? The apostle Paul struggled through more hardships than his modern counterparts will ever see. Paul explains in Colossians 1:28–29, "We proclaim him, admonishing and teaching everyone with all wisdom, so that we may present everyone perfect in Christ. To this end I labor, struggling with all his energy, which so powerfully works in me."

Your Desk and Your Files

It's important to look at the relationship between your files (see Chapters 17 and 18) and your workspace in general. Filing is a dynamic process. Items that you place in your file folder today may find their way onto your shelves, reemerge in some other form, or be chucked. What's on your shelves may (in some mutant form) find its way into your files.

If you have a big reference book on a shelf, you may want to extract a few pages from it, discard or recycle the larger volume, and retain only a few essential pages in a folder in your filing cabinet. The relationship among all your storage areas is dynamic; your prevailing quest is to boil down what's crucial for you to retain— keep only the essence.

Are you fearful about tossing something because you "know" you're going to need it tomorrow? Accept this: If there are no discernible negative consequences to tossing something, toss it. Most of what you're retaining is readily replaceable anyway. Efficiency experts claim that 80 percent of what executives file, they never use again. Even if that's only partially true, it still means that a significant chunk of what you're retaining is deadwood.

Caution Corner

If you can't find what you've saved, it's of no value to you. Worse, the time you took to read and file the items was wasted.

Caution Corner

The great paradox of keeping house is that getting things in shape takes time.

Clearing this deadwood out of your desk, files, and surrounding areas keeps your workspace in shape. That enhances your capacity to properly handle new demands. It also improves the odds that you'll be able to locate those items you actually need.

Consider the cumulative time savings you could potentially chalk up if you cut your search time in half. Let's say you'll save 12 minutes per day, at minimum. That adds up to an hour per week and 50 hours per year. That's like creating an extra week for yourself. As a bonus, others around you get a clear message that you're someone who is able to remain in control, find things quickly, and stay on top of situations. So, you get a multiple payoff for keeping your files (and your work space in general) in shape.

Persevere. The small time investment you make in developing your newfound efficiency in managing household affairs will pay off repeatedly down the road.

Part

5

Organizing New Information

It's one thing to get your existing documents in order. It's quite another to effectively integrate the volumes of new information that comes into each of our lives on pretty much a daily basis. The three chapters in this part help you to become a master at identifying and ingesting new information so that it serves you and your family to the best advantage.

Chapter 20

Reading and Information Aids

Most people today contend with all types of information in great quantities. A single superstore bookseller offers more than 150,000 titles (none of which addresses Information Fatigue Syndrome!), stocks nearly 2,500 domestic and international newspapers and periodicals, and can easily order an additional 200,000 book titles from national distributors.

The children's section of this bookstore may include 15,000 titles; the music section includes 25,000 CDs and cassettes. And this is but one outlet for producers and publishers, who generate up to 10 times that many products.

In the over-information society we all face today, keeping pace with important as well as elective reading materials has become a major challenge for many people. The amount of reading that you do to further your career can be staggering.

In this chapter, we discuss ways to take a more organized approach to both your professional and personal reading—and, by extension, ways in which your entire family can benefit as well.

Approaching Reading in New Ways

In the course of a week, you may find yourself spending anywhere from 10 to 20 hours just on reading "to keep pace." Add to that any reading that you do to enhance your domestic life or for pleasure, and you quickly see how the hours add up.

Fortunately, you can employ a variety of techniques to assist you in getting through your reading quickly, gleaning what is necessary and still feeling as if you have a family life:

- **Evaluate the source.** The best sources routinely provide the best information. Rather than plowing through dozens of industry journals, pick the best two or three, extracting articles of importance. You'll cut down on the total volume to which you are exposed, while relatively ensuring that you're being exposed to the best and latest of what's going on in your industry or profession.

- **Skim.** This involves looking at the first couple sentences of each paragraph within an article or chapter in a book. By skimming, you get to quickly find out whether you should read the article or chapter in greater depth. Often simply skimming the first sentence or two is sufficient to gain the essence of the information provided.

- **Scan.** If you encounter a large volume of reading such as a sizable book or a large report, it is often impractical to attempt skimming. An alternative method is scanning, which involves reviewing any lists, charts, or exhibits in the book; the index; the table of contents; some of the chapter leads; and an occasional paragraph. In short order, you learn enough about the book or document to determine if it merits even greater attention.

- **Park it.** As you learned in Chapters 17 and 18, if you park a large amount of the materials you encounter into creatively labeled file folders, when you withdraw it later, you often find that you don't need to read it at all.

Divine Guidance

If you don't have many books on the Christian faith and not much time to find them, go online. Websites such as www.focusonthefamily.org, www.crosswalk.com, and other faith-oriented efforts exist; a quick Google search yields thousands of them. Secular retail sites by Amazon.com, Borders, and Barnes and Noble also offer a host of faith-based texts.

- **Line up your tools.** If you use a stick-em pad, paper clips, felt-tip pens, magic markers, scissors, and the like to assist you in your efforts when you read, have them nearby. When you can deftly extract or highlight the information you want to retain, the overall reading burden is greatly reduced. Then you can maintain a lean, mean, potent file consisting of information and items that you will actually act upon.

- **Read at the start and end of the day.** Undoubtedly you know the value of doing your reading early in the morning before others are stirring. The same holds true in the evening, after everyone has left work or at home and has retired. Anytime you find yourself unable to sleep, particularly for more than a 30-minute stretch, fill in the time with reading. The sleep specialists say that this is as worthwhile a technique as any and has no adverse effect. Simply read until you feel drowsy again and can no longer continue because you are going to nod off.

- **Mix and match.** If you have a lot of reading to do, sometimes it is more effective and easier mentally to mix some of the longer, involved articles with the shorter, easier ones. By alternating back and forth between the complex and the simple, you continue to mow down the pile without taxing your intellect too much.

Divine Guidance

Through scanning, you often can identify the handful of relevant passages or pages that are worth photocopying and then recycle the book or report. If you are concerned about the legality of photocopying, generally if it is for a limited personal use, you are not violating any copyright laws.

Caution Corner

When was the last time you opened the Bible? Can you list the Ten Commandments? What are the fundamental beliefs of your denomination? If you're stumped, even a little, your reading selections could use some spiritual additions.

The quieter the place is where you read, the faster and easier you will be able to finish the pile. Still, if you have some familiarity with what you are reading, even a somewhat noisy place can be suitable. Do find a quiet sanctuary whenever you are reading about highly technical issues, item with which you have little familiarity, and heavy philosophical or think pieces—anything that requires you to pause and reflect before proceeding. It is too difficult to do this kind of reading when surrounded by distractions.

Extract the Best, Leave the Rest

Many people lament the lack of opportunity to tackle some of the current full-length nonfiction books available. The huge online vendors make it abundantly clear how many new books are regularly available. An article or slim report is one thing, but a 280- or 300-page book is a whole other story. It's predictable that there will be more full-length books than you want to read. Here are some ideas for sorting through the possibilities in a highly productive manner:

- Read the back jacket first in detail. Here is where you will see what others have said about the book.

- Read the inside flaps. This material is usually written by the author but is presented as if written by the publisher. This is what the author wants you to know about the book and about himself or herself.

- Read the foreword to the book, if there is one. The foreword is usually written by a friend of the author expressing things about the author and the book that the author wanted to have said. A well-written foreword often serves as an executive summary to the entire book. It also often gives some insights on the author's slant or bias.

- Read the table of contents. You may decide to read some chapters immediately. Likewise, you may determine that you can safely skip other chapters.

- Read the introduction, which is usually written by the author. It provides an executive summary of sorts.

As you proceed to the chapters you have decided are worth some attention, now try the following:

- Read at least the first two paragraphs of each chapter. This will tell you if you want to read the rest of the chapter. For those chapters you don't want to continue to, the first two paragraphs will at least give you a reasonable idea of what was covered.

- Go to the last page of each chapter, and read either the last paragraph or any summary or highlights list that is presented. These can be invaluable and, in some cases, can serve as a substitute for reading the entire book.

- Review any resource lists, reference lists, charts, or graphs that strike your fancy as you are flipping through the book. When you are trying to save time, such features can be worth the attention invested.

Divine Guidance

Always, always, always photocopy the handful of key pages that have future value for you.

- Go to the last chapter and read the last two or three pages. The author's major conclusions and observations are presented here, and this will save you from having to read at least the last chapter, possibly the last section of the book, and maybe even the entire book.

Read and Discuss

To develop a regular reading habit, join a local book discussion club. Book clubs are a great way to meet other book readers. Many people find that they learn more from a book when they hear other people's points-of-view on it.

Most book clubs read and discuss one book per month. Book clubs are organized by all sorts of people, such as groups of friends and acquaintances, co-workers, and members of neighborhood associations. Some book clubs are devoted to specific themes, such as religion, politics, or genre fiction. Remember, you want to exercise your mind, so seek out a book club that will be reading books that fit the bill.

Book clubs that are seeking new members usually take out ads in the classified sections of local newspapers. Also be sure to look in monthly, weekly, and semi-weekly papers as well as the daily paper. Other good places to look are public-notice boards at libraries and bookstores, or anyplace where flyers are posted. In addition, reference librarians and bookstore employees are good people to ask about book clubs in your area.

That's the Spirit

The written word is vital for religious causes, too—perhaps even more than for the secular. Billy Graham explained the importance of books and magazines: "Once a radio program or a film is over, its impact is largely finished," Graham said. "Books and magazines, however, go places a spoken sermon will never reach, and they can continue to have an impact long after their author is gone."

Look It Up!

When you are reading those classic novels, you may run into words you don't know. This presents the perfect opportunity to work on your vocabulary. First, you'll need a good, useful dictionary on hand. This means something larger than a typical pocket dictionary, which usually has 50,000 entries or less—the English language has more than 450,000 words. Invest in a dictionary in the middle of that range, something that has around 100,000 to 150,000.

When you come across a word you don't know, either look it up right then or write it down and look it up later. The more you read, the more likely it is that you'll encounter these words, and the faster you'll build your vocabulary. You can take your vocabulary-building efforts a step further by giving yourself vocabulary tests. Once you've accumulated 20 new words, write their definitions.

If you use the Internet frequently, check out the Merriam-Webster website at www.m-w.com/home.htm. Save it as a favorite or bookmark. It's quick and can give you synonyms at the click of the mouse.

Let Go of Subscriptions

When you suspect that a subscription is perhaps still worth the money but not worth your time, let it go with the last issue. If you don't miss it, you are ahead of the game. If you do miss it, the publication will take you back, often at a reduced rate. Perhaps you can gain the same information online, or visit the library periodically and peruse three or four issues of the same publication at high speed.

Divine Guidance

Anytime you can come across a review of a book, an excerpt, a critique, or anything else that gives you the essence of what the books says without having to read the whole book, you are ahead of the game.

Many libraries stock books and lectures on tape, and in most cases these represent abridged versions of the longer tome. You can safely listen to a cassette as you drive (an entirely different activity than talking on a cell phone). This is a relatively easy way to gain information, avoid eye strain, and still arrive on time.

Key Newsletters

Newsletters cut down on your overall reading time because the implied mission is to supply you with succinct, well-crafted, critical information specifically so you don't have to go and round it up.

By scanning a couple key newsletter directories often found in the reference section of your library, you can determine the key newsletters in your industry or profession. The *Oxbridge Directory of Newsletters*, *The Newsletter Yearbook*, and the *National Trade and Professional Organizations* each give information about key newsletters that are available for a fee or for free.

Traveling and Reading

Been in any airport lines lately? An article appearing on two or three pages can be folded into sixths, by first folding it in half and then folding what is left into thirds. This is a convenient organizing ploy, since the article will now fit in your pocket. Then the next time you are stuck in any kind of line, pull out the article and read for a couple of minutes. You feel a little better about any delays because you are being productive. Sometimes you'll finish the whole article. Sometimes you will hardly get started when you find yourself at the head of the line. No problem—put the article back in your pocket and save it for the next line.

Whenever you are a passenger to someone else's driving, this represents a wonderful time to do some reading. Pull out your article and continue on. This can work for a bus, train, plane, or taxi ride, depending on where you are going and how long it takes to get there.

Be careful not to take too much reading material with you when you're traveling for business, though, because you inevitably end up creating more tasks for yourself than you can act upon when you are on the road. Do take the thin files representing the few key articles and few key pages you want to handle. The pack will be relatively slender and will only get lighter as you chuck the pages you no longer need.

Listen Instead of Read

One of the most brilliant ideas for keeping pace with certain kinds of information involves making great use of your drive time or commute time. If you drive to work, there are many ways to address your professional and personal reading and information needs. Install a CD or tape player to control your environment to and from work. When it comes to cassettes and CDs, you have several broad-based areas from which to choose. You can …

- Listen to Books on Tape via subscription, or by patronizing your local library, which may also offer lectures, plays, and books, on cassette.

- Listen to programs on a variety of other topics, such as self-improvement, leadership, sales, and career advancement. Skillpath, Nightingale-Conant, and Dartnell are the leading producers in this category.

- Learn a foreign language with programs such as those by SyberVision or Berlitz.

- Keep up with the latest business books and articles through summaries offered by such groups such as Executrak and Audio Summaries.

In a little more than a year, you could achieve the equivalent of having audited five college courses, which is an entire semester. The beauty of such an experience is that you get to pick what you want to hear, you make an otherwise purposeless commute meaningful, and there are no quizzes, term papers, or final exams.

An Organized Approach to E-mail

In all walks of life and in all professions, people are increasingly reporting that they feel overwhelmed by the volume of information and communication that they are exposed to on a daily basis.

If information overload makes you feel overwhelmed and powerless, take heart—you're not alone. The information revolution has reached pathological proportions for many individuals.

In this chapter, we'll focus on a key contributor, information overload: the rise of e-mail.

Send and Receive

The odds are good that you send and receive e-mails each day. The advantages of e-mail are abundantly clear. E-mail is fast; it's transmitted nearly instantaneously after you push the Send button; No paper, no toner cartridge, no stamps, no envelopes, no trip to the mailbox, no second-guessing whether you had the right postage, no nothing. It just goes—which is why, as you've already undoubtedly concluded, you receive so many every day. It's too convenient! You can send anything to anybody!

The number of e-mails you receive is probably growing at a frightening pace. Actually, among those with e-mail accounts, the number of e-mails everyone is receiving daily is escalating. That's what happens when anybody can send to anybody with the click of a mouse!

Despite software filters and ISP crackdowns on offenders, mass delivery from spammers has risen dramatically. Using unsecured, third-party servers, a spammer can target nearly every e-mail address found on the Net at practically no cost, since the ISP pays for the transmission.

Divine Guidance

It should come as no surprise that e-mail can be used for Christian purposes as well as commercial offers. Yes, the message of salvation can be found in e-mail. Siam Rogers, Southern Baptists' first national missionary to the Internet, said, "The power of the (Internet) is that while we're sleeping, the Lord is using that (Internet) to reach people who are looking for answers." (www.accessjesus.org)

Spam in a Can

E-mail spam has become such a problem that the U.S. House of Representatives has introduced four bills to stop spammers in their tracks. Nearly all the four bills introduced require spammers to provide inclusion of easy opt-out instructions and forbid them to employ false or misleading headers or subject lines. Violators could incur civil and potentially criminal penalties, be barred from using ISP lists, and be subject to individual suits for damages.

Independent of which bills become law and what effect they may have on your inbox, undoubtedly you need strategies for dealing with spam right now. It's vital to understand that responding to spam increases the volume of spam you receive. Try the following:

- **Ignore all offers.** Although it may seem like a good offer, resist the temptation to respond to any spam. If you respond to a spam message by choosing Opt Out, you only confirm that there is an actual person behind your e-mail address, which *increases* the amount of spam you receive. Maddening, isn't it? Do not respond to the spammer in any way.

Divine Guidance

If you send any spam messages you receive to your ISP's abuse e-mail address, along with the source code from the original spam message, your ISP may be able to take action.

- **Use complex addresses.** Spammers' lists run alphabetically. Since they're often cut off when an ISP notices an attack, addresses at the end of the list tend to receive less spam than those at the beginning. Therefore, Zach@xdomain.com gets fewer spam messages than Allyson@zdomain.net. The more complex the e-mail address is, the less spam it receives. BillJ@yahoo.com or Quatrina67@Hotmail.com, for instance, will get more spam than 23rxt98@yahoo.com or dfW32ly668@hotmail.com.

- **Watch where you go.** By posting your e-mail address on the Internet through chat rooms, message boards, directories, and web pages, you're making it available to spammers. Thus, do so sparingly. It may also be useful to have a second, more private mail account.

- **Register sparingly.** Different websites have different policies about the privacy of your e-mail address, so be selective when registering online. When in doubt, don't.

- **Watch the "language."** Any time you receive mail that has lots of X's or all capitals (which is regarded as shouting), or that otherwise makes excessive claims, don't waste a nanosecond on it.

- **Time your checks.** Unless you're specifically waiting for an e-mail, it's best to check your mail about twice a day, and perhaps a third time, if you're feeling particularly ahead of the game. The people who get obsessed with checking their e-mail at every spare moment are often the ones who tend to dawdle anyway.

Caution Corner

Doctors have started diagnosing a new psychological disorder called "communicative enslavement." This disorder is characterized by obsessively checking and rechecking e-mail for new messages. It's also characterized by refusing to leave the vicinity of the computer, so as to always be available to someone else via chat or e-mail. The desire to stay in constant communication has mushroomed in importance to the point that it interferes with the activities of daily living. Some people check their e-mail hundreds of times a day. Some incessantly send mail merely to receive mail. Some spend significant time actually pondering the legions of spam they receive.

The 6-D System

In terms of deftly handling e-mail, management trainer Laura Stack advocates a "6-D" system to handle e-mail regardless of what type of package you use:

1. **Discard it.** Delete the e-mail as soon as you receive it.

2. **Delegate it.** Forward it to someone else who can take care of it.

3. **Do it.** Respond to the e-mail and then delete it.

4. **Dungeon it.** File it so that you can retrieve it again if you need to.

5. **Don't see it again.** Call the sender and get off the routing list.

6. **Decide.** When are you going to deal with it?

> **That's the Spirit**
>
> We should not fear technological change, because change allows God to work in new ways. "Weep not that the world changes—did it keep a stable, change-less state, it were a cause indeed to weep."
>
> —William Cullen Bryant

Notice that the 6-D system is related to the four-part system for handling paper files cited in Chapter 18:

1. Act on it.

2. Delegate it.

3. File it.

4. Recycle it.

Some people find it comforting to print each e-mail they can't handle at once. This only adds to the clutter around you. Nevertheless, if you can stay in control of your hard-copy e-mail file, go ahead and print your messages.

Be Precise

Most people dash off e-mails at high speed. I'm not knocking the high rate of typos and grammatical errors—that is not a huge issue regarding e-mail use. However, have you ever teed off anyone because of an e-mail? Did you ever receive a disappointing or questionable e-mail from someone you like? Put a little more thought into your writing, and you can avoid the potential for confusion or misunderstanding.

Think about the e-mail messages that you receive that go on and on for far longer than the first screenful. Especially among those that are unsolicited, do you read them all? If you do, how many of them do you actually save? Chances are, the longer ones become discarded more quickly.

Occasionally you'll get an e-mail from someone who uses such cryptic language, chops so many keywords from sentences, and uses so many abbreviations that the meaning of the message is all but lost. For example: looking fw'rd 2 c'ing u this eve. is 7 gd, or do u thk earlier is btr? Also, R U getting tix or me? I'll B in to 5. later, TGB.

If Internet abbreviations were universally known, used, and understood, they'd represent tremendous savings in terms of composing and reading e-mail messages. But Internet abbreviations are not universally known, used, or understood. When you use such abbreviations, you'll likely confuse the other party—and that's not a time-saver for anyone.

Don't be among those who prune beyond reason—and beyond the recipient's ability to extract your meaning. And forget all those semi-neat Net abbreviations you see in other books, such as BTW, which means "by the way." You're more likely to confuse the other party than effectively communicate.

> **Divine Guidance**
>
> Undoubtedly, you can shorten many of your messages—and maybe you already do. If you don't, it's time to start practicing. Prune your prose. Say it once and be done.

Unknowingly Curt

Sometimes an e-mail message can make you seem as if you're curt or abrasive. It's not that you intended to ruffle any feathers; it's that e-mail, unless worded carefully, can sometimes come off as impersonal, cold, and uncaring.

"The Send button can prove an irresistible temptation to propel thoughts on their way to impress or titillate or even inflict pain," says Michael Eisner, CEO of the Walt Disney Company. Too many people apparently are ignoring the draft box and clicking the Send button nanoseconds after typing the last letter in their message.

As with traditional writing, when possible, perhaps it's best to park e-mails for a day and revisit them before sending. With some e-mail service providers, you have the option to delay sending until a prearranged time. With most providers, you have the option either to park an e-mail message in the Draft Message box or to send it.

> **That's the Spirit**
>
> Even in the Internet Age, it's wise to remember the basics of right and wrong. So before you send an angry e-mail message or give someone else's e-mail address to an online marketing site, remember the Golden Rule: "So in everything, do to others what you would have them to do you, for this sums up the Law and the Prophets." (Matthew 7:12)

Responsiveness Under Pressure

With a multitude of e-mail messages piling up in your inbox, even a brief time away from your PC means you'll have scads of e-mails to respond to upon returning. A mere two days away could mean coming back to at least two to three times the normal number of e-mail messages you encounter.

Triage is the method of quickly poring over a variety of items and allocating them based on what needs to be handled immediately, what can be handled later, and what can be ignored altogether. I advocate practicing triage for all e-mail messages all the time. First, you want to quickly eliminate the inane. These include all forms of spam.

Quick Considerations

After eliminating the obvious, the next question is which e-mails you can place in a holding folder, bin, or file. Some are entirely worth saving but simply are not urgent. Some are from friends and loved ones, and you want to pore over what they've written. Some have told you in the letter that the reply time need not be immediate.

The last category concerns e-mail messages you receive that require quick to immediate action. *Quick* means sometime during the day. *Immediate,* as I use it here, means reply right now, while you're online. The number of messages you get that fall into the quick or immediate categories should be small.

See and Send

Even if a message isn't urgent, if you're able to respond to it quickly and effortlessly, why waste time parking it? If the message is staring you in the face, all you have to do is hit the Reply button, type a few words, and then send it.

For e-mails that mandate your present, earnest, and rather speedy attention, do your gut-level best to handle them so that they're out of the way and you're mentally—as well as physically—clear of them.

Some Response Is Better Than Stone Silence

If you've returned from several days away from your PC, or if the number of e-mail messages in your inbox is ganging up on you, here's a viable temporary solution to this dilemma: Have stock messages ready—such as that you have returned from traveling and will respond by midweek, or anything else that conveys your sense of responsiveness.

When I receive an acknowledgment message from someone (even an automated acknowledgment), I regard that person highly. At least he took the time (or set up his system) to let me know that he received my message and intends to do something about it. That's a far cry from those you don't hear from for days, much of the time suspecting that you'll never hear from them.

> **Divine Guidance**
>
> E-mail filters find and delete e-mail that contain specific keywords or that were sent from specific addresses.

Any of the customized e-mail programs on the market enable you to save stock messages and easily retrieve them as needed. Also, many feature filters, which automatically sort e-mail as it arrives.

Receiving Before Sending

When I first log on, before sending my drafted letters to their intended recipients, I press Get Messages. Sometimes the messages received supersedes the messages I was ready to send to someone. A new message might resolve the issue altogether. As the new e-mails appear on my screen, I take a few minutes to review them, scanning the essence of what's involved and then moving on. I eliminate spam immediately.

> **That's the Spirit**
>
> *Adaptive* means changing your strategy to meet the information needs in the new digital world. "Instruct a wise man and he will be wiser still; teach a righteous man, and he will add to his learning." (Proverbs 9:9)

Once I've reviewed the array of new messages, I turn to my draft files and launch all the e-mail waiting to be sent. In most cases, this includes all the drafts, but occasionally I delay or eliminate one because of the new e-mail messages that I've received.

I then return to the messages that I recently received and handle them individually. I quickly reply to messages when not much effort is needed. Those that can be answered with a short message and sent by simply hitting the Reply button are best handled in that fashion.

Sometimes Your Answer Appears

Some e-mails contain information that I want to save to my hard drive. Often these contain attachments. In this case, I open the attachment, save the item in the appropriate folder on my hard drive, and return to my e-mail screen. Now I'm left with the handful of e-mails that are urgent and perhaps require significant attention. To handle the issue, I may have to round up information, cut and paste files from my hard drive, make a telephone call, or create a new directory.

When it may take me a while to resolve a particular issue, I sometimes send a stock message or short note back to the sender saying, "I'm working on it and will be back in touch on such and such day." This lets the sender know that I received the message, that I regard it as important, and while I can't resolve the issue or meet the request at this moment, I certainly am working on it.

Organize at the Outset

Create plenty of online file folders. Communication software packages enable you to create as many file folders and subfiles as you choose. Assign a file folder for each of your major projects and for each broad topic important in your work and your life, such as Vacation, Family, School, and so on.

In addition, you can create a variety of folders on a temporary basis, when an issue or project is at hand, and eliminate the folder when the significance of the issue recedes.

Because you can rename, combine, or submerge folders with the click of a mouse, and because the nature of your family life is probably constantly changing, it makes sense to move folders in some way at least once a week. If you are not doing so, chances are good that you're not using e-mail as effectively as you could.

One-Way or Two-Way?

Everything discussed up to this point leads to the inevitable issue: Is the message you want to convey appropriate via e-mail? The answer is not always so clear-cut. Sending e-mail, like leaving a voice-mail message for someone, is a one-way media. When you leave your message, communication is flowing in only one direction. Jaclyn Kostner, Ph.D., based in Denver, Colorado, offers the following list of *inappropriate* messages for one-way media, such as e-mail and voice mail:

- The complex
- New ideas
- Issues requiring clarification
- Solicitation for agreement
- The emotionally charged
- Material that has a strong personal impact on the recipient

Other than these, it's probably okay to engage in one-way messaging. Once you've determined that your message is suitable for one-way media, Kostner observes that you have one more choice: Should you relay your message by e-mail, or is voice mail preferable? Let's review her guidelines.

Kostner advocates choosing e-mail (not voice mail) in these situations:

- When a written record is needed.
- When language is a barrier. In multilanguage teams, written words are frequently easier to understand than spoken ones, especially when accents are heavy or language skills are less than fluent.
- When the team's normal business hours in each location do not match.
- When you've been unable to reach the person interactively but you know the person needs the details right away.

The following also can represent appropriate use of e-mail:

> **That's the Spirit**
>
> Life isn't logical or sensible or orderly. Life is a mess most of the time. And theology must be lived in the midst of that mess.
>
> —Charles Colson

- One-word or short answers
- Approval or disapproval
- Forwarding vital information to appropriate parties
- Articles, reports, outlines, and guidelines that have been specifically requested by the recipient
- Updated information, such as price quotes, progress reports, and summaries of activities, again when the other party is expecting or requesting it

Coming to Your Hand Soon

Palmtops provide wireless links to the Internet, e-mail, and fax capabilities to users around the globe. Palmtops can store thousands of addresses, years' worth of appointments, multithousands of memos, and multithousands of to-do items, all uniquely arranged based on user preferences. Data exchange between a PC and a handheld device in general has become as easy as touching a single key.

What else do these miniature wonders provide? The ability to ...

- Add memory as the need for storing more addresses, phone numbers, to-do lists, and so forth increases.

- Support a variety of software applications.
- Link automatically with a variety of hardware devices, peripherals, and accessories.
- Access any information quickly.
- Offer battery life exceeding five hours.
- Provide ultraconvenient, ultrapowerful address books, to-do lists, a memo pad, calendars, trip logs, and expense calculators.
- Present enhanced, full-color, high-clarity screens.

Regardless of the device you use, a variety of techniques enable you to quickly and easily ensure that you maximize your use of time when engaging in such functions as voice mail, e-mail, Net surfing, and faxing.

Whether or not you currently use a hand-held computing device, the odds are astronomical that within a few short years you will. Soon enough, the computing power on your wrist will exceed what was possible on a desktop in the early 2000s.

All Too Easy

It's easy to receive many more e-mails than you can possibly respond to. It's also easy for you to send e-mails to others when no message is needed or wanted. The more you send, the more you get in return. As a guiding principle, send as few as possible and still have a life. And remember, simply because you can send to anyone doesn't mean you should.

Chapter 22

Search and Ye Shall Find

Let's face it, the Internet has become a staple of family life and its impact continues to grow. In this chapter, we'll discuss using search engines, scouting good websites, maintaining privacy, and using newsgroups.

Sensational growth in web use has impacted virtually every aspect of society: By 2001, 58 percent of the United States, representing 165 million people, had home Internet access, up from 39 percent two years previously. Those who go online are doing it more frequently and are spending more time staying online. The average user spent 10 hours and 19 minutes in the first half of 2001, up from 7 hours and 39 minutes two years before.

Based on research conducted by Google.com, an astounding figure of more than 70 percent of web pages are less than one year old, as of 2001, and more than 89 percent are less than one to two years old, as reported by the web servers. (The actual age can be greater.) For the far-reaching future, the rate of new data posted each day will continue to explode.

The Internet Prevails

With millions of websites now accessible and user-friendly applications becoming available all the time, the Internet is taking over as the dominant form of entertainment, communication, and information vehicle in society. Concurrently, it can become a major time drain. Searching for the precise information you seek can tie up as many as five hours a week. Your ability to stay organized by gathering the information is hampered by too many alternatives, regardless of what you're seeking. Hence, you need to clearly establish your searching/browsing objectives by posing the following questions:

- Who are you trying to reach?
- What are you seeking to learn/gain?
- To what effect?

For all the news and information it provides, it's important to remember that the web is primarily a marketing vehicle for those who host websites. Think of the World Wide Web as an information guidebook and advertising directory with more than 100 million entries that is updated or changed every picosecond.

Much of the web is self-serving hype about the web itself. Many people are trying to show off the "cool" graphics they can make, offering little else. That won't improve your life or end your workday any quicker.

Your house and garden plants need to be regularly shorn of dead leaves and stems to promote healthy growth. Likewise, you need to trim yourself of deadweight thinking: believing that you need to endlessly strive to keep informed and up-to-date. The web beckons at all hours. You know it's there—like television, it's an "informational" drug available in unlimited quantities, ready to rob you of your time at any moment.

Caution Corner

Don't waste your time on "cool site of the day" selections. Too often, such sites, while graphically interesting, offer little in the way of concrete benefits to you.

Before you face the mounds of new information, delete outdated documents and unnecessary downloaded files from your computer. Download from the Internet only the information that will truly support you in your work. Instead of downloading files that you'll use occasionally, record their addresses and leave the information on the Internet.

Seek and Ye Shall Find

Search engines are probably the best tools invented in the last 50 years for finding information quickly. They are a tremendous boon to the Christian family seeking to find information quickly, without having reams of paper around in the form of newspapers, pamphlets, guides, and directories. Indeed, no volume of hard-copy directories that you can maintain, trips to the library, calls to research specialists, or other information-gathering strategies quite match the power, speed, and breath of simply typing keywords into a search engine and letting them do their magic!

Divine Guidance

"Cyberfaith" is growing in popularity. By May 2001, 8 percent of adults and 12 percent of teenagers went online for religious or spiritual experiences, according to Barna Research Online. More than two thirds said that they would likely engage in future Internet use for religious experiences on a regular basis as the decade progresses. Among the most appealing Net-based religious activities were archived teachings, online devotionals, and religious products and resources for sale.

From www.google.com, which generates more results than any other search engine on the web (and does it in seconds flat) to a variety of other well-designed, highly useful search engines, you can go online when you want to …

- Get quick background in a topic area.
- Find a mailing address, phone or fax number, or e-mail address.
- Determine where a phrase or line of lyrics originated.
- Review what has been written about a particular place, item, or person, including yourself. The service that search engines provide is unprecedented and unrivaled.

Most search engines are basically indexes. You type in words, and the search engine finds the web pages in its index with those words. To do this, search engines use what are called "robots" to index tens of millions of web pages. The "hits" that search engines provide, unfortunately, are not always based on objective search results.

Many of the hits that you are likely to see within the first 10 results that you have obtained may be based upon paid arrangements. A vendor pays the search engine to be among the first entries listed when certain key terms are entered by web users (such as yourself!). This unfortunate state of affairs has prompted congressional inquiry to examine the matter and suggest legislation mandating that such search engines conspicuously post consumer caveats.

Divine Guidance

Each search engine is a bit different, so look for the buttons labeled Options, Help, Hints, Tips, or Advanced for online assistance on how to use the site.

Although some search engines do not stack their results based on payment arrangements with other web vendors, they will nevertheless "adorn" your results page. You'll encounter banner ads, special links, and other enticements designed to have you click onto the sites of selected vendors who have entered into deals with the company behind the search engine.

These types of search engine "results" tend to be a little more obvious because they do not necessarily taint the primary roster of hyperlinks that you are provided.

Search Engine Strategies

You can use several strategies to most efficiently employ search engines. One is to use a variety of engines with the same search criteria until you settle on the few that give you the best results consistently. A few of the more popular ones include these:

- www.google.com

- www.lycos.com

- www.infoseek.com

When seeking a product, service, or simply information on the web, entering one keyword or a set of them might bring up thousands of sites. You may need to use more precise terminology. The more keywords you use, generally the more accurate your results will be.

Caution Corner

Thousands, if not tens of thousands, of Christian and religious websites exist on the Internet. A short list from which to start includes www.christianitytoday.com, www.crosswalk.com, www.focusonthefamily.com, www.accessjesus.org, www.Christianity.com, and www.biblegateway.org. If you are interested in filtering out objectionable content, most ISPs offer filters, or you can use companies on the web, such as www.familyclick.com.

Virtually all search engines use quotation marks to identify phrases. For many, you can put the plus sign before any word you need to find included on the web page, and you can use the minus sign for those you want to omit from your search results. For example, when searching for entries on professional speakers, you might want to make sure to exclude the words *stereo* and *car*, or you'll get entries on sound systems.

How Results Are Derived

Depending on what search engine you use, it makes sense to understand how their results are derived. Different search engines employ different criteria in assembling information, ranking results, and providing links to you. Hence, you may end up with widely desperate rosters of results.

The variations among popular search engines such as www.yahoo.com, www.lycos.com, www.infoseek.com, www.altavista.com, www.hotbot.com, and others are numerous and varied. You have to literally visit each site and individually discover each one's specific criteria.

Some search engines rely heavily on the keywords that individual website owners purposely employ, both visible on the site and in code invisible to the typical website user. In this manner, web owners can "doctor" their site by adding a combination of words that will increase the probability of receiving a high ranking within a given search engine's results roster. When a user types in a specific word or word grouping, it will seem as though such a site matches the query more exactly than it actually does.

Some search engines index only home pages; others index the entire site. For the pages they do index, some search engines catalog every word on the page, some catalog only the title, and others fall somewhere in between. Hence, your results among different search engines can vary greatly.

Metasearch engines submit your search criteria to a number of different search engines for you. One such metasearch engine is www.metacrawler.com.

Google.com Stands Apart

As a shortcut to finding the information you need with relatively unbiased rankings, it makes sense to employ sites such as Google.com, which do not pick up metawords, metatags, or other web owner options. Google.com is based on how many and how often other sites link to a particular site. In other words, Google's listings are based on the popularity of sites as deemed by other sites that link to them. This approach offers a type of "search results" insurance not featured by sites that rely on metawords, metatags, and other website owner options.

If you are looking for information on, say, astronomy, wouldn't you want to have a search results roster that reflects the most popular sites on the Internet? The short answer is, yes, you would.

The possible risk here is that a site may have many references to it from other sites but may not necessarily contain the in-depth or rigorous information that you are seeking. Nevertheless, the long-term odds are that someplace within your first 10 hits, and certainly within the first 20, you will be exposed to 1, 2, 3, or more sites that are entirely relevant to your information quest.

Use the Best and Forget the Rest

Good websites, whether they be search engines or other types of sites, have certain features in common. If you find a site that offers most of the features listed here, it will help to optimize your time online:

- Keeps visitors from getting lost. A good website includes multiple links that take you back to the home page, to the previous page, or to another value-packed page of your choice. It ensures that you can quickly return to something familiar or move forward to something new.

- Goes easy on the graphics. Many websites truly are works of art by master graphic artists. However, smaller graphics and text-only hyperlinks help you navigate much faster.

- Includes multiple contact links. Good sites contain clear links that point you to contact information such as e-mail addresses, fax numbers, snail mail addresses, and phone numbers, if appropriate.

- A good website is visitor-focused. It centers on your needs, ensuring the most direct access to the information that is most valuable to you.

That's the Spirit

Whether you're online, on the job, or on call, don't forget the big picture: Focus on God. When God counseled Moses, he told him of trouble to come with the Israelites after they left Egypt. But God reminded Moses to persevere. "Do not throw away this confident trust in the Lord, no matter what happens. Remember the great reward it brings you. Patient endurance is what you need now, so you will continue to do God's will." (Hebrews 10:35–36)

What Time Is It?

Much of what you find on websites is time-sensitive or is updated on a daily or weekly basis. Top media sites such as USAToday.com, FoxNews.com, and the like may update their sites dozens of times daily, and certainly when a story is breaking. With most other sites, checking back weekly is probably all most people need. Other sites post information for the long run. My site, www.BreathingSpace.com, includes both dynamic and static information. One feature called Book Digest summarizes nearly 100 books. Visitors may download book digest selections of their choice each month for free. I add to the digest periodically, but it is basically a static portion of the site.

Specialty Information Sites

Increasingly, websites and information services are available that enable you to cut down on bulky newspaper and magazine subscriptions by receiving your news and information in customized, byte-size portions. Some sites, such as *The New York Times*, at www.NYT.com, ask you to disclose personal information in exchange for free daily news and updates.

Somewhat similar to *The New York Times*, CNN, at www.CNN.com, requests information about you, your business, and your interests in exchange for allowing you to custom-design how your news is delivered.

Other sites, such as *The Wall Street Journal*, at www.WSJ.com, enable newspaper subscribers to add an online component for a modest fee, while nonsubscribers must pay roughly double the cost.

A Little Privacy Please!

One of the more annoying developments on the web is the constant invasion of privacy. Websites plant cookies on your hard drive so that when you visit them more than once, your interests—as determined by what you visited previously—can be quickly catalogued by the site owner. However, chances are good that it is simply a mechanized catalog and there may not be someone in particular who monitors your visits.

On a positive note, Harris Interactive Surveys conducted a study in June 2000 revealing that 39 percent of respondents knew what a cookie was and how to disable it. Men were twice as likely as women to know this information. A cookie is an electronic marker that a website places on your hard drive so that if and when you revisit the website, your PC is electronically recognized and you are shunted to site features that presumably lie within your area of interest.

The banner advertising you encounter, and even some of the features on the site itself, can literally change in nanoseconds based on what cookies have been stored on your hard drive, arguably a gross form of manipulation. Fortunately, all browser software comes with the capability to screen for cookies or eliminate them at the end of each visit or each day. The Help menu offers instructions.

Divine Guidance

Life has changed drastically since the World Wide Web made the Internet more accessible. We don't recognize change as it happens. We just cope, according to the book *The Internet Church*: "Radical Discontinuity—a phrase that best describes the condition of a world in such rapid change that we don't have answers readily available for what we see going on around us."

Buying Online

Ordering online will only get easier—it has to! After 12 years of languishing, the idea of using electronic money has taken hold. CheckFree and PayPal have become standard payment options for many online shoppers. Websites are lining up to secure shoppers' ability to pay over the Internet, slicing days off traditional bank transaction times.

E-cash transfer services act as seamless intermediaries in the exchange between merchant and buyer. To open a PayPal account, for example, you need only provide your name, your e-mail address, and a password. Once you register, you're issued a credit, debit, or checking account number, and then you're free to send and receive funds. Both parties in a transaction have to subscribe to the service.

These Are My Rules!

If you choose to do business at a particular website, make sure it is a secure site. That means if you transmit any important information, like credit card data, third parties would have an exceedingly hard time finding it.

If you are unsure of how the information you submit to a web vendor will be used, send that party an e-mail first and ask. You want to protect your privacy, and you also don't want to waste your time dealing with annoying or exploitative vendors.

Newsgroups: An Alternative Information Source

A network called Usenet originally started as an electronic bulletin board served by two sites: the University of North Carolina and Duke University. Today Usenet newsgroups have grown into a global collection of thousands of discussion groups where people post messages and replies on specific topics of interest.

Usenet—short for "users' network"—is a connected network of people. Usenet newsgroups reside at specific, accessible computer sites and originally were operated independently of the Internet. People stopped by, read comments and added their own, and checked replies much like a community bulletin board in a public hallway.

Start Your Readers

The major web browsers come with built-in newsgroup readers that let you view, write, and reply to the postings of the groups you specify. Two basic categories comprise newsgroups: the first, most highly controlled, category contains the following headings:

- **Comp:** Computers and related topics (hardware, software, technical discussions)
- **News:** Usenet itself (announcements, software, and other information)
- **Rec:** Recreation and hobbies, entertainment, and the arts

- **Sci:** Science (excluding computer science)
- **Soc:** Social issues
- **Talk:** Debates on controversial topics
- **Misc:** Everything else, including "help wanted" postings

The second, less stringent, set of categories includes these:

- **Alt:** Alternative groups
- **Bionet:** Biology
- **Bit:** The most popular topics from Bitnet electronic mailing lists
- **Biz:** Business, marketing, and advertisements

The major group headings under each category are further broken down into subtopics, each separated by a period in the address of the group. As the separators grow, the topic area shrinks. For example, you may see a newsgroup identified as biz.books. Here you would expect to see information about all kinds of books on business. People participating in biz.books.technical, however, would be specifically interested in technical business books.

Discussions Abound

Deja News, at www.dejanews.com, is a useful site for uncovering discussion groups. The Deja News search engine is devoted entirely to newsgroups, and the site contains information and tools to help you find and use the groups that interest you. After you've visited a few and gotten a feel for how they work, you may find the best to suit your needs.

By following groups in a certain field, you can gauge trends regarding particular issues, products, or services. You can join a group and get to know it, and then let group participants know you exist. Offer information that they'll value. When you become comfortable in the group, ask questions, solicit ideas, and request feedback.

Part

6

Organizing in Everyday Life

This last part of the book offers specific guidance for staying organized in specific situations. At least annually, you have to file tax receipts, and most people do not find this to be a pleasant or simple undertaking. If you make any type of purchase of an appliance or electronic gadget, you undoubtedly know that manuals, registration cards, and packaging materials need to be handled. So, too, you must handle any service contracts, guarantees, or warranties. Fortunately, the chapters in this part guide you to a successful conclusion. Finally, we discuss the important notion of not volunteering to be overwhelmed and avoiding the all-too-common maneuver of inviting clutter into your life. As you'll learn, all other things being equal, when your household is organized, you have a better chance of a better quality of life.

Chapter 23

Organizing Your Income Tax Receipts

Before the war on terrorism—when the United States was experiencing budget surpluses each year—the U.S. Internal Revenue Service (IRS) audit section had less incentive than in previous years to wield their might. Now, as we hover around the middle part of the decade, deficits are back. Keeping accurate, complete tax information is a fundamental component in the life of the organized Christian family.

I've worked with various departments of the Internal Revenue Service over the years, primarily as a speaker or seminar leader at its conferences and conventions. As such, I have met IRS agents as individuals and find that they are much like you and me. They are concerned about their families, their respective communities, and the future. While there may be a rogue agent here and there, the vast majority of IRS agents are not "out to get" anybody and often feel as if they are the ones being picked on.

You don't have to be concerned about the IRS if you take simple steps, described in this chapter, to ensure that you have the documentation necessary to back up your tax returns.

Get Organized Before the Tax Year Begins

Organizing your income tax receipts is an easy undertaking if you take simple steps at the start of each tax year. Any office supply store today sells a variety of notebooks, binders, folders, dividers, and a variety of other office supplies that enable you to quickly and easily house the various documents, receipts, and vouchers related to both your income and your expenses.

Some families maintain all their deductible tax receipts in a Pendaflex folder that has a compartment for each month of the year. Other more involved folders allow you to file receipts on a weekly basis over the course of 52 weeks. Personally, I find that a three-ring notebook works as well as anything. You can insert dividers for each month and add three-hole punched plastic sleeves that enable you to both store and view the receipts and documentation you accumulate. With three-ring binders, if your expenditures in any given month are considerable, simply use more than one sheet for that month.

That's the Spirit

The Bible has more than 1,500 references to the word *give*. There are no references for *donation* and only one for *donate*. The not-so-subtle message is that donating is fine for tax purposes, but giving is for the soul. Jesus instructs his disciples that worldly wealth should not be our focus: "Give to the one who asks you, and do not turn away from the one who wants to borrow from you." (Matthew 5:42)

If you own property, you can make room within your notebook specifically to record and house transactions related to such ownership. Do the same for other types of tax-related issues such as expenditures for child care, employee business expense, job search, and depreciable assets.

Your best guide for setting up your "tax" notebook often comes from reviewing previous year's tax returns. Notice what kinds of forms you filed and the likelihood that you will need room in your notebook for that particular tax-related area for the coming year.

Some people use financial-management software to record all income and expenses soon after the transactions occur throughout the year. This is fine if you can maintain that kind of diligence. I've found that to stay organized and effectively organize your taxes on time, it is unnecessary to use such programs. For most families, the majority of expenditures made can readily be traced through the family checkbook and major credit cards.

Divine Guidance

Increasingly, the major vendors, especially American Express, automatically issue a convenient, concise compendium by category of all expenditures that you made using the respective card in the past year.

Obviously, if you make any cash expenditures that may be tax deductible, you need to get a receipt. This could include cash donations to charitable organizations, supplies that assist you in any of the aforementioned tax-related areas, or any other out-of-pocket disbursements. To keep things easy on yourself, however, establish the practice of paying by credit card or check for everything that remotely could be deductible on your tax return. That way, you will have complete documentation at the end of the year between these two major sources of financial information.

The All-in-One File

If setting up a monthly tax-receipt notebook seems too involved, there is an even easier method, one that I have favored for several years. All you need is one basic file folder to collect your receipts and another file folder for any pay stubs or documents related to income. The file folder for expenses will, of course, grow at a faster pace.

Starting on January 1 of the tax year, place any expense receipts in the file folder. In chronological order throughout the year, keep adding to the pile. Hence, at the end of the year, the last few expenditures you make, around December 29, 30, and 31, will be at the top of the file folder. The expenditures you made at the beginning of the year will be at the bottom.

Delving into the File

One winter afternoon, on a large table, take out the file folder and begin allocating the receipts into like areas, such as Airfare, Hotels, Work Supplies, School Supplies, Utility Bills, and Auto Maintenance and Repair. You already know these categories because you have been dealing with them for years!

You may end up with 15 or 20 piles on the table before you. Completely allocate the entire file until every single shred of paper is filed someplace. For items that are difficult to classify, create a file called Miscellaneous.

Divine Guidance

If you opt for a container even as crude as a shoebox, you're better off than not having a folder or container specially earmarked at the start of the year to capture your tax receipts.

Because you plowed through this file from the top to the bottom—that is, you started with December 31 and moved toward the start of the year—when your individual piles are fully assembled, they will be in chronological order from start to finish of the calendar year. Now paper clip, staple, or otherwise fasten them together so that you have 15 or 20 neat piles.

With a calculator, you can derive the sum for each category. Write that sum on a Post-It pad attached to the first receipt. Then create a summary page of all the categories and all the sums.

Reviewing Your Itemized Statements and Checkbook

Carefully review your itemized statement from your major credit card company to include any expenses that showed up on its concise roster that weren't otherwise in your year-long file folder. Afterward, do the same with your checkbook.

If you wrote a check for an item that is deductible, but you have no other documentation for it, be sure to add that sum to the appropriate category. When you are done, you will have all the expense information you need to successfully make complete and accurate claims on your tax returns.

About Your Income

Open the file folder that contains information on your income for the year. Proceed in the same way, categorizing, fastening, summing, and ultimately producing a single sheet that encapsulates your yearly income.

Now you have clear, complete documentation with which to file your taxes. No reason to be concerned about possible audits—if you can document it, you can claim it.

Even for a family of four to six people, the volume of paper that you accumulate in these file folders in the course of a year remains rather manageable.

Other advice that you may have encountered, perhaps suggesting things such as putting your receipts in a shoebox, ends up making a lot more work for you. You have to then allocate all the items into their respective piles and arrange each pile in chronological order.

Caution Corner

Make sure that any religious organization soliciting donations and claiming to be a legitimate tax-exempt enterprise can give you a verifiable tax ID number. Such groups are required to file annual reports. Get one before you give. Without the ID number and proof of actual charitable work, it's possible that your donation might go to good use, but the government won't recognize it as a tax deduction for you. Also, if you donate more than $250 a year to your church, the business office should issue a statement for your tax records.

Slugging It Out Manually

When it comes to preparing your tax returns for submission to the IRS, it often is helpful to examine your tax returns from previous years. If you are not using tax-return software (discussed later in the section "Tax-Preparation Software," and definitely recommended), examining past returns can aid you in completing this year's return. Categories and calculations and allocations that you made in previous years, particularly if you know you were right (or at least didn't get audited!) can serve as guide posts for completing your taxes this year.

Caution Corner

Attempting to file this year's tax returns without the benefit of reviewing past tax returns is always a bit more difficult because you have to reintroduce yourself to how the various forms are completed, your various savings and investment accounts, and other useful information listed on your previous returns.

Past tax returns also save you time because you have already listed financial institutions where you have money invested, Social Security numbers of people in your family, and other financial and family historical data that may prove relevant for the current year's tax return.

To be sure, each year there are at least minor modifications to many of the major tax forms. So, you have to be careful. You simply can't follow the procedures line for line that you used in previous filing years.

For past returns, if you received any notices from the IRS or your state's department of taxation, reread the notices especially if they involved a correction to your statement. In that way, you can minimize the chance of making the same error for the current year's statement.

Tax-Preparation Software

Tax-preparation software is available and has been perfected! If you are already using it, you know how much faster and easier it is to prepare your taxes than it was in the days when you had to tediously proceed line by line for each of the tax forms you were obligated to file.

If you haven't used tax-preparation software, the next few paragraphs may be among the most important for you in this book.

> ### Divine Guidance
>
> Two major vendors manufacture tax-preparation software: Kiplinger's TaxCut (www.kiplinger.com/software) and Quicken's TurboTax (www.quicken.com/taxes/products). Such software can save you hours of time and frustration when completing your tax returns.

> ### Divine Guidance
>
> For any family in any tax year, with the variety of income and expense categories that are possible, there is no one fundamental way that your taxes have to be filed. You nearly always have options as to how to classify and list various forms of income and expenses.

Commonalities Among Tax Software Programs

The variations among software programs are not great. Each has a friendly user interface. You start off listing basic information and then simply click the Next button. As you answer one question after another, the software assembles your information for appropriate and highly accurate use throughout your tax returns.

Based on the answers to the questions you provide, you proceed down one path or another. The software is designed so that you automatically file those forms that you need to be filing based on your tax situation.

Each of the software programs contains options that allow you to easily go back to a previous screen, change data or information, prepare a tax worksheet on the fly, or examine an actual return information.

What If ...?

Tax-preparation software allows you to pose "what if" types of questions. In other words, if you elect to file one-way versus another, you can quickly see the ramifications of your selection.

The amount you owe to the IRS will vary depending on ...

1. How you classify an expense. Many are subject to interpretation.
2. What income or expenses can justifiably be deferred.
3. Other elections, such as taking a standard deduction or making an itemized deduction.

Attempting to do such calculations by hand is time consuming, tedious, and largely inaccurate. By saving your tax return under various file names, you can literally experiment with a variety of elections to see what combination gives you the most favorable return.

Roll Forward

If you use tax-preparation software from the same vendor year after year, much of the data that you entered earlier, including the list of financial institutions with whom you have investments, is automatically brought forward to the current year's tax returns. Increasingly, even if you use a different vendor's software from one year to the next, much of the data can be brought forward, thereby saving considerable time.

Help That Actually Helps

The help functions are routinely well constructed. You can look up a topic, type in a keyword, examine frequently asked questions, or consult a helpful index. All the major tax-preparation software vendors also have online assistance, directing you to their respective websites where even more help is provided. Some also enable you to ask questions via e-mail or via telephone, although the terms—and possible costs—vary.

That's the Spirit

However you file, resist the obvious temptation to pay a little less than you really owe. Jesus taught his followers and critics that lesson in Matthew 22:15–21: "Then the Pharisees went out and laid plans to trap him in his words. They sent their disciples to him along with the Herodians. 'Teacher,' they said, 'we know you are a man of integrity and that you teach the way of God in accordance with the truth. You aren't swayed by men because you pay no attention to who they are. Tell us then, what is your opinion? Is it right to pay taxes to Caesar or not?' But Jesus, knowing their evil intent, said, 'You hypocrites, why are you trying to trap me? Show me the coin used for paying the tax.' They brought him a denarius, and he asked them, 'Whose portrait is this? And whose inscription?' 'Caesar's,' they replied. Then he said to them, 'Give to Caesar what is Caesar's, and to God what is God's.'"

To get you started on the high road to using tax-preparation software, the sections that follow contain brief descriptions of the products and services provided by a few of the major vendors in the field.

TaxCut by H&R Block

Kiplinger's TaxCut is designed by H&R Block, the accounting and income tax service with 40 years of experience. The vendor observes that with hundreds of tax law changes each year, it pays to acquire TaxCut Deluxe. The program comes complete with one free electronic filing (after mailing in a rebate).

Ad copy for the product states: "TaxCut is packed with tax expertise and guidance from the experts at H&R Block and Kiplinger! Plus, we've added a ton of new features to make your tax preparation even easier, including: Tax Law Assistant, Auto Entry, and our Comprehensive IRA Advisor. "TaxCut asks you simple questions, automatically selects and completes the forms you'll need, and double-checks your return. Electronically file your return and get your refund faster, or print and mail your return." For more information, visit www.taxcut.com.

TurboTax by Quicken

Ad copy from the vendor states: "The TurboTax line of products delivers everything you need to file your federal and state taxes quickly and easily. Plus, new features help maximize your personal and small business tax savings."

Quicken reports that TurboTax Premier is the company's most powerful TurboTax product and "is the ultimate way to manage and prepare your taxes! It helps increase your retirement savings, forecast tax liability, and more! Ideal for investors, rental property owners and anyone seeking maximum tax savings."

TurboTax for the Web, advertises the vendor, "specifically helps one to quickly and easily prepare and file a tax return without downloading or installing any software. From the easy-to-use interview to features such as Instant Data Entry, also found in the TurboTax desktop products, TurboTax for the Web offers easy, fast, and customized tax preparation." For more information, visit www.quicken.com/taxes/products.

Handling State Income Taxes

In nearly every state in the union, you also have to file state income taxes. These forms are somewhat less rigorous than the forms from the IRS. Completing your state income taxes takes but a fraction of the time required to file the federal income taxes. Again, use your returns from past years to serve as reasonable guides for what goes where on your current year's state return.

It may be to your benefit to buy the state versions of tax-preparation software. Many of the vendors will give you a discount of the state version if you have already bought their federal version. At around $19.95 per state version, you will have to consider whether it is worth it to you. If you are already adept at handling them manually, doing your state taxes takes less than 25 minutes.

Nevertheless, when you use state tax-preparation software, your overall transaction time is greatly reduced, often to 10 minutes or less. You have the satisfaction of knowing that there is a decent probability that the forms have been filled out correctly. Your printer spits them out in rapid fashion, and as with the federal forms, they are neat, complete, and ready to be mailed.

To File Online or Not to File Online

The IRS and many of the state departments of taxation accept online filing. Online filing has the advantages of reducing the need to handle paper, being much speedier than mailing the forms, and, if you are receiving a refund, getting the money to you much faster. You can even request that your refund be directly deposited into your bank account.

Some people who are leery of filing online ask, "What if they lose my file or it comes over as gobbledygook?" Generally this isn't a problem. First, you have your complete tax returns saved on your hard drive, and you can elect to have hard-copy backup as needed. Within minutes—and often moments—you get online verification that your file has been received. You can both store that communiqué and make a hard-copy backup of it. So, you're covered on all bases.

Divine Guidance

You've paid the government what you owe in taxes—whether you paid with your return or expect to receive a refund. But did you make as many tax-deductible contributions as your income allows? There's no shame in paying the government the taxes you owe—and no honor in skimming a little off the bill even if you don't get caught—but wouldn't you like to know that you had a hand in helping someone in need? And it really didn't cost you any more than you paid in taxes last year.

Moreover, filing online is no more risky or prone to electronic mishap than is sending a standard e-mail with a moderate-size attachment.

Filing the Old-Fashioned Way

Many people who use tax-preparation software opt to print and mail their tax returns "the old-fashioned way." This is desirable if your source of income is diverse. Suppose that instead of simply working for one employer who gives you a complete wage and tax statement at the end of the year, you derive your income from a variety of sources. Perhaps you work for two or more employers, or you run a small business and have several clients or customers sending you checks. In such cases, you may end up collecting a variety of W-2 statements.

When you submit your taxes via mail, on the left side of the top page of your tax return some variation of a Form 1040, there is an indication of where you are to staple your W-2 statements. Also, if you have extenuating circumstances related to an investment and want to provide the IRS with such documentation, it is easier to mail your returns than attempt to convey this information by electronic means.

Avoid the April Rush

If you send in your returns before March 15, you are reasonably assured of receiving a refund in a reasonable amount of time. After April 1, you are competing with the masses who have procrastinated up until this time. Approaching April 15, you are but one of a flood of taxpayers nationwide who are racing to get theirs turned in on time.

Most employers and most financial institutions comply with the law and send you the various W-2s, 1099s, and other required statements by the end of January. So, you have the full month of February and most of March to gracefully prepare your taxes and get them in on time, whether you opt for electronic or mail submission.

> **Divine Guidance**
>
> To be sure, not all people who pay taxes are procrastinating, some wait until the last day before filing because being self-employed, they tend to always owe, and hence pay at the last moment possible.

Time, Not Payment, Extensions

If you cannot complete your taxes by April 15, you can opt to file an extension that gives you an additional four months to complete your tax returns. Filing the extension, however, doesn't give you any grace when it comes to submitting any funds that may be due on or before April 15.

When you file an extension, don't make the mistake of unnecessarily incurring a tax penalty because you failed to pay sums due on the fifteenth. You can make the logical argument that if you haven't prepared your taxes by the fifteenth, how can you determine exactly what sum you owe by April 15? Good point. In most cases, you have a fair idea of what is due—and if you are going to err, err on the side of the IRS. Pay a little more, to increase the likelihood that you have at least paid your share.

If you have paid extra, you will get it back in the form of a refund. If you haven't, you will hear about it soon enough anyway.

Support the IRS

This may sound funny in a book on organization, but seek to help the IRS as much as you can. While it may seem to be a monolithic, uncaring organization, essentially one person reviews your tax returns. So, any explanations you can offer above and beyond the miniscule amount of space provided on the form can prove to be quite helpful. Moreover, it shows the IRS agent that you are a conscientious citizen and taxpayer and that you are trying to be helpful. This can only work in your favor.

List the phone numbers where you can be reached and even your e-mail address. Any agent can find this information about you if he so chooses; you might as well provide it upfront.

After you've sent in your tax return, relax. You have earned the right.

Chapter 24

Organizing Your Purchases

You see an advertisement for an appliance on television or in a magazine, and you are completely enticed! You can't wait to buy the item, bring it home, and use it. Then, between the initial enticement and the actual operation, the stark reality hits.

Much of what you buy today comes with lengthy instruction manuals, warranty cards to be completed and mailed, and papers to file. How can you get optimal use of your purchases, master some of the more complex features, file the appropriate papers and packaging, and otherwise stay organized? In this chapter we examine these issues!

The Show Room Floor Is Too Late

Before ever stepping foot in somebody's store or ordering something online, determine in advance what you actually want the product to be able to do. If you wait to ascertain the functions and features that you want in an appliance or gadget when you are on the showroom floor, it is way too late!

Develop a checklist of associated benefits and features of doing business with ventures that are attractive to you. I use a purchasing checklist to help ensure that I am getting the best deal if ever I am going to spend money on something:

- ❏ Are there quantity discounts or special terms?
- ❏ Are there corporate, government, association, or educators' discounts?
- ❏ Do they give weekly, monthly, quarterly, or seasonal discounts?
- ❏ Do they give off-peak discounts or odd-lot discounts?
- ❏ Do they offer a guaranteed lowest price?
- ❏ Do they accept major credit cards?
- ❏ Do they give an additional discount for opening up a store credit card?
- ❏ Does opening a store credit card provide any additional financing benefits?
- ❏ Do they accept orders by fax?
- ❏ Do they accept orders by e-mail?
- ❏ Do they offer a money-back guarantee or some other guarantee?
- ❏ Do they have a toll-free ordering line and customer service line?
- ❏ Do they guarantee the shipping date?
- ❏ How do they ship?
- ❏ Do they offer free delivery?
- ❏ Are their shipments insured?
- ❏ Are there shipping and handling charges?
- ❏ How long for delivery?
- ❏ Do they offer free installation?
- ❏ Will they keep your name off their mailing list (unless you want to keep up with special sales)?
- ❏ Do they intend to sell, rent, or transfer your purchase information to others?
- ❏ Are their prices guaranteed?
- ❏ Is there tax?
- ❏ Are there any other charges?
- ❏ Do they have free samples?
- ❏ Are authorized dealer/repair services in your area?

❏ Are references or referral letters available?

❏ Are there satisfied customers in your area?

❏ How long have they been in business?

❏ Who are they owned by?

❏ Is gift-wrapping available?

❏ Does the product come with a warranty?

Once onsite, with a single, slim piece of paper in my hand, I am focused and ready. Most consumers don't take any of the steps that I take because they don't think about it—or if they do, perhaps it seems like too much work. For me, it is far less work to ensure that I acquire the right appliance, model, make, and capabilities than to acquire something only to discover that it doesn't do what I sought.

Divine Guidance

Procrastination is often defined as the art of putting off until tomorrow what you should do today. Cliff Cole says procrastination clutters up our lives with an appalling number of half-done things. As you look at the previous exhaustive list for appliances, you may be tempted to complete only about half. Don't give in—go the whole way because the very item you ignored may come back to hurt you later.

Test-Drive It There and Then

Onsite, in a store is the time you want to give the appliance a good workout. For example, with the salesperson present, run through the various product functions. Ensure that you understand how the darn thing works, not when you get it home, on your own, alone, without guidance.

The salesperson is there to serve you, the consumer, not the other way around (although increasingly it seems like that in many of today's retail operations). Come with the mind-set that you are there to gather information, not necessarily to buy. If you gather the information you are seeking and are fortunate enough to encounter a manufacturer's make and model that fits the bill in all respects, then you can consider a purchase.

Too Complex for You? Don't Blame Yourself

If you can't understand how to operate the unit and run through its basic functions while you are in the store, then perhaps the fault lies not with you, not with the salesperson, but with the manufacturer.

The manufacturer had many decisions to make before the product was ever shipped from the plant. These decisions involved the quality of materials to be used and the design and layout of the various switches, buttons, and dials that adorn the appliance. The intelligence with which engineers designed the product largely dictates how easy or difficult it will be for the typical consumer to use it.

Think about clothes dryers, microwave units, blenders, combination radio/alarm clocks, and CD players. Mysteriously, some of them seem to have instructions that are too ponderous to fathom, while others seem easy to operate. Did you luck out, or did the design engineer back at the plant have something to do with it?

> **Caution Corner**
>
> As Vance Packard told us more than 40 years ago in his book *The Waste Makers*, much of what we think represents our own shortcomings when it comes to operating an appliance is erroneous.

Eschew Thick Instruction Manuals

When it comes to the instruction manuals accompanying appliances, you have undoubtedly noticed that some are thick, densely written, and all together unwieldy. Others are slimmer, written in everyday language, loaded with diagrams, and prepared so that even highly nontechnical types can easily proceed through them.

Yet when you are in a store contemplating an important appliance purchase, how often do you ask to see any accompanying manuals? Some manufacturers think it is impressive to strap you with a 180-page instruction book. Increasingly, however, such literary productions are symptomatic of appliances that have not been designed for ease of use.

In our over-information society, in which you are bombarded with instructions on a daily basis, can you afford to expend the mental energy required to master the nuances of a particular appliance, even one that you have vigorously sought?

That's the Spirit

It's not uncommon to feel like you're having "sensory overload." Computers with monitors and printers, faxes, cell phones, PDAs, DVD players, VCRs, and TVs .... Technology is at hand every second, and all forms of it are desperate for your attention. Ever wonder what might happen if you turned off all electronics for a day or even a few minutes? The next time you have the opportunity, get alone with God. Remember this simple passage from Psalm 46:10: "Be silent and know that I am God."

Designed for Ease of Use

From now on, seek products designed with intelligence. Recognize that having fewer switches, buttons, or dials does not necessarily mean that the product is less sophisticated or offers fewer benefits or features. Indeed, the opposite may be true.

I own a video camera from the mid-1990s that still confounds me. I suppose that if I wanted to kill a half-day and learn how to actually employ the various editing functions, it certainly would be within my capability. But when is that half day going to come? Meanwhile, other units are available that have simplified the process for the rank and file user who simply wants to fade in or fade out, turn the sound up or down, and do so without having a Ph.D. in video camera operations.

Are PCs a Special Case?

What about instructions when it comes to operating a PC, notebook, or palmtop computer? Granted, these devices require far more time and consternation than your typical household appliance. I have college students as helpers. Some of them major in computers, or whatever they call it. They help me navigate the maze of new software. We establish sequences and routines that I can follow. We type those "instructions" onto my hard drive and save them in a file I can easily recall.

Instead of becoming enmeshed in all the features of a new software program, I focus on mastering the handful of capabilities that I want to use. We then write and save the instructions in a master file of all the other instructions that I have saved. I often keep the immediate instruction nearby as I complete the learning phase.

Divine Guidance

Bringing in some knowledgeable other, even if it is for pay, is a far better strategy than trying to organize your schedule to accommodate the spate of self-instruction sessions you will need to master a given appliance.

You have to consider that the true cost of operating an appliance—or, for that matter, a computer—effectively is not merely your dollar outlay for its acquisition. Effective use of the product also exacts a cost. This principle can be extended to appliances. I've found that some people are much more adept at setting up and using a VCR than I am. The same is true of cameras, DVD players, and many of the increasingly digital appliances that populate one's home.

Instructions Designed for Ease of Use

As you pursue the packet of papers that comes with your appliance—including the instruction manual, diagram or schematic, and a warranty card—be on the lookout for the at-a-glance instructions. These represent a single page or card, often laminated, that mercifully lists the 5, 8, 10, or 12 basic functions that 98 percent of buyers will use on a regular basis. If this card is illustrated or uses symbols or icons, all the better.

Taking the card in hand, see how easily you can operate the showroom model. Perhaps you need help from the salesperson at this juncture. That is okay; run through the card once with help and then a second time without it. If you can master what is on the card, you've likely got it made.

Ideally, on the second run without help, you should be fairly adept at making the appliance operate per the simple instructions. If not, maybe another make and model on the next shelf is even easier to operate and still addresses the basic functions that you're seeking.

Caution Corner

It doesn't take long for our possessions—including household appliances and gadgets—to control our lives, according to Walter P. Wilson. "Our culture sweeps us along with the tide as if we were in the middle of a river in a small raft," Wilson explains in *The Internet Church*. "The water appears to be still all around us, but a glance at the shore reveals we're moving along at a rapid pace."

Keep Your Purchases Organized

To stay organized following the purchase of each of the appliances, equipment, or gadgets you acquire, you have several options, including the following:

- Use the plastic see-through notebook sleeves.
- File the documentation, but keep the instruction manual close by.
- Farm out the manuals.
- Adopt a *laissez faire* approach.

Use Plastic See-Through Notebook Sleeves

Using the plastic see-through sleeves that are so valuable for organizing tax receipts (described in Chapter 23), store the receipt, instruction card, and any thin diagrams or schematics that will comfortably fit in the plastic sleeve.

> **Divine Guidance**
>
> The typical magazine holder can house at least 8 such instruction manuals, and perhaps as many as 12 or 15 if most are mercifully thin.

Tuck that sleeve into the pages of the instruction manual, and put that instruction manual in a magazine holder (as described in Chapter 16), along with the other plastic sleeve and instruction manuals from the other appliances you have acquired.

The magazine holder itself can go in one of your unused kitchen cabinets, under the kitchen counter, in your den, on working shelves in a utility closet, or any place where you know that you will be able to readily retrieve it as necessary.

File the Documentation and Keep the Instruction Manual Close By

File the receipt, diagrams, or schematics and any other associated paperwork as you normally would with a purchase, but keep the instruction manual and the at-a-glance instructions near the appliance itself. This works particularly well for DVD and video players since, in many cases, you can simply place the instructions under the unit.

For other types of appliance, it may make sense to temporarily house the instruction manual and at-a-glance instructions near the appliance for the first several weeks of ownership. Then transfer the instruction manual to the aforementioned magazine holder or a kitchen or desk drawer where you keep other instruction manuals.

You may want to keep at-a-glace instructions near the unit for the long haul. I found, for example, that keeping the at-a-glance instructions for my telephone answering machine under the unit itself works well. I can never keep track of the remote commands for turning the machine on or off, replaying a single message or all messages, changing the message, and deleting messages. Having the card under the unit itself and another in my briefcase (which I take with me) enables me to quickly refer to the instructions as necessary. Fortunately, I don't have to look at the card more than, say, once a month.

Farm Out the Manuals

Another option for organizing your instruction manuals and accompanying documentation is to give them to your trusted assistants. Have your assistant read them and become the guru to you for that particular appliance. This is my preferred approach because I don't even want to open one of those manuals!

At the outset, the assistant takes the manuals with him or her. Thereafter, once this person has mastered the piece, perhaps it makes sense for you to once again house them, since if you do need any onsite counseling in the future, your assistant may need to refer to the manual. So, it makes sense to have it handy.

It is hard to describe the sheer joy of casting off the manuals in this way. You feel so free, you don't know why you proceeded in any other way in the past.

If you have children old enough to assist you in these maneuvers, by all means recruit them. While you are empowering your children to advise and counsel you, go for the double win and solidify your relationship with them through this new joint effort. I know many a mom or dad who has a son or daughter who is the household appliance guru, cheerfully instructing them how to operate this or that, which button to push, which dial to turn, how to modify default settings, and so forth.

While organizing the many little instruction books in your life, it's a good time to take stock of spiritual materials. You might not think you have much to organize, but where do you keep your Bible or Bibles, for instance? Are they handy for everyone to see and use? You also should post an accessible list of numbers for your faith life:

- Church phone number and address
- Minister's phone number
- Church prayer chain contact
- Sunday school coordinator
- Members of your Bible study or small group

It goes without saying that you should give extra priority and detail to church and family events as you organize your life. As someone said, "God first, family second, you third. The formula for joy is Jesus, others, you."

Laissez Faire (Hands Off)

Another option is simply leave the manual in the original box and store the box in an attic, basement, or other storage area.

These days, you need to keep the box if you want to make any kind of return or if you want to resell the item at a later date. Returning the box always is a powerful selling point for those in the secondhand buyer market. If you followed much of the advice at the beginning of this chapter for certain items at certain times, you may never need to refer to the manual. That's the best of all worlds!

> **Divine Guidance**
>
> Why have manuals in your life to begin with, if you don't have to have them? In other words, if you can learn how to do something via someone's instruction, or can use a single sheet of instructions, then large manuals are unnecessary.

Most homes have Internet access, so one viable option for bypassing the manuals altogether is to go on the Internet and visit the vendor's website. The site may have frequently asked questions (FAQs), a reference to a hotline, or it may provide assistance by e-mail. There may be a forum or chat room where product users have continuing running conversations with one another.

More Tips on Using the Web for Consumer Instructions

Sites such as www.dejanews.com and www.tilenet.com essentially serve as search engines to the Usenet function of the Internet. Newsgroups (officially known as Usenet newsgroups) distribute messages called articles on specific subjects using the Internet. They are popular sources of information that contain an estimated one million new articles posted each day.

Newsgroups are grouped by subject. When you post an article, you post it to the newsgroups of your choice and it becomes viewable by all users. You can also send a reply to the author of a message to address a question, concern, or complaint. You can read articles in newsgroups without posting anything. To conduct research, you can search for newsgroups with names that relate to a product or service.

You can use www.google.com or any of the other popular search engines to simply type in your query, such as how to use the XYZ feature on the ABC appliance. It's helpful to put such a question in quotes because then the hits that you receive will contain that actual question as you posed it.

If you don't get enough hits, reword your question and pose it more generally until you do get viable hits. Then visit those sites and voilà—often you will be surprised to see that someone has already addressed the issue that you are seeking information on. Some sites, such as www.ConsumerReports.com and eopinions.com, maintain product reviews and user comments on a wide variety of appliances.

Many types of electronic gadgets and popular appliances have their own user groups. These are individuals spread out across the country—and, in some cases, the globe—who are enthusiastically devoted to the product. The palmtop series comes to mind, but there are also user groups for GameBoys, XBox, and even John Deere lawn mowers and the like.

To find such groups, simply type the name of the appliance or product and then "users group" into the search engine. You will probably get immediate hits, but if not, put quotes around the request, as in "GameBoy users group." You will likely get more than you hoped to find.

Divine Guidance

Some sites offer no-holds-barred analysis and commentary that can prove to be quite illuminating! When you read the opinions of actual users, you can gain great insights as to a product's reliability and how well that product might suit you.

Chapter
25

Service Contracts, Guarantees, and Warranties

When it comes to dealing with service contracts, guarantees, and warranties, remaining organized can pay off in major ways. How often, however, do you even pay attention to them? In this chapter, we'll look at what service contracts guarantee and what warranties are all about and how to use them to your advantage.

Service Contracts

The mere concept of a service contract poses a dilemma to the befuddled consumer. If you are buying an appliance of reasonable quality with a warranty of sufficient length, why would you need to shell out extra money for a service contract?

Consumer Reports has studied the issue extensively from several different angles and largely concludes that in nearly all instances, for most appliances, service contracts are unnecessary. Most items you buy (with the exception of clothing) will have some type of limited warranty, usually for one year after the date of purchase.

Chances are, if something is significantly wrong with the product, it'll break down within one year and you can have it replaced. Moreover, purchasing extended contracts generally takes money out of your pocket that doesn't need to go anywhere.

Caution Corner

The incidence of breakdown after the warranty period is not so great with a product from a reliable vendor that it justifies the cost of a multiyear service contract.

Usually, if you need a repair or two, your out-of-pocket expenditure will not equal the cost of the typical service contract that you are often induced to buy. At the rate of product obsolescence, with new models perpetually forthcoming, if you hold on to an appliance—especially a smaller-ticket item—for several years, the cost of any significant repair in most cases will rival that of simply buying the latest model.

That's the Spirit

Christianity is not the latest model. It doesn't require an extra service contract. There's a real danger in "Cafeteria Christianity"—taking the most convenient aspects of different faiths and bending them to fit your life. Don't expect that the latest chic faith to get you closer to God or prepare you for death and what comes after. In a warning against adultery, Proverbs 6:20–23 explains the value of God's laws. "My son, keep your father's commands and do not forsake your mother's teaching. Bind them upon your heart forever, and fasten them around your neck. When you walk, they will guide you; when you sleep, they will watch over you; when you awake, they will speak to you. For these commands are a lamp, this teaching is a light, and the corrections of discipline are the way to life."

On Occasion

All the foregoing is not to say that there are not circumstances when it may make sense to sign up for the service contract. For expensive items that you will be using extensively and for which it would be otherwise a great burden to find appropriate repair specialists, service contracts may be advisable.

Always proceed with caution: A service contract may cover only certain parts of the product or specific repairs. Read the contract carefully. If it does not list something as specifically covered, assume that it is not. Service contracts do not cover repairs resulting from misuse or failure to maintain the product properly. Also, you may be obligated to take certain action, such as notifying the company of problems, to ensure that the service contract is not voided.

Consider what the service contract gives you that the warranty will not. Carefully compare the coverage of your warranty to the coverage offered by the service contract, to decide if the service contract is worth the additional expense.

Be wary of other expenses after you buy a service contract. Some service contracts, like insurance policies, often have deductible amounts. Or, you may be charged each time the item is serviced. Some expenses are limited or excluded. In addition, you may have to pay cancellation or transfer fees if you sell the covered product or want to end the contract.

When a service contract is offered by a local retailer or dealer, you may be able to get only local service. Consider the possibility that problems may develop while you are traveling or after you move away from the area. Service contracts that provide onsite assistance can prove attractive if you live in a relatively rural area and would find it a hardship to have to tote an item to a repair center.

You may be better able to decide if you need a service contract after you have owned the product for some time.

> **Divine Guidance**
> If the vendor offers the option of acquiring a service contract after your original warranty has expired, then you could certainly wait until your warranty period expires to buy a service contract.

Stay Organized and Win

If you do opt to acquire a service contract, keep those papers with all the other afore-mentioned papers associated with your appliance purchase. Here's the mantra: Use a plastic see-through sleeve to store the service contract, the product purchase receipt, and instruction cards. Tuck that sleeve into the pages of the instruction manual, and put that instruction manual in a magazine holder, as described in Chapter 16.

Alternatively, keep all service contract information, printed guarantees, and warranties (discussed later in the chapter) together in a separate folder or book. This is especially true for high-dollar items such as electronic equipment and *anything* that has a written lifetime warranty. Some items that parents tend to overlook are children's backpacks and book bags. Many of these have a lifetime warranty, so when the product is worn out, you can send off for a new one and save the expense of buying new backpacks every year.

Too many people who acquire service contracts forget that they have done so, haven't filed the papers accordingly, and then, when the equipment malfunctions, don't know that they are already covered. As such, service contracts represent a lucrative profit center for vendors:

1. In many cases, the equipment doesn't malfunction.

2. In other cases, people can't remember that they acquired a service contract.

What a racket!

Guarantees

A printed guarantee is a wonderful thing, whereas an oral guarantee is not worth the paper it is printed on.

One frequently hears advertisements, particularly telemercials and advertorials, boasting a "30-day money-back guarantee." What exactly does this mean? Mass marketers have long known that even if they offer an iron-clad guarantee, such as, "You must be completely satisfied or your money will be cheerfully refunded," only a small fraction of buyers will ever take them up on such an offer.

Divine Guidance

Worldly matters can often remind us of our faith. Guarantee—to agree to be responsible for obligation or performance. We get guarantees—valid and invalid—on nearly everything we buy. With many of those guarantees, you have to read the fine print, which will tell you that the guarantee is good only if you meet extreme conditions and regulations. It's a shame that the business world can't pattern more guarantees after God's guarantee: Do one thing, have total belief in me through my son, Jesus Christ, and you will have salvation. No fine print.

The Odds Are …

The vendors have already figured the odds. Most people do not have the wherewithal to retain the box, original packing materials, and all other elements necessary to successfully return an item. Among those who are sufficiently organized to retain and are able to retrieve all the aforementioned items, most people are not sufficiently motivated to package and mail the item and return it to a physical location by the expiration date of the guarantee. Guarantees by and large are a marketing ploy and have little relationship to the quality of the product.

If the vendor is selling enough of the product at a healthy profit per unit, then historical return rates all but ensure that offering a tremendous guarantee will not cut into profitability. Actually, the opposite is true. The guarantee induces many more people to buy who would not otherwise have purchased. These extra sales more than offset any modest increase in the number of people who end up returning the item. As you guessed, the guarantee serves as a profit generator.

Use Guarantees to Your Advantage

You can use guarantees and your ability to stay organized to set yourself apart from the rest. In the case of a 30-day money-back guarantee for which you must be "completely satisfied," take advantage of such an offer for what it's worth. When you acquire an item, carve out the time and energy to give it a full workout in the first couple days after installation. That way you have the highest probability of ascertaining whether it makes sense to retain it.

Caution Corner

If you wait for the tenth or fifteenth day of a 30-day money-back guarantee, you narrow the odds that you will return the item within the terms of the money-back guarantee period.

If the guarantee is not printed on the packaging but instead comes with an accompanying letter or card, keep it in sight during the trial period. You want the opportunity to review the guarantee as you put the appliance through its paces.

Divine Guidance

If you end up returning the appliance, keep a copy of the guarantee and also include the original at the top of the package.

Particularly for purchases that you bought on speculation, you might not be sure if it was something that you wanted to retain, but the guarantee made the offer enticing. Do not put away the packaging! Keep it out in the open. In the short run, it is better for one room in your house to be a little cluttered while you are evaluating your desire for long-term retention of the product than to risk retaining a product that you would rather not keep.

The Secret Price You Pay

If you order a product with a strong guarantee from a direct-mail catalog or website, be wary. Even if you return the product within the specified time and you prove to be a highly unsatisfied customer, your name goes on a list and you will find yourself inundated with catalogs and new product announcements despite your protestation. This happened to me when I bought an item from a vendor's catalog. When I used the item, it turned out to be an utter disappointment. I mailed it back immediately, with a note expressing my dissatisfaction.

The vendor dutifully refunded my payment. About six weeks later, however, I got a catalog in the mail from the vendor. I was surprised since, from my point of view, I would be one of the last people on earth that they'd seek to do business with. Soon I started receiving more of their catalogs and solicitations on a regular basis. The inundation became irritating. It took somewhere between four and six months to remove myself completely from the system—far more costly than the item I had first purchased. If I had it to do over again, I would never have acquired the item in the first place—but, hey, live and learn.

That's the Spirit

One of the hardest things to do is to pray for people who wrong you. It doesn't seem to be a natural reaction—and it certainly argues the Old Testament adage of "an eye for eye." But it's absolutely necessary. The well-known passage from John 8:6–7 explains it: "They were using this question as a trap, in order to have a basis for accusing him. But Jesus bent down and started to write on the ground with his finger. When they kept on questioning him, he straightened up and said to them, 'If any one of you is without sin, let him be the first to throw a stone at her.'"

If solicitation inundation following a purchase becomes problematic, here are some strategies:

- When you are besieged by third-class mail from repeat or gross offenders, and if such offenders have included a self-addressed bulk mail reply envelope, feel free to use the envelope to request that your name be removed from their lists. Also review their literature to see if you can use an 800-number to make such a request at no cost.

- For those who don't heed your request, file a complaint with the Direct Marketing Association, the U.S. Postal Service, or the Office of the General Counsel of the offending group.

- Sometimes the fastest way to deal with repeat offenders is to write the words "Speed Reply" right on the communication you've received. Underneath those two words, write the message, "Please remove me from your mailing list now and forever." Sign your name, date it, and send back the same items or communication that you received. Be sure to address it to the mailing list manager of the offending organization.

- At all times and in all places, inform the parties with whom you do business that you do not appreciate having your name added to mailing lists and being inundated by catalogs, announcements, brochures, and fliers. This is necessary if you place an order by fax, make a purchase by credit card, fill out a magazine subscription form, or procure any other type of good or service.

Guarantees: The Bad and the Good

To be satisfied is a strong consumer privilege. Satisfaction is a highly subjective issue. What satisfies me would utterly disappoint me.

Caution Corner

Be wary of any guarantee that is not based on your being happy with the product. There are too many ways to go wrong when performance level is the criteria for the guarantee!

Any guarantee that does not refer to your satisfaction, but instead to some performance level, may end up being an undesirable purchase. How can this be so? Suppose that a product does perform at the level guaranteed by the vendor, but some other level or aspect of operation is totally disappointing or frustrating for you. What if it performs at the quantity level indicated, but not at the desired quality?

Here are some appropriately worded guarantees taken from actual products:

1. If XYZ product ever fails due to a defect in materials or workmanship, we will either repair it, without charge, or provide a replacement. As your satisfaction is our goal, we will also endeavor to ensure that our service matches your expectations.

2. If you are not completely satisfied with the performance of our products, you may return them within 90 days of purchase for replacement or refund. (See return policy for restrictions and terms.) We guarantee our products to be free

from manufacturer defects. Liability under this pledge is limited to the replacing of any product found to be defective under normal use. We cannot guarantee against damage resulting from improper storage or other misuse.

3. Your absolute satisfaction is guaranteed. We're confident that you'll be delighted with your purchase. That's why every product purchased from us is backed by our satisfaction guarantee: If you are not absolutely satisfied with your purchase for any reason, let us know. We will promptly replace the item or give you a refund.

4. One hundred Percent Product Guarantee. It's plain and simple: No questions asked! If for *any* reason you are not completely satisfied with *any* of our fine products, simply return them within 14 days for an exchange *or* a complete refund. We are proud of all our products' quality, design, and value—and we are sure you will be also. We stand behind them 100 percent.

> **Caution Corner**
>
> Most warranty cards require more information than is necessary for the vendor to duly authorize your warranty. So feel free to omit sections that you feel exceed what the vendor needs to know. This will not imperil your warranty.

> **Caution Corner**
>
> Questions not related to your specific purchase are entirely for the vendor or distributor's market research department and have nothing to do whatsoever with ensuring that your warranty is duly authorized.

Warranties

If you carefully read the product information you receive when you purchase a new item, most items carry a limited warranty regardless of whether you send in a card. In fact, many of the items you buy carry a warranty that goes into effect *the moment you make a purchase*. Hence, in many instances you have nothing to fill out, sign, or send. When an otherwise legitimate warranty card accompanies the appliance, review it carefully.

Never give away more information on such cards than is absolutely necessary. For example, requests for your Social Security number when buying a product are unwarranted. I refuse to state my e-mail address on such cards, and I do not offer my personal fax number, either. I refuse to check off anything related to income level. I rarely give occupation information, often checking the Other box, and I absolutely won't list what other purchases I have made or am thinking of making.

The Bogus Warranty Card

Some appliance vendors include a bogus "warranty," card making a marketing research survey card appear as if it is a warranty card when, indeed, your warranty has already gone into effect as a result of your purchase! The card is nothing more than free and easy market research information that the vendor gathers from gullible consumers.

Many vendors title such a card as a "product registration card," but what does that actually mean? With whom are you registering? Complete purchase information is already on file with the vendor, whether it be a retail, wholesale, or manufacturing outlet that deals in retail transactions.

If you choose to fill out such cards, convey personal information sparingly. Keep a copy of everything that you send, including front and back sides. In filling out the warranty card, also make sure to check any boxes referring to your desire not to receive product announcements and updates, and to not be put on mailing lists. I attach a label that I created myself which reads: "I don't want my name placed on any mailing lists whatsoever, and I forbid the use, sale, rental, or transfer of my name."

Over the years, I have found that probably 90 percent of the vendors are deterred from inundating me with their product information as a result of my stern message affixed to warranty and registration cards.

If sending in a card makes you feel more comfortable, and if there is no box to check to stay off mailing lists, attach a note saying that you don't want your name and address to be distributed to other companies. You can do the same when registering online. Send an e-mail to the manufacturer requesting that your information be kept confidential.

Divine Guidance

Don't get mad. You've requested once, twice, three times for a company to take you off its mailing list. Still the mailings come. You can continue to ask the company to stop, but guard against investing angry energy in the effort. Anger doesn't make you more effective. It might make you believe that you're being fueled by hate for the company. The customer service representative you call doesn't get personally involved and likely won't perform any better because you're angry. Instead, look at the situation as another opportunity to pray. Each opportunity to pray gives you a little one-on-one time with God and gets you closer to where you want to be.

Code Your Address

Code your address to help ensure that your contact information is not being distributed to direct mail, online, and other mass-market vendors. Here is how coding works. To trace who might be selling your name and contact information, when you make a purchase, add a code to the end of your street address, such as 1A or 2D. Later, if you receive mail with your coded address, you know who sold your name to whom.

In an era when each piece of mail adds to environmental glut, it's your civic duty, as well as an effective technique for staying organized, to reduce the amount of junk mail you receive. You can eliminate 40 percent of your junk mail with one letter. Write to:

Mail Preference Service
Direct Marketing Association
P.O. Box 9008
Farmingdale, NY 11735-9008

Tell them: "I would like my name removed from your direct mail lists." Sending this letter will effectively reduce your junk mail by 40 percent for three to six months. Thereafter, keep sending them the same letter.

Warranties and the Timing of Product Failure

Is it necessarily a coincidence that for some of the products you purchase, repairs seem necessary soon after the warranty period has expired? Once again, this phenomenon is more a function of design than happenstance.

As Vance Packard so deftly observed in his book *The Waste Makers,* a product is only as sturdy as its weakest link. If some inferior material was used within the design and construction of the product, that is the item that will give out first. The operating life of that component is generally known by the manufacturer and is on file in its engineering department. For this reason alone, it makes sense to pay a little more at the outset for quality; in the long run, costs prove to be far less.

Simple math tells us that a product that costs $200 and lasts five years for a yearly cost of $40 is a better buy than a product that costs $150 and lasts three years, all other things being equal.

> **Caution Corner**
>
> Based on how a manufacturer designs and builds a product, it is predictable that certain parts will give out at particular time intervals.

Parting Advice

When it comes to staying on top of appliance service contracts, guarantees, and warranties, the most prudent advice might be to make your purchases at reasonable intervals. If you buy too many items in a concentrated period, your proclivity to organize the accompanying packaging, instruction manuals, and return mail cards goes down markedly. You find that you don't have the energy to deal with all that stuff, and often it merely sits there.

When you don't carve out time in your schedule to master each of the items you buy, if you feel the need to return one of them, you'll likely miss the money-back return deadline. You're also more likely to feel overwhelmed.

When you buy items at manageable intervals, you have a much better chance of staying organized, achieving optimal use of the item, and keeping your home or work space relatively clutter-free.

What about Christmas, your birthday, and other occasions when you predictably receive several appliances around the same time, each with its own set of instructions and accompanying paperwork? In that case, carve out time in advance for the several weeks following the event to integrate the appliance or device into your life as smoothly as possible, with a minimum of clutter. That is the Christian way to get optimal value from your new possessions, stay organized, and enjoy the surrounding events.

Chapter 26

Make Time for Living

The days pass by, seemingly more speedily for each of us as we proceed into the future. Change is ever accelerating on many fronts: communication, technology, product-development, and information flow.

Unquestionably you can quickly add more information, more items, and more technology into your home, but toward what end? Greater family unity, health, or fitness? Greater reverence to God?

"No" for an Answer: A Parable

I was called once by a marketing representative from a well-established investment company. Usually I listen for a minute and then find a polite way to end the conversation. This particular caller seemed to know his subject well, so I listened and even responded. He talked about his company's various investment options and told me that he could send a brochure listing the 35 different investment vehicles available, plus his company's annual report and prospectus.

"Wait a second," I told him, "I have no interest in reading about 35 different investment options. Please do me and yourself a favor by boiling down your information to a single page. Then send a paragraph on the three options that you think would be best for me." I also told him that I was not going to read his company's annual report, so there was no reason to send it.

If I liked what he sent me on the single page, I could always get the annual report at another time. I told him that while I'm an MBA, am certified as a management consultant, and have worked with hundreds of companies, "I'm not fond of reading prospectuses, so please don't send that, either."

At the end of our conversation, I repeated to him that I needed to see only a single page with the three investments he thought were best for me, and perhaps one slim brochure about his company.

Several days passed, and I forgot about the call. When Monday's mail came, I noticed a thick package from his investment house. I cringed. I opened it, and voilà: a brochure on the 35 investment vehicles, an annual and a quarterly report, the company's thick prospectus, and other useless brochures and fliers.

I grabbed the pile and tried to rip the whole thing with one flick of my wrists, but it was too thick. I tossed it and (rest assured) did not become a client. If that broker had sent me what I had asked for, who knows? I might have made his day. The point for all Christian families is this: Never volunteer to be overwhelmed, and never unnecessarily invite clutter into your home. The quality of your life partly depends upon it.

That's the Spirit

One of the main benefits of being better organized is that you have more time to spend on spiritual disciplines—such as praying, fasting, enjoying solitude with God, being active in your church, and attending Bible study groups. Don't squander the extra time saved from being more efficient on frivolous things. In this regard, check out the spiritual organizers and planners in your Christian bookstore. The *Believer's Life System* (Moody Press) is an excellent resource to help you here.

Organized Enough for Leisure

If the late twentieth and early twenty-first centuries have taught us anything, it is that while technology may increase particular aspects of life and work, and the frequency of communication between parties at a distance, it doesn't necessarily promote a more balanced life or encourage in-depth relationships. Material goods in general and technology in particular have not …

- Brought families closer together.
- Helped to decrease the rate of divorce in society.
- Conclusively resulted in increased scores on standardized tests among school children.
- Brought spiritual revival or a better understanding of the Gospel.

As the world in general and your family, in particular, become ever more dependent upon communication technology for information, education, and entertainment, it becomes that much more important to get away from it periodically. No virtual-reality device, at least in the foreseeable future, will provide a quick substitute for all the sensations, physical exercise, and beneficial effects on your psyche of talking a walk in the woods, doing the backstroke in a tranquil lake, skating through the park, or being alone with God in prayer.

You need to withdraw from technology on a daily and regular basis to keep things in perspective. Technology is a tool to help you accomplish goals that support your chosen priorities. Too many people in society apparently become fixated in front of TV screens and computer screens, allowing their level of fitness and, perhaps, health to decline. This de facto abdication in maintaining balance in their lives yields an ominous warning.

Creative Leisure

The amount and quality of leisure in your life may be one telling indication of how organized you are. Have you ever noticed that some families, independent of family income, seem to able to make frequent weekend vacations or engage in extended domestic or international travel?

The trend in America in the last 15 years or so has been toward frequent but shorter vacations, often boxed around holiday weekends. If you use a contrarian approach and take time off when the rest of the world doesn't, then holiday weekends are a good time to stay at home and let everybody else compete for highway lanes and parking spaces. In any event, be sure to get the quality leisure you need to keep your life in balance.

In my previous book on reaching your goals, I offer a variety of possible social, leisure, and lifetime goals. The following is but a small subset of the lists contained in that book, with some extended explanation.

Join the Church Choir

Undoubtedly there's an opportunity for you within a local group or at your place of worship to open your mouth and make a joyful noise. Through the ages, singing has been beneficial to health. After all, you have to breathe more deeply, expand your lungs, and exercise your lower facial muscles.

If you've found a group that meets at a time that is comfortable for you, many benefits await. You open up a creative space in your brain that perhaps you haven't tapped recently.

> ### Divine Guidance
>
> Most groups choose songs that are among the world's favorites. You get to participate with others who potentially are at the same place in life as you, or who are at the same place as you at least for those few moments during the week. Spread the Good News of Christ's love by not only evangelizing, but also serving the material needs of those less fortunate than you. Volunteer to help the widows and orphans that the Lord so often talks about in the Bible.

The Rainy Day File

Here is a file to keep in one of your desk drawers or filing cabinet drawers to review on a rainy day. You can include handwritten notes from other people, pictures, memos, jokes, cartoons, and anything else that helps brighten your day. It could even include …

- Performance appraisals, evaluations from speeches or presentations you have made, or simply your boss's handwritten words of praise accompanying something that you have submitted.
- Love letters, ticket stubs, or program mementos.
- A lucky medallion, coin, or dollar bill.
- A flight itinerary, vacation brochure, postcard, or picture from a magazine.

Anything and everything that will lift your spirits is fair game for your rainy day file.

> **That's the Spirit**
>
> In your rainy day file, include some faithful reminders of God's presence. You might keep a special reminder or sermon topic that you scribbled on the church bulletin one Sunday, or even a photo of the church from the day you were married or when one of the kids was baptized. Maybe you have a favorite Bible verse, such as Philippians 4:13: "I can do anything through him who gives me strength."

Spectator Sports: Taming Longer Games

If you're watching on TV any of the big three sports—baseball, basketball, or football—especially for weekend games, recognize that the inundation of longer commercial breaks all but guarantees that the contests could run three hours from start to finish. Don't get caught up in this syndrome. What are your options?

- You can begin watching exactly at the start of games and skip the 30 minutes of commentator and expert analysis.

- If you don't need to see the game in real time, tape it and then fast forward through the commercials when you finally view it.

- Although I am not a fan of multitasking in the least, it may make sense to have tasks ready during the long commercial breaks, such as straightening up the house or reading magazines that require your attention only in short spurts.

- Most popular: Tune in from the start of the third quarter or, in baseball, from the fifth inning on.

Engage in Creative Writing

Either by turning on your PC or simply by taking out a pen and paper, you have the opportunity before you to let your creative juices flow. How about a short story? Some well-crafted short stories are less than 100 words. Could you write one?

How about writing poetry? You may have tried it when you were in high school. Think about how much more wisdom you have acquired and how that could impact your ability to wax poetic. No one is saying that you have to get published or even show your work to anyone else. You may keep your writing in a log or journal for your own benefit.

Teach a Course You've Mastered

When you teach a course in which you're already a master, there is less effort on your part. You may not need to read up or prepare a lot of notes or outlines. Particularly if you're teaching in an adult education or university extension environment, you can walk in and let the sparks fly. The reward comes in your ability to share with people who want to benefit from your wisdom.

It's been said that you don't learn while talking to others; you learn only while you listen. Actually, that's not entirely true. Sometimes you say things in new ways, or you say things that you didn't know you were going to say, and you actually learn as a result of your own articulation. If you are growing in your faith and have a good knowledge of Scripture, volunteer to teach Sunday school to adults or children, or lead a Bible study.

When you're teaching a course, you're opening yourself up for the chance to learn. As students ask questions, pose their views, and offer insights that represent new ground for you, you are learning as well.

That's the Spirit

When you think of the image of a teacher, what comes to mind? Maybe your favorite elementary school teacher, Mrs. Whatshername. But who's the greatest teacher ever? It's easy: Jesus. The Gospel of Matthew is particularly concerned with depicting Jesus as a teacher "A man came up to Jesus and asked, 'Teacher, what good thing must I do to get eternal life?'" (Matthew 19:16) If you teach, model your methods after the greatest of teachers—because if your life and words reflect those of the ultimate teacher, you may lead others to him.

A Grander Notion

Some people like to combine their leisure time with intellectual improvement. Maybe you're one of them. Have you ever considered educational travel? This is when people travel to a location with the primary purpose of learning something that's directly related to the location. So, if you go to Stonehenge, or the pyramids, or the Falkland Islands off the coast of Argentina, you act as both tourist and student.

Take a trip to the lands where Paul went on his missionary journeys, and learn more about the Book of Acts. And when our prayers are answered for peace in the Middle East, go to the Holy Land and walk where your teacher, Jesus, walked.

The Smithsonian Institution in Washington, D.C., routinely offers educational travel. Such trips are cited within the first couple pages of each issue of the monthly magazine the *Smithsonian*. Other institutions offer them as well, primarily universities, conservation societies, and even some professional associations.

> **Divine Guidance**
>
> Educational travel allows you to immerse yourself in whatever you're studying and come back a better person.

Educational travel makes perfect sense. You can study archeology, the environment, art, architecture, or natural history by actually going onsite and examining subjects in their original location or natural condition.

Some Parting Ideas

Here are some additional ideas on how to make the most of your leisure:

- Take airplane trips that are only one-flight, nonstop on your vacation. Anything else taxes you in ways you don't need to be taxed.

- Go to the store and buy bubble bath today, even if you're not sure exactly when you'll use it.

- Install a hammock in your backyard. Never mind when you think you'll actually use it (see the advice about bubble bath).

- Take on new friends who engage in leisure activities that you find alluring and who will teach, guide, train, and include you in their activities.

- Open your home more frequently to others via parties, receptions, meetings, and brief visits.

> **Divine Guidance**
>
> Consider taking up a sport you've never attempted, such as golf, archery, hiking, or snorkeling. Or, take a class on crafts, be it pottery, metals, ceramics, leather, stained glass, jewelry, or woodworking.

- Frequently take walks in shopping malls, along city sidewalks, down nature trails, and anyplace else you feel safe.

- Go to the library one evening a week, and read whatever magazines appeal to you. Join a monthly book review discussion group.

- Jesus says what you do to the least of these you do for him. Volunteer in a nursing home, drug rehab center, food pantry, or crisis pregnancy center, or share the Gospel with those in jail.

- Take an impromptu weekend trip to someplace you haven't visited.

- Become an amateur geologist and go on your own "fossil" hunts. This could be as simple as finding rocks and breaking them open, or looking for petrified shark's teeth, troglodytes, or minerals embedded in stone.

- Buy a telescope and start watching the sky.

- Train a hamster, a gerbil, a cat, or a dog.

- Get on the committee that sponsors a festival, holiday parade, street fair, or exposition.

- Take a course in handwriting, calligraphy, or sketching.

- Visit one new restaurant a month or, if the spirit moves you, once a week. With your mate or friend, go to a restaurant much earlier than usual some evening and linger over appetizers, the entrée, and dessert; take your sweet time leaving as well. By the time you're out of there, the world will have changed. So will your attitude.

Get close to God starting now because he loves you unconditionally.

That's the Spirit

Human nature being what it is, there's always a danger that you will drift too far away from God. Sometimes it's called backsliding. Remember the priority of God first, and don't get discouraged. If you find yourself sleeping in on Sundays and not reading your Bible, or living like the worldly people, you've gone too far. Remember these important words from Mother Teresa: "Yesterday is gone. Tomorrow has not yet come. We have only today. Let us begin."

It All Starts with You

Being sufficiently organized to have ample leisure time; maintaining a clean home that is well stocked; supporting a happy, healthy home and family life; and being able to get closer to God and serve him starts with the basic notion that with his help you are in control. As we observed in Chapter 1, you steer the rudder, flip the switch, pull the lever, call the shots, and have the power within you to take steps to make your life more organized.

Whether or not you specifically seek to have a neater home, more time, greater peace of mind, less stress, less clutter, less to clean, and/or less to maintain, God has suffused you with the power to prevail. Your quest to become and remain organized is a worthwhile pursuit that will benefit you and your family in wondrous ways.

Appendix

Resources

Crabb, Larry. *Finding God.* Grand Rapids, MI: Zondervan, 1993.

Davidson, Jeff. *Breathing Space: Living & Working at a Comfortable Pace in a Sped-up Society.* New York: Mastermedia, 2000.

——. *The Complete Idiot's Guide to Assertiveness.* Indianapolis, IN: Alpha Books, 1997.

——. *The Complete Idiot's Guide to Managing Stress.* Indianapolis, IN: Alpha Books, 1999.

——. *The Complete Idiot's Guide to Managing Your Time.* Indianapolis, IN: Alpha Books, 1999.

——. *The Complete Idiot's Guide to Reaching Your Goals.* Indianapolis, IN: Alpha Books, 1998.

——. *The Complete Idiot's Guide to Reinventing Yourself.* Indianapolis, IN: Alpha Books, 2001.

Fritz, Robert. *The Path of Least Resistance.* New York: Fawcett Columbine, 1989.

Goldbeck, David. *The Smart Kitchen.* Woodstock, NY: Ceres Press, 1994.

Harwin, Ronald, and Colin Haynes. *Healthy Computing.* New York: AMACOM, 1991.

Hawkins, Kathleen. *Spirit Incorporated*. Marina Del Rey, CA: DeVorss & Co., 1973.

Hillman, Os. *Today God Is First*. Shippensburg, PA: Destiny Image Publishers, 2000.

Kostner, Jaclyn. *Virtual Leadership*. New York: Warner, 1996.

Lakein, Andrew. *How to Get Control of Your Time and Your Life*. New York: Wyden, 1973.

Lewis, C. S. *Mere Christianity*. New York: Touchstone, 1996.

MacArthur, John. *What the Bible Says About Parenting*. Nashville, TN: Word Publishing, 2000.

Miller, Donald. *Prayer and the Art of Volkswagen Maintenance*. Eugene, OR: Harvest House, 2000.

Packard, Vance. *The Waste Makers*. New York: Mackay, 1960.

Packer, J. I. *Knowing and Doing the Will of God*. Ann Arbor, MI: Servant Publications, 1995.

Reese, William L. *Dictionary of Philosophy and Religion*. Atlantic Highlands, NJ: Humanities Press, 1980.

Salsbury, Glenna. *Art of the Fresh Start*. Deerfield Beach, FL: Health Communications, 1995.

Stanley, Charles. *How to Listen to God*. Nashville, TN: Thomas Nelson, 1985.

Sugarman, Joe. *Success Forces*. Chicago, IL: Contemporary Books, 1980.

Tenner, Edward. *Why Things Bite Back: Technology and the Revenge of Unintended Consequences*. New York: Vintage Books, 1997.

Wilson, Walter P. *The Internet Church*. Nashville, TN: Word Publishing, 2000.

Index